Frommer's®

Prague
day BY day™

1st Edition

WILEY
Wiley Publishing, Inc.

Contents

Published by:

Wiley Publishing, Inc.

111 River St.
Hoboken, NJ 07030-5774

ISBN: 978-0-470-19404-1

Editor: Christine Ryan
Production Editor: M. Faunette Johnston
Photo Editor: Richard Fox, with Photo Affairs, Inc.
Cartographer: Elizabeth Puhl
Production by Wiley Indianapolis Composition Services

For information on our other products and services or to obtain technical support, please contact our Customer Care Department within the U.S. at 800/762-2974, outside the U.S. at 317/572-3993 or fax 317/572-4002.

Wiley also publishes its books in a variety of electronic formats. Some content that appears in print may not be available in electronic formats.

Manufactured in China

5   4   3   2   1

A Note from the Publisher

Organizing your time. That's what this guide is all about.

Other guides give you long lists of things to see and do and then expect you to fit the pieces together. The Day by Day guides are different. These guides tell you the best of everything, and then they show you how to see it *in the smartest, most time-efficient way*. Our authors have designed detailed itineraries organized by time, neighborhood, or special interest. And each tour comes with a bulleted map that takes you from stop to stop.

Would you like to follow in Kafka's footsteps or spend a day exploring Prague castle? Planning a walk through Prague's Old Town? Hoping to sample some Czech beers at a traditional pub? Whatever your interest or schedule, the Day by Days give you the smartest routes to follow. Not only do we take you to the top attractions, hotels, and restaurants, but we also help you access those special moments that locals get to experience—those "finds" that turn tourists into travelers.

The Day by Days are also your top choice if you're looking for one complete guide for all your travel needs. The best hotels and restaurants for every budget, the greatest shopping values, the wildest nightlife—it's all here.

Why should you trust our judgment? Because our authors personally visit each place they write about. They're an independent lot who say what they think and would never include places they wouldn't recommend to their best friends. They're also open to suggestions from readers. If you'd like to contact them, please send your comments my way at mspring@wiley.com, and I'll pass them on.

Enjoy your Day by Day guide—the most helpful travel companion you can buy. And have the trip of a lifetime.

Warm regards,

Michael Spring, Publisher
Frommer's Travel Guides

About the Author

Journalist, photographer, and freelance writer **Mark Baker** has lived in Prague off and on since 1991. He was one of the original editors of *The Prague Post* and a long-time radio correspondent with Prague-based Radio Free Europe/Radio Liberty. He is a frequent contributor to the *Wall Street Journal Europe* and *National Geographic Traveler,* among other publications.

An Additional Note

Please be advised that travel information is subject to change at any time—and this is especially true of prices. We therefore suggest that you write or call ahead for confirmation when making your travel plans. The authors, editors, and publisher cannot be held responsible for the experiences of readers while traveling. Your safety is important to us, however, so we encourage you to stay alert and be aware of your surroundings.

Star Ratings, Icons & Abbreviations

Every hotel, restaurant, and attraction listing in this guide has been ranked for quality, value, service, amenities, and special features using a **star-rating system.** Hotels, restaurants, attractions, shopping, and nightlife are rated on a scale of zero stars (recommended) to three stars (exceptional). In addition to the star-rating system, we also use a **kids icon** to point out the best bets for families. Within each tour, we recommend cafes, bars, or restaurants where you can take a break. Each of these stops appears in a shaded box marked with a coffee-cup-shaped bullet .

The following **abbreviations** are used for credit cards:

AE	American Express	DISC	Discover	V	Visa
DC	Diners Club	MC	MasterCard		

Frommers.com

Now that you have this guidebook to help you plan a great trip, visit our website at **www.frommers.com** for additional travel information on more than 3,600 destinations. We update features regularly to give you instant access to the most current trip-planning information available. At Frommers. com, you'll find scoops on the best airfares, lodging rates, and car rental bargains. You can even book your travel online through our reliable travel booking partners. Other popular features include:

- Online updates of our most popular guidebooks
- Vacation sweepstakes and contest giveaways
- Newsletters highlighting the hottest travel trends
- Online travel message boards with featured travel discussions

A Note on Prices

In the "Take a Break" and "Best Bets" sections of this book, we have used a system of dollar signs to show a range of costs for 1 night in a hotel (the price of a double-occupancy room) or the cost of an entree at a restaurant. Use the following table to decipher the dollar signs:

Cost	Hotels	Restaurants
$	under $100	under $10
$$	$100–$200	$10–$20
$$$	$200–$300	$20–$30
$$$$	$300–$400	$30–$40
$$$$$	over $400	over $40

An Invitation to the Reader

In researching this book, we discovered many wonderful places—hotels, restaurants, shops, and more. We're sure you'll find others. Please tell us about them, so we can share the information with your fellow travelers in upcoming editions. If you were disappointed with a recommendation, we'd love to know that, too. Please write to:

Frommer's Prague Day by Day, 1st Edition
Wiley Publishing, Inc. • 111 River St. • Hoboken, NJ 07030-5774

12 Favorite
Moments

12 Favorite **Moments**

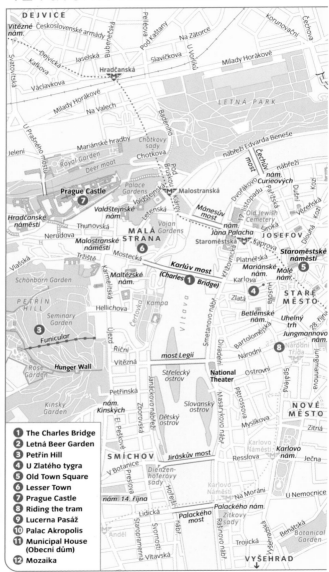

DEJVICE

LETNÁ PARK

Prague Castle ❼

Hradčanské náměstí

MALÁ STRANA

Karlův most (Charles ❶ Bridge)

Staroměstské náměstí ❺

STARÉ MĚSTO

❹

PETŘÍN HILL

Seminary Garden

❸ **Funicular**

Hunger Wall

Kinsky Garden

most Legii

National Theater

NOVÉ MĚSTO

❽

SMÍCHOV

Jiráskův most

Palackého most

VYŠEHRAD

❶ The Charles Bridge
❷ Letná Beer Garden
❸ Petřín Hill
❹ U Zlatého tygra
❺ Old Town Square
❻ Lesser Town
❼ Prague Castle
❽ Riding the tram
❾ Lucerna Pasáž
❿ Palac Akropolis
⓫ Municipal House (Obecní dům)
⓬ Mozaika

Previous page: The Charles Bridge at dawn.

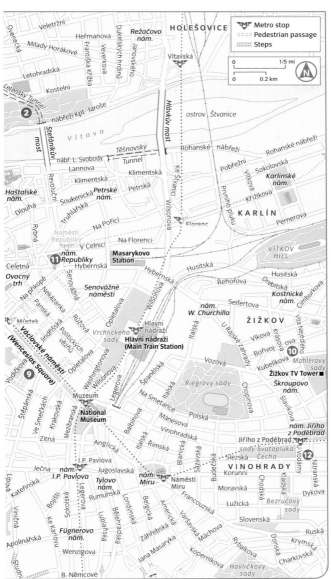

Prague's breathtaking beauty has been discovered. The city now ranks among the most popular in Europe. That's great news for the economy and for people who live from the trade, but for me it means I need to plan my special moments carefully. I am a recluse by nature, and I love the feeling of having a place to myself. These are my tips for moving away from the masses. I hope you enjoy them too.

Relaxing at the Letná Beer Garden.

① **Walking across the Charles Bridge.** It doesn't matter if it's early in the morning, late in the evening, in the rain, in the fog, in the snow . . . anytime but on a hot, crowded day in summer. The bridge is best when you have it nearly to yourself. It's only then that you really notice the eternal spirit of the bridge, the breeze coming in off the river, and the subtle play of lights and shapes among the statues, the domes of Malá Strana, and the castle off in the distance. *See p 13.*

② **Spending a summer evening at the Letná Beer Garden,** perched around a table of old friends. If you want to know where the whole city seems to go for that after-work beer in the summer, look no further than Letná. Bankers, lawyers, students, mothers with kids, people with dogs—they're all here, sitting at picnic tables and drinking 20 Kč beer out of plastic cups. The spectacular views out over the Old Town lend a special feeling to the night. *See p 89.*

③ **Walking across Petřín Hill.** It's the most inspiring view in the city, yet on a typical weekday it seems everyone else is too busy to notice. When I get the chance to slip away, I take the funicular up to Petřín and then make this trek across the top of the meadow toward Prague Castle. There's a little trail to follow and several benches to rest on. Occasionally, I run into another Prague resident, usually walking his or her dog, who loves this place just as much as I do. *See p 85.*

④ **Drinking Pilsner Urquell at a real Czech pub like U Zlatého tygra or U Černého vola.** The new watering holes in town are nice, but nothing beats the simplicity of a wooden table, a crowd of friends, and a half-liter of the beer that conquered the world. It's true that the stodgy food at these places could stand some improvement, but no one really comes for the food anyway. *See p 115.*

5 **Hanging out on Old Town Square.** Yes, it's touristy, filled to overflowing most days with tour groups, dubious street musicians, festivals, and lots and lots of (admittedly) average restaurants. Still, somehow it works. No place in Prague feels more lively or connected to the outside world. Any time of day or night is fine, but evenings are my favorite. There's something about entering the square from the Malé náměstí side, rounding the Clock Tower, and catching those floodlighted towers of the Týn Church and the dark Baroque facades below. Every night feels like a street party. *See p 65.*

6 **Getting lost in the Lesser Town.** Malá Strana is special. It doesn't have the sheer number of traditional tourist sites that Old Town does, and it draws far fewer visitors. My favorite area is Kampa Island and the little bridges across the Čertovká that connect with the mainland. If I have lots of time and sunshine, I pack a lunch, book, and blanket and head for the grassy meadow of Kampa Park. From there, I like to walk back along the river off Na Kampě toward the Charles Bridge. The entire district feels timeless. *See p 59.*

The Old Castle Steps in Malá Strana.

7 **Enjoying the splendor of Prague Castle,** especially strolling through St. Vitus Cathedral. If you've got the energy, climb the 287 steps of the South Tower for some inspiring views of the Castle complex below, and Malá Strana and Old Town out in the distance. When I come on my own, I rarely buy a ticket to go inside the Royal Palace. It's enough for me just to amble around the courtyards and soak in the atmosphere. And don't forget, you can enter St. Vitus for free. *See p 31.*

8 **Riding the tram.** It doesn't have to be in any particularly scenic area. The trams are to Prague what the subways are to New York—the lifelines of the city. Each car is a microcosm of society and wonderfully democratic, ferrying everyone from students to government ministers. When I have a few hours of time, I sometimes hop a tram heading in any direction just to see what's out there. 20 Kč gets you 90 minutes of travel (except at rush hour). That's enough to cover a lot of ground. *See p 50.*

9 **Poking around Lucerna Pasáž.** I am not much of a shopper, but I love coming here. It's not for the stores—most of them seem to sell impractical, one-of-a-kind items like antique cameras. It's more the 1920–1930s feel. Modern shopping malls promise

A tram passing by the National Theater.

Lucerna Pasáž.

a lifestyle experience, but this place actually delivers, with several great cafes, an old-fashioned movie theater, a big hall for balls and dances, and a great rock and jazz club in the basement. It's amazing that it's withstood the test of time. I fully expect in a few years it will be filled with lifeless chain stores, but for now, Lucerna is still something special. *See p 23.*

🔟 **Catching a show at the Palac Akropolis.** Prague's changed a lot in the nearly 20 years since the fall of communism. Most of the changes have been for the better, but it sometimes feels like the city has lost its edge. This longtime nightclub and social staple in Žižkov still pulls in its share of great rock and folk acts. On quieter nights, it's good for just chilling out in the restaurant or cafe

The Czech National Symphonic Orchestra performing at the Obecní dům.

upstairs, or listening to the DJs spin tunes in the basement. This is the place to come when I want to feel that vibe that brought me to Prague in the first place. *See p 131.*

⓫ **Getting tickets for a concert at the Municipal House.** It's a rare treat to snag a good seat in the opulent Smetana Hall at the Obecní dům. Locals complain that concert programmers sometimes play it too safe, loading the card with crowd pleasers like Smetana, Janáček, and Dvořák. That's fine by me, and I'm sure by most visitors as well. Czech composers are too rarely played abroad, so come and hear them when you've got the chance. If you can't book something at the Smetana, the Rudolfinum will do just fine. *See p 9.*

⓬ **Having a dinner out in "new Prague."** Part of the thrill of watching a city recover and develop is witnessing the explosion of new businesses, places to go, and things to do. Nowhere is this dynamism more apparent than in the restaurant business. And you don't need to drop a lot of money to eat well. My favorite place at the moment is Mozaika (p 105). I also love Oliva (p 106), Černý Kohout (p 102), and Aromi (p 98). They all revel in good food and know that to succeed in Prague it's not enough to cater only to the tourists. ●

The Best **in One Day**

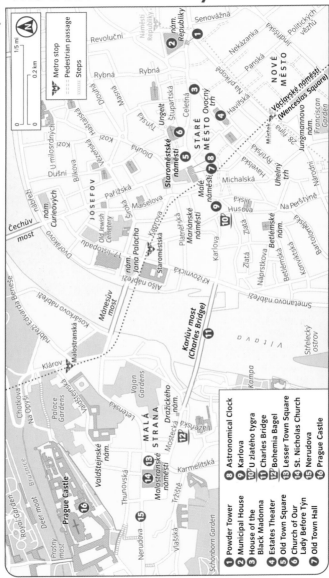

Metro stop
Pedestrian passage
Steps

1/5 mi
0.2 km

1 Powder Tower
2 Municipal House
3 House of the Black Madonna
4 Estates Theater
5 Old Town Square
6 Church of Our Lady Before Týn
7 Old Town Hall

8 Astronomical Clock
9 Karlova
10 U zlatého tygra
11 Charles Bridge
12 Bohemia Bagel
13 Lesser Town Square
14 St. Nicholas Church
15 Nerudova
16 Prague Castle

Previous page: Old Town Square.

This one-day tour follows the ancient coronation route of Bohemian kings. It's impossible to see all the major sights in a day, but this walk comes as close as humanly possible. You can do it in 3 or 4 hours without stops. If you decide to poke your nose in here or there, it can stretch into a whole day. Be forewarned: There's a lot of ground to cover from the Powder Tower to Prague Castle, so get an early start and wear comfortable shoes. START: **Náměstí Republiky.**

① ★ Powder Tower (Prašná brána). The late-Gothic Powder Tower is one of the last standing remnants of the Old Town's original fortification system and marks the start of the Royal coronation route. The name derives from the tower's early purpose: to hold gunpowder for defending the city. The tower dates from the 15th century, but the trademark golden spires were a relatively late addition from the 19th century. You can clamber up to the top for a view out over the Old Town, but better to save your strength for one of the many other towers that lie on the road ahead. ⏱ *10 min. 50 Kč. Daily 10am–6pm.*

② ★★ Municipal House (Obecní dům). Before proceeding down Celetná and starting the Royal Route, take a peek inside this ornate Art Nouveau building from the early days of the 20th century. The Municipal House was built as an expression of Czech nationalism (at a time when Czechs and Germans were rivals for cultural supremacy). The architects consciously mimicked the elaborate Parisian variant of Art Nouveau over the more subdued "Secession" style favored in Vienna. Today, it's home to one of the leading orchestras, the Prague Symphony Orchestra (see chapter 8), as well as a cafe,

Powder Tower.

French restaurant, traditional pub, and cocktail bar. Fans of Art Nouveau should take a guided tour of the interior. ⏱ *15 min., 1½ hr. with tour. Náměstí Republiky 5. ☎ 222-002-121. 150 Kč (adult), 250 Kč (family). Metro: Náměstí Republiky.*

Detail of stained glass on Municipal House exterior.

The National Theater performs an experimental version of Don Giovanni at Estates Theater every year.

③ ★ House of the Black Madonna (Dům U černé Matky Boží).

This former department store—now housing a Museum of Czech Cubism and a beautiful 1920s-era cafe—is one of the best examples of Cubist architecture from the first decades of the 20th century. Cubism is a style that most people associate with painting, but Prague architects saw in the style a modern alternative to the boring historicist trends of the 19th century. The small Museum of Czech Cubism shows how eye-catching, angular Cubist styles could also be adapted to sculpture, textiles, furniture, and household goods. ⏱ 30 min. Celetná 34. ☎ 224-211-746. Tues–Sun 10am–6pm.

④ ★ Estates Theater (Stavovské divadlo).

A short detour along the Ovocný trh (the pedestrian zone leading off to the left) brings you to this historic theater, which in 1787 saw the world premiere of Mozart's opera *Don Giovanni*, conducted by Mozart himself. ⏱ 15 min.

⑤ ★★★ Old Town Square (Staroměstské nám.).

Returning to Celetná and continuing the walk soon takes you into the heart of Old Town: "Staromák," as Czechs affectionately refer to Old Town Square. The square has been at the center of the city's economic life for nearly 1,000 years and is one of the most beautifully preserved Gothic and Baroque spaces in Europe. To get your bearings, stand with the

Brightly-painted facades in Old Town Square.

One of Old Town Hall's intricate windows.

twin-spire Church of Our Lady Before Týn (or simply "Týn Church") to your immediate right; a statue of Czech Protestant reformer Jan Hus stands in the middle. Diagonally across is the white St. Nicholas Church (not to be confused with the church of the same name in Malá Strana). Straight ahead is the Old Town Hall (Staroměstská radnice), with a clock tower on top and fascinating medieval astronomical clock on the side. ⏲ *20 min.*

⑥ ★★ Church of Our Lady Before Týn (kostel Matky Boží před Týnem).
There's something undeniably bewitching about this Gothic church's spires rising up over a row of Baroque facades below. At night, brilliant floodlights illuminate the towers, making the effect even more powerful. The church dates from the 14th century and was once Prague's leading Hussite (Protestant) church. In fact, its spires once held a giant golden chalice (the sign of the Hussites) between them, which the Catholics promptly melted into a golden Madonna (still visible on the front of the church). The interior is

largely Baroque. To the right of the main altar you'll find the tomb of famed Danish astronomer Tycho de Brahe of the court of Rudolf II. Enter through the arcades under the red address marker 604. ⏲ *30 min. Staroměstské nám. Free admission. Tues–Sun 10am–1pm, 3–5pm.*

⑦ ★★ Old Town Hall (Staroměstská radnice).
If you have legs for only one tower climb,

Týn church.

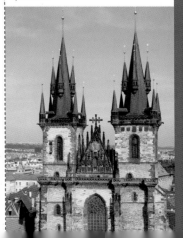

Huge crowds gather in front of the astronomical clock every hour.

make it this one. The view to the square below is beloved by photographers everywhere—one of the signature views of Prague. There's an elevator if you're not up for the narrow steps. The Old Town Hall occasionally hosts art and photo exhibitions. It's also home to a branch of the tourist office. Before leaving, walk over to where the Town Hall fronts the square. On the ground you'll find 27 X's marking the spot where in 1621 the Hapsburgs beheaded 27 Bohemian noblemen in hopes of frightening the local populace into accepting Austrian rule. Austria remained in control for 300 years until the end of World War I. ⏱ *30 min. Staroměstské nám. 1/3.* ☎ *724-508-584. 60 Kč (tower). Apr–Oct Mon 11am–6pm, Tues–Sun 9am–6pm; Nov–Mar Mon 11am–5pm, Tues–Sun 9am–5pm.*

8 ★★★ **Astronomical Clock (Orloj).** If it's close to the top of the hour, race over to the city's number one crowd pleaser: the medieval astronomical clock. The clock was not used to tell time; instead it was meant to mark the phases of the moon, the seasons, and the Christian holidays. At the top of the hour, the brief, eerie, medieval morality play unfolds. Two doors slide open and the 12 apostles glide past, while the 15th-century symbols of evil—death, vanity, corruption, and greed—shake and dance below. Legend has it that Master Hanuš, one of the clock's designers, was blinded by the Municipal Council after he finished repairing the masterpiece so that he couldn't build an even more spectacular clock somewhere else. ⏱ *15 min.*

9 ★ **Karlova.** From the astronomical clock walk toward the adjoining Small Square (Malé nám.), passing the ornate Renaissance sgraffito of the "House at the Minute" (Dům u minuty). Franz Kafka lived here as a kid. Karlova street begins at the corner of the Small Square and wends its way eventually to the Charles Bridge (Karlův most). Not long ago this street was filled with student cafes and pubs. Now, with the massive influx of tourists, it's mostly T-shirt and glass shops, but still fun to meander. Astronomy buffs will be interested in the house at no. 4, once the residence of Johannes Kepler. It was Kepler who finally figured out the paths of the planets, settling once and for all the debate over whether the earth or the sun lies at the center of the solar system. ⏱ *20 min.*

10 **U zlatého tygra.** If it's after 3pm, stop at the intersection of Karlova and Husová for a quick beer or a light meal at one of the few remaining authentic Czech pubs in the center of the city. The Pilsner Urquell beer here is rumored to be the freshest in the city. It's still considered an "old man's pub," so you'll need to show respect for the regulars. This pub's place in Prague lore looms so large that Václav Havel even invited U.S. president Bill Clinton to have a beer here in 1994. *Husová 17.* ☎ *222-221-111. $.*

⓫ ★★★ Charles Bridge (Karlův most). Karlova eventually deposits you at the start of what is arguably Prague's most stunning architectural attraction. When this bridge was first built in the 14th and 15th centuries, it was considered one of the wonders of the known world. It was commissioned by Charles IV and laid out by Peter Parléř, one of the original architects of St. Vitus Cathedral. The Baroque statues that lend the bridge its unique character date from the 17th century. The stark religious imagery

was the work of the conquering Hapsburgs and represents their attempt to re-Catholicize the stubbornly Protestant Czechs. Before crossing the bridge, stop first to admire the Old Town Bridge Tower (Staroměstská mostecká věž). The eastern side of the tower, facing the Old Town, shows the original facade of the coats of arms of the Bohemian kings and the Holy Roman Empire. The western side was damaged in battle by Swedish troops at the end of the Thirty Years' War. If you're up for a climb, there's a picture-perfect view of the bridge waiting for you at the top. Most of the 30 or so statues that line the bridge are reproductions. Not all are considered artistic masterpieces, but each has a story to tell. The statue of the Bronze Crucifix (third on the right) is the oldest on the bridge and stands on a spot once occupied by a wooden crucifix. Legend has it the Hebrew inscription that reads HOLY, HOLY, HOLY GOD was

Karlova street.

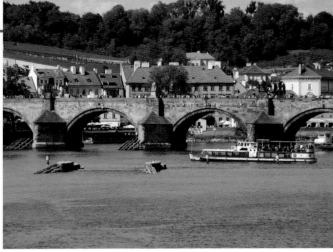

Charles Bridge.

forcibly paid for by an unknown Jew who had mocked the crucifix. The statue of St. John of Nepomuk (eighth on the right) is the most popular. He was allegedly tossed from this bridge and drowned; touching

St. Nicholas Church in Malá Strana (not to be confused with the church of the same name in Old Town Square).

his relief on the statue (now shiny gold) is said to bring good luck. Art critics judge the statue of St. Luitgarde kissing Christ's wounds (12th on the left), done by Baroque master Matthias Braun, as the most valuable. ⏱ *45 min. 60 Kč (to climb the Old Town Bridge Tower).*

12 **kids** **Bohemia Bagel.** There are several places within easy reach of this side of the Charles Bridge to have a full course meal with all the trimmings (see chapter 6), but if you're just looking for a quick and easy sandwich or bowl of soup, try this local branch of the Prague-wide Bohemia Bagel chain. Very good bagels with the standard toppings, or American-style sandwiches (steak and cheese, chicken salad) served on bagels, baguettes, or focaccia bread. Soups are often vegetarian and made fresh daily. They serve excellent full-course breakfasts until late morning. *Lázenská 19.* ☎ *220-806-590. $*

13 **Lesser Town Square (Malostranské nám.).** Walk below the Lesser Town Towers

(Malostranské mostecké věže), noting the smaller tower on the left. It was built in the 12th century and actually predates the bridge itself. Mostecká is the picturesque street that leads you to the focal point of the Lesser Town, Malostranské náměstí. There's not much to see here, but the square continues to function as an important transportation junction. 🕐 *10 min.*

⓮ ★★ **St. Nicholas Church (Kostel sv. Mikuláše).** This 18th-century church, the work of Killian Dienzenhofer and his son, is considered a masterpiece of high Baroque. In general, Czechs tend to favor Gothic over Baroque, associating the latter with the Austrian Hapsburg occupation, but nearly everyone loves this church. The voluptuous marble columns, the statues, and the frescoes are over the top in almost every way, but the exuberant interior somehow works. The exterior dome is especially lovely when viewed from the Charles Bridge. The church is one of the better venues for concerts. 🕐 *20 min. Malostranské nám. 1.* ☎ *257-534-215. 50 Kč. Daily 9am–5pm.*

⓯ ★ **Nerudová.** From St. Nicholas Church, follow this street uphill for the trek to Prague Castle. The street takes its name from Czech author Jan Neruda, who was born here in the 19th century. The Nobel prize–winning Chilean poet Pablo Neruda so admired Jan Neruda's writings that he adopted "Neruda" as a pen name. The street is lined with stunning Baroque palaces. Many have been given cute descriptive names. The house at no. 12, for example, is "The House of

Fighting giant statues atop Prague Castle's main entrance gate.

the Three Violins" (U tří housliček). My favorite is no. 11: "The House of the Red Lamb" (U červeného beránka). 🕐 *20 min.*

⓰ ★★★ **Prague Castle (Pražský hrad).** At the top of Nerudová are steps leading to Prague Castle. The castle complex, including the Royal Palace and St. Vitus Cathedral, has been the seat of political and religious authority in the Czech lands for nearly as long as there have been Czech lands. Unless you've jogged the entire Royal Route, it's unlikely that you'll have the time to make a full tour. Instead, save a more in-depth exploration of the castle for Day 2 (see the tour starting on p 30), and just take a peek inside to get your bearings. If this is your only chance to see the castle area, be sure check out St. Vitus. Entry into the cathedral is free. 🕐 *30 min.*

The Best **in Two Days**

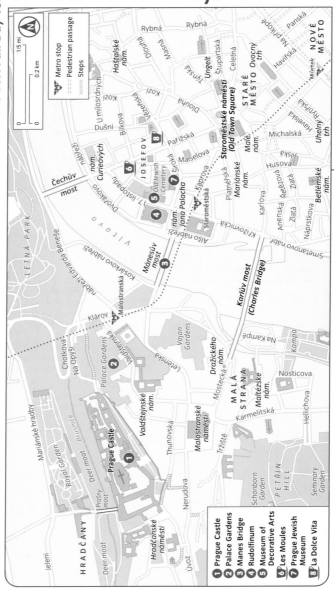

N

➊	Prague Castle
➋	Palace Gardens
➌	Manes Bridge
➍	Rudolfinum
➎	Museum of Decorative Arts
➏	Les Moules
➐	Prague Jewish Museum
➑	La Dolce Vita

Metro stop
Pedestrian passage
Steps

0   1/5 mi
0   0.2 km

The one-day tour of Prague was all about covering ground. This second-day tour is more about drilling down and focusing on the city's two world-class attractions: Prague Castle (Pražský hrad) and the Prague Jewish Museum (Židovské muzeum v Praze). Both tend to attract hordes of visitors, but are well worth any minor inconvenience. The tour is set up to begin at the castle and move across the river to the Jewish Museum, but it can easily be done in reverse. The important thing is to get an early start and don't try to push too hard. Budget a half-day for each and reward yourself with a nice lunch in between. This walk can easily be combined with the neighborhood tours of the Castle District (Hradčany) and the former Jewish Quarter (Josefov) described in chapter 3, but bear in mind that the more you tack on, the more time you'll need to finish.

START: Hradčanské nám. in front of the main castle entrance.

① ★★★ Prague Castle (Pražský hrad). The Prague Castle complex includes both the Royal Palace (Královský pálac), the residence of the early kings, and St. Vitus Cathedral (Chrám sv. Víta), the country's spiritual center. You can wander the castle grounds and enter St. Vitus for free, but to fully explore the major attractions and see the royal crypts and tower at St. Vitus, you need to buy a combined entry ticket. Two types of tickets—full-price and reduced admission—are available; which to choose depends on the amount of time you have and your level of interest. Both tickets are valid for the major attractions, including the Royal Palace, St. Vitus Cathedral, St. George's Basilica (Kostel sv. Jiří), and Golden Lane (Zlatá ulička). A full-price ticket also includes the Prague Castle Picture Gallery (Obrazárna Pražského hradu) and a special permanent exhibition in the Royal Palace titled "The Story of Prague Castle." If you're not well versed in the ups and downs of Czech history, consider renting a portable headset "audioguide." The English-language commentary runs long but provides badly needed context. For help navigating the castle, see the Prague Castle tour on p 30. ⏱ *3 hr. Hradčanské nám.* ☎ *224-372-423. www.hrad.cz. Full admission 350 Kč adults, 175 Kč children, 500 Kč family; reduced admission 250 Kč adults, 125 Kč children, 300 Kč family. Audioguide 300 Kč (full day), 250 Kč (2 hr). Daily Apr–Oct*

Stained glass window in St. Vitus Cathedral in the Prague Castle complex.

9am–6pm; Nov–Mar 9am–4pm. Metro: Malostranská (plus tram 22 or 23, two stops).

② ★ **Palace Gardens (Palácové zahrady).** Exit the castle complex on the lower end, beyond the Dalibor tower, and find the entrance to these five interconnected Baroque gardens that run downhill toward Malá Strana. One admission price gives you entry into all five gardens. The gardens are more fully described in the tour "The Gardens of Malá Strana" on p 90. Make your way downhill and exit on Valdštejnská. 🕐 45 min. ☎ 257-010-401. 79 Kč. Apr–Oct daily 10am–8pm.

③ **Manes Bridge (Manesův most).** From Valdštejnská walk past the Malostranská metro station and cross the Vltava River via this modern bridge. The Manes Bridge has nothing on the Charles Bridge in terms of beauty, but it provides a nice perspective on the impressive length of the Charles Bridge, which is quite a structure given the engineering limitations of the 14th century. 🕐 20 min.

④ **Rudolfinum.** Standing on your left as you leave the Manes Bridge on the Old Town side, the

neo-Renaissance Rudolfinum is the leading concert house in the Czech Republic and home to the Czech Philharmonic Orchestra (p 128). It's not normally open to the public for a look inside, but it's well worth trying to snag tickets to a performance. 🕐 10 min. Náměstí Jana Palacha. ☎ 227-059-227.

⑤ ★★ **Prague Museum of Decorative Arts (Uměleckoprůmyslové muzeum v Praze).** If you have a little time before lunch and want a quick diversion, this often-overlooked museum across the street from the Rudolfinum is worth a detour. The collection covers applied arts from the 16th to the 20th century, but the strong suit is the collection of early-20th-century Cubist, Art Nouveau, and Art Deco jewels, glass, textiles, and posters. Also be sure to head upstairs to the Votive Hall (Votivní sál) to see a set of 14th-century silver ornaments that were discovered hidden in the walls of Karlštejn Castle. The museum has a great if small gift shop and a popular onsite cafe that's a lifesaver when you're starting to wear down. 🕐 45 min. 17. listopadu 2. ☎ 251-093-111. 80 Kč. Daily 10am–6pm.

The Rudolfinum.

The Old Jewish Cemetery.

6 **Les Moules.** Before tackling the Jewish museum, have lunch at this Belgian-style bistro just around the corner from the museum's entrance. The specialty is mussels, but there are plenty of decent pork and steak entrees. Good Belgian beer on tap (and, naturally, excellent Czech beer as well). *Pařížská 19.* ☎ 222-315-022. $$.

7 ★★★ **Prague Jewish Museum (Židovské muzeum v Praze).** After Prague Castle, this is arguably the second most important tourist attraction in town. The Jewish Museum is a collection of surviving synagogues and the Old Jewish Cemetery (Starý židovský hřbitov) that date from the 15th to the 19th century, when Jews were forced to live in this tiny parcel just north of Old Town Square. The city of Prague cleared the Jewish Quarter and razed most of the buildings at the end of the 19th century after it had become a slum. Each of the four synagogues (Maisel, Pinkas, Klaus, and Spanish) has a separate exhibition on Jewish life, but the real highlight is the somber but spiritual Old Jewish Cemetery, crammed with

some 12,000 tombstones. A combined entry ticket gets you into the museum's four synagogues, plus the cemetery and the adjoining Ceremonial Hall. A separate ticket is required to visit the Old New Synagogue, the oldest still-functioning Jewish place of worship in Europe. For help navigating the Jewish Museum, see the Jewish Quarter tour on p 52. ⏱ *3 hr. U Starého hřbitova 3a.* ☎ *222-317-191. www. jewishmuseum.cz. Jewish Museum 300 Kč adults, 200 Kč children; Old New Synagogue 200 Kč adults, 140 Kč children; combination ticket 480 Kč adults, 320 Kč children. Apr–Oct Sun–Fri 9am–6pm; Nov–Mar Sun–Fri 9am–4:30pm. Closed on Jewish holidays.*

8 **La Dolce Vita.** After a grueling but fascinating day of sightseeing, it's time to repair for some coffee and refreshments. This is a local favorite with the shoppers and shop clerks from fashionable Pařížská street, who come for the espresso, cakes, sandwiches, and the chance to chill out. *Široká 15.* ☎ *224-226-546. $.*

The Best **in Three Days**

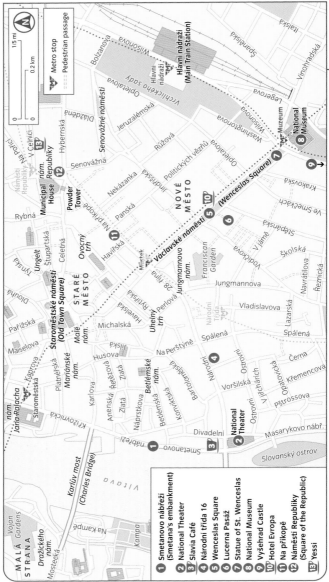

Metro stop
- - - Pedestrian passage

1/5 mi
0.2 km

1. Smetanovo nábřeží (Smetana's embankment)
2. National Theater
3. Slavia Café
4. Národní třída 16
5. Wenceslas Square
6. Lucerna Pasáž
7. Statue of St. Wenceslas
8. National Museum
9. Vyšehrad Castle
10. Hotel Evropa
11. Na příkopě
12. Náměstí Republiky (Square of the Republic)
13. Yessi

You can congratulate yourself at this point. If you've followed the previous days' tours, you've definitely hit the major sights, but what's missing is a feel for the modern city—that part of Prague life that takes place outside the tourist strongholds of the Old Town Square and Prague Castle. This tour is a grab bag—a little relaxing, a little shopping, and a little taste of the big city. START: **Staroměstská metro station.**

View from Smetanovo nábřeži.

① ★ Smetanovo nábřeži. (Smetana's Embankment).

From the metro station, find the tram stop on Křižovnická ul. and follow the street in the direction of the Charles Bridge. Pass the bridge and continue walking south, finding the sidewalk that takes you along the river. This is the Smetana embankment, named for Czech composer Bedřich Smetana, author of probably the best-known piece of Czech music outside the country: *The Moldau (Vltava)*. This also happens to be the place for that killer photograph, the one with the Charles

Bridge to the right and the castle above and behind. The best time to catch the view is mid-morning with the sun over your shoulder as you look out over the water. 🕐 *20 min.*

② ★ National Theater (Národní divadlo).

Continue walking until you reach the main cross street, Národní. You can't miss this neo-Renaissance masterpiece of a theater, a symbol of Czech nationalism, dating from the late 19th century. The theater took decades to build, but when it finally opened in 1881, it was destroyed by fire after

The National Theater.

Wenceslas Square.

only 12 performances. It was quickly rebuilt and opened again in 1883. Smetana composed the opera *Libuše* for the occasion. It's still the leading theater in the country and maintains a rotating program of theater, opera, and dance. It's rarely open to the public, but try to get tickets for something here (p 126). ◷ *10 min. Národní třída 2.* ☎ *224-901-668.*

③ **Slavia Café.** Stop for coffee at this legendary dissident cafe that has the added advantage of a perfect view over the river toward Prague Castle. The Slavia was once a meeting point for Václav Havel and other dissident intellectuals from the theater and film worlds. At one point in the 1980s, half of the cafe would be filled with dissidents and the other half with secret police. Now it's mostly for tourists, but serves good coffee and light meals. *Smetanovo náb. 2.* ☎ *224-218-493. $$.*

④ **Národní třída 16.** Stop here under an arcade to see a small plaque honoring the students who started the Velvet Revolution in 1989 that overthrew the communist government. The "Communist Prague" tour on p 38 goes into more detail, but it was at this point where the police stopped a group of student demonstrators on that fateful night of November 17, 1989.

That marked the beginning of the end for the authorities, as the demonstrations each night grew bigger and bigger. Ultimately there were hundreds of thousands of protesters. ◷ *10 min. Národní třída 16.*

⑤ ★★ **Wenceslas Square (Václavské náměsti).** Follow Národní to the end and then along a pedestrian walk to the base of Wenceslas Square. After Old Town Square, this upwardly sloping boulevard is the most famous "square" in the city. It began life in the 14th century as Prague's horse market but has since evolved into the commercial heart of the city and also the symbolic center of the nation's conscience. Crowds have gravitated here to celebrate every milestone, or protest every defeat, for the past 200 years—independence from Austria in 1918, the Nazi occupation in 1939, the Soviet-led invasion in 1968, the funeral for student martyr Jan Palach in 1969, and finally the Velvet Revolution in 1989. The square was built up in the 19th and 20th centuries and lacks the harmony of the Old Town Square. Nearly all of the fashions in vogue during this time can be seen here, from the neo-Renaissance National Museum at the top of the square to the turn-of-the-century Art Nouveau style of the Hotel Evropa (no. 25) and the functionalist style of the

1920s and 1930s (Bata shoe store, no 6). 🕐 *30 min. Václavské nám.*

6 ★★ **Lucerna Pasáž.** Walk up the square on the right-hand side. Fans of the 1920s and 1930s will love the retro styling of the Lucerna Pasáž shopping center, the most attractive of the many shopping arcades on both sides of the square. There's not much to buy here, but there are a number of interesting cafes, a 1920s-era cinema, and even a statue of St. Wenceslas riding on an upside-down horse hanging from the ceiling, courtesy of Czech artist David Černý. You can enter the Lucerna Pasáž from either Vodičk-ová or Štěpánská streets. 🕐 *15 min. Štěpánská 61.* ☎ *224-224-537.*

7 **Statue of St. Wenceslas.** At the top of the square stands the very equestrian statue that Černý was poking fun at. St. Wenceslas, a former Bohemian prince, is one of the patron saints of the Czech lands, and it was from the base of this statue that the proclamation of Czechoslovak statehood was first read out in 1918. Love it or loathe it, the statue plays a practical role as the most popular meeting spot in the city—if a Prague resident suggests that you meet "at the horse," this is where you should go. 🕐 *10 min.*

Statue of St. Wenceslas, with the National Museum in the background.

8 ★ **National Museum (Národní Muzeum).** Like the National Theater and the Rudolfinum, the construction of the National Museum was closely tied up in the Czech national revival movement of the 19th century. The stern neo-Renaissance facade was badly damaged in the 1968 Warsaw Pact invasion when it was fired on by Russian troops. Today, the museum houses enormous collections of minerals, remnants from archaeological digs, folk costumes, pottery, coins, textiles, sheet music—nearly everything that a museum can collect. More interesting than the collections themselves perhaps is the enormous Pantheon interior. 🕐 *15 min to view the facade, 2 hr. to visit. Václavské*

Viewing the National Museum's elaborate interior might be worth the visit alone.

nám. 68. ☎ *224-497-111. 120 Kč. Daily May–Sept 10am–6pm; Oct–Apr 9am–5pm (closed every first Tues of the month).*

⑨ ★★ Vyšehrad Castle. If it's a beautiful day and you feel like getting out of the city, skip the rest of the tour and instead hop the metro (C line) two stops south to the ruins of Vyšehrad Castle. Vyšehrad was the seat of the first Czech kings in the Přemyslid dynasty going back to before the turn of the first millennium. Legend has it that well over a thousand years ago, Princess Libuše (of Smetana opera fame) looked out over the Vltava river valley from this spot and predicted the founding of a great city. Today, the main fortifications remain on rocky cliffs, blocking out the noise and confusion from below. It's a perfect place to drop a blanket and have a picnic or just take the day off. The Vyšehrad Cemetery (Vyšehradský hřbitov) on the castle grounds is one of the most important in the country. It's the final resting place of composers Antonín Dvořák and Bedřich Smetana and Art Nouveau painter Alfons Mucha, among others. *Soběslavová 1.* ☎ *241-410-348. www.praha-vysehrad.cz. No admission. Metro: Vyšehrad (plus a considerable walk).*

Hotel Evropa.

⑩ Hotel Evropa. If you decide not to head out to Vyšehrad Castle, continue the tour here. From the top of Wenceslas Square, turn back toward the lower end walking along the opposite side of the square. The cafe of this glorious Art Nouveau hotel is the perfect perch to take a break. In the summer, sit on the terrace; in winter, relax amid the turn-of-the-century splendors. It's the most ornate interior on the square, bar none. *Václavské nám. 68.* ☎ *224-215-387. $.*

⑪ Na příkopě. Turn right at the bottom of Wenceslas Square onto the broad pedestrian street Na příkopě. The name of the street means "at the ditch," referring to a time when this street was a moat separating the Old Town (Staré Město) to the left from the New Town (Nové Město) to the right. Despite its humble name, today it commands some of the highest office-rental prices in Europe, and is home to some of the city's best shopping. ⏱ *20 min.*

⑫ Náměstí Republiky (Square of the Republic). Na příkopě leads to Náměstí Republiky and numerous tram and metro connections. Though Náměstí Republiky itself holds two of Prague's finest buildings (the Powder Tower and the Municipal House), it's an architectural potpourri that's never really worked as a public square. As this book was going to press, an enormous shopping mall, the Palladium, had just opened at the far end of the square. ⏱ *10 min.*

⑬ Yessi. The slogan at this sandwich shop/deli is "positive eating," meaning they use healthful, fresh ingredients. Excellent sandwiches, wraps, and a well-tended salad bar are nice ways to end a long walk. *V Celnici 4.* ☎ *222-212-585. $.* ●

Kafka's Prague

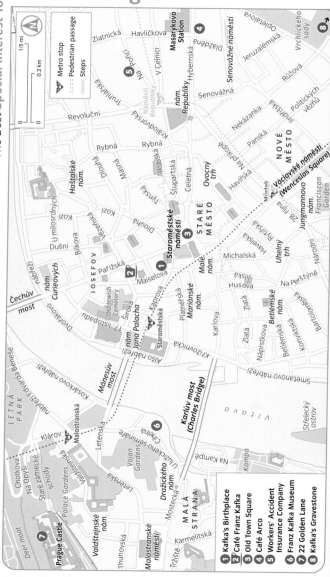

Legend:
- Metro stop
- - - - Pedestrian passage
- Steps

0 — 1/5 mi
0 — 0.2 km

Previous page: Detail of Vyšehrad Castle door.

1 Kafka's Birthplace
2 Café Franz Kafka
3 Old Town Square
4 Café Arco
5 Workers' Accident Insurance Company
6 Franz Kafka Museum
7 22 Golden Lane
8 Kafka's Gravestone

Map labels:
Zlatnická, Havlíčkova, Masarykovo Station, Opletalova, Vrchlického sady, V Celnici, Dlážděná, Jeruzalémská, Na Poříčí, náměstí Republiky, Truhlářská, nám. Republiky, Revoluční, Králodvorská, Senovážná, Hybernská, Senovážné náměstí, Růžová, Politických vězňů, Rybná, Rybná, Nekázanka, Panská, NOVÉ MĚSTO, Dlouhá, Masná, Jakubská, Na příkopě, Havířská, Ovocný trh, Václavské náměstí (Wenceslas Square), Haštalské nám., Kozí, Týnská, Celetná, Štupartská, STARÉ MĚSTO, 28. října, Jungmannovo nám., Franciscan Garden, U milosrdných, Vězeňská, Dušní, Bílkova, Kozí, Staroměstské náměstí, Melantrichova, Rytířská, Michalská, Uhelný trh, Národní, nábřeží, JOSEFOV, Pařížská, Maiselova, Malé nám., Jilská, Na Perštýně, náb. Curieových, Čechův most, Dvořákovo nábřeží, Old Jewish Cemetery, Široká, Kaprova, Platnéřská, Mariánské nám., Husova, Betlémské nám., Zlatá, nám. Jana Palacha, 17. listopadu, Staroměstská, Karlova, Náprstkova, Betlémská, Zlatá, Konviktská, Bartolomějská, Alšovo nábřeží, Křižovnická, Smetanovo nábřeží, Mánesův most, Karlův most (Charles Bridge), VLTAVA, Střelecký ostrov, LETNÁ PARK, nábřeží Edvarda Beneše, Kosárkovo nábřeží, Klárov, Malostranská, Letenská, U lužického semináře, Čihelná, Na Kampě, Kampa, Chotkova, Na Opyši, Staré zámecké schody, Valdštejnská, Palace Gardens, Vojan Gardens, Dražického nám., Mostecká, Prague Castle, Deer moat, Valdštejnské nám., Malostranské náměstí, MALÁ STRANA, Karmelitská, Thunovská, Tržiště

The former communist government was never entirely comfortable with Franz Kafka, the German-Jewish writer who was born here in 1883. Kafka's themes of bureaucracy and alienation were too close to the grim reality of day-to-day life of pre-1989 Prague, and Kafka was all but ignored by the powers that were. All of that changed after the Velvet Revolution, and a caricature of Kafka's familiar face—complete with his overly elongated ears—can be found on posters, T-shirts, and coffee mugs in every souvenir shop in town. Perhaps it's ironic that a somber German-Jewish intellectual—the father of the modern novel—should somehow be adopted by the tourist industry as one of the faces of new Prague. On the other hand, given the city's turbulent history of Nazi occupation followed by communist dictatorship, perhaps it's more than fitting. Kafka died fully 15 years before the start of World War II, but in retrospect, his novels seem eerily prophetic of what was to come. START: **Old Town Square (Staroměstské nám.).**

① ★ **Kafka's Birthplace.** Just beside the St. Nicholas Church (Chrám sv. Mikuláše) stands the house where Kafka was born. At the time, the neighborhood was still pretty seedy, just on the edge of the then-Jewish ghetto. The actual house was destroyed by fire and the only element remaining is the impressive doorway. The plaque on the side of the house reads in Czech FRANZ KAFKA WAS BORN HERE ON JULY 3, 1883. Part of the house now holds a small permanent exhibition of Kafka's writings. The gift shop is better than the exhibition itself. ⏱ *20 min. Expozice Franze Kafky. U radnice 5. No phone. 40 Kč. Daily 10am–6pm. Metro: Staroměstská.*

② **Café Franz Kafka.** Perfectly in keeping with the Kafka theme, this little cafe around the corner from Kafka's birthplace feels almost like a shrine. They serve excellent coffee drinks and light food options like sandwiches and salads. The beautiful photos of old Prague on the wall will put you in the mood for a literary crawl. *Široká 12.* ☎ *222-318-945. $.*

③ ★★★ **Old Town Square (Staroměstské nám.).** Kafka spent many of his formative years on Old Town Square and the surrounding streets. Kafka's father, a haberdasher, married well, and the family was moving up the social ladder. One of their

This plaque marks Kafka's birthplace.

nicer apartments was at Staroměstské nám. 2 (the Renaissance house "U Minuty") just beside the Astronomical Clock. As a boy, Kafka attended the German grammar school across the square at the bright-pink Kinský Palace (Staroměstské nám. 12). His father ran a haberdashery in the same building (commemorated by a plaque on the courtyard wall). Later in his life, ill with tuberculosis, Kafka lived again with his family at Staroměstské nám. 5. Here he worked on probably his most famous book, *The Castle,* and several short stories. My favorite Kafka memorial is found at Staroměstské nám. 17, the former home of socialite Berta Fanta, who ran a weekly salon in her drawing room. A plaque on the house reads: HERE IN THIS SALON OF MRS. BERTA FANTA, ALBERT EINSTEIN, PROFESSOR AT PRAGUE UNIVERSITY IN 1911 TO 1912, FOUNDER OF THE THEORY OF RELATIVITY, NOBEL PRIZE WINNER, PLAYED THE VIOLIN AND MET HIS FRIENDS, FAMOUS WRITERS, MAX BROD AND FRANZ KAFKA. Wow. ⏱ *20 min. Metro: Staroměstská.*

Einstein plaque at Staroměstské nám.

④ ★ Café Arco. Leave the square walking down Celetná, passing another of the Kafka family residences at no. 2. Continue straight beyond the Powder Tower, following the street Hybernská to find the Café Arco. Unfortunately, little remains of this once-illustrious cafe, one of the centers of German-Jewish intellectual life in the early years of the 20th century. The Arco now houses a depressing cafeteria for police officers and some other random offices. It was also a favorite of Max Brod, Kafka's faithful friend and the man arguably most responsible for Kafka's posthumous fame. On his death, Franz Kafka asked that his writings be destroyed. Brod instead cobbled them together,

edited them, and sought out a publisher. The rest is literary history. The Arco was not the only cafe Kafka frequented. He occasionally favored the Café Louvre at Národní třída 22 and the now-defunct Café Continental at Na příkopě 17. ⏱ *10 min. Hybernská 16. ☎ 974-863-542. Metro: Náměstí Republiky.*

⑤ ★★ The former Workers' Accident Insurance Company. Franz Kafka lived a double life. By night he was the consummate haunted intellectual, scribbling about alienation and the modern condition. By day, he was a mild-mannered claims adjuster for the insurance company that once stood at Na poříčí 7. The original building still exists, but today houses the Mercure Hotel. Kafka's office was located where room 214 now stands, and the receptionist will happily show you the room if it's empty. Real fans can book the room for the night, but it's not much different from any other room. ⏱ *15 min. Hotel Mercure. Na poříčí 7. ☎ 221-800-800. Metro: Náměstí Republiky.*

⑥ ★★★ Franz Kafka Museum. The tour picks up across the river in Malá Strana. The easiest way to get here is to catch the metro at Náměstí Republiky (Line B), changing lines at Mustek (Line A) and continuing to Malostranská. From Malostranská

Photograph of Franz Kafka.

Kafka once lived in this blue house at 22 Golden Lane.

station, the Kafka Museum is about a 10-minute walk. This relatively new museum is a more serious treatment of Kafka's life and works than the exhibition at Kafka's birthplace (see above). The museum has two sections, one focusing on the influence of Prague on Kafka's work and the other a video display of Kafka's Prague. 🕐 *1 hr. Hergetova Cihelná. Cihelná 2b.* ☎ *257-535-507. 120 Kč. Daily 10am–6pm. Metro: Malostranská.*

7 ★ 22 Golden Lane (Zlatá ulička 22). The next stop is within the Prague Castle complex on a tiny street that once housed castle artisans. From the Kafka museum, you can return to the Malostranská metro station and then hike up the steps that lead up to the castle from the right of the station—though it's best to combine your visit here with a full castle tour (see "A Day at Prague Castle," below) since the admission price to Golden Lane is included in the ticket. Kafka's sister rented this tiny room from 1916 to 1917 and allowed her brother to live and work here for a time. During the early years of the 20th century, Golden

Lane was a kind of eclectic Bohemian ghetto filled with eccentrics and creative types. Now it's mostly T-shirt and glass shops. There's a small gift shop here and a tiny marker on the house that states in Czech: FRANZ KAFKA LIVED HERE. 🕐 *30 min. Zlatá ulička 22. Hradčany. Metro: Malostranská (plus tram 22 or 23, two stops).*

8 ★★★ Kafka's Gravestone. Kafka died in 1924 at a sanatorium in Vienna of tuberculosis. He was only 41 years old. He's buried in the New Jewish Cemetery in the Prague suburb of Strašnice. From Malostranská or Hradčanská metro stations take the A line to Želivského. From here it's just a short walk to the cemetery and signs will point you along the way to sector 21, where Kafka's grave marker stands. "Dr. Franz Kafka" is buried under a simple white stone

along with his parents, Hermann and Julie Kafka. A small plaque below is dedicated to Kafka's three sisters, all of whom died in Nazi concentration camps during World War II. 🕐 *30 min. New Jewish Cemetery (Nový židovský hřbitov). Metro: Želivského.*

Kafka's gravestone, in the New Jewish Cemetery.

A Day at Prague Castle

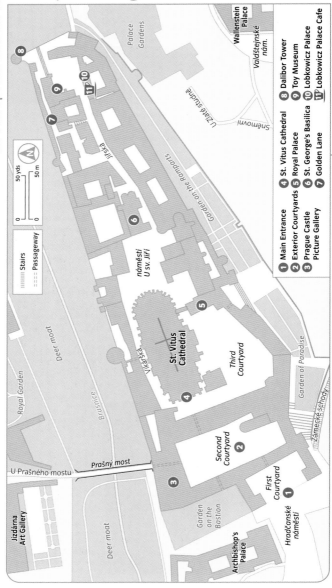

1 Main Entrance
2 Exterior Courtyards
3 Prague Castle Picture Gallery
4 St. Vitus Cathedral
5 Royal Palace
6 St. George's Basilica
7 Golden Lane
8 Dalibor Tower
9 Toy Museum
10 Lobkowicz Palace
11 Lobkowicz Palace Cafe

Stairs
Passageway

N

0   50 yds
0   50 m

Touring Prague Castle can be a bewildering proposition. First there's the sheer size. It's the largest castle complex in the world. Then there's the fact that the historical events and personalities behind the buildings are not well known to most visitors. You may have some dim recollection of Charles IV or Rudolf II from a past European History class, but what about Adalbert or Sigismund or the Přemyslid dynasty? Still, the castle complex—which includes St. Vitus Cathedral, the Royal Palace, St. George's Basilica, Golden Lane, and other major sights—is such a treasure-trove of art, architecture, jewels, tombs, and jaw-dropping views that it's well worth the effort. Be sure to leave yourself at least good half a day to do it justice. See the box "Prague Castle: Practical Matters," later in this chapter, for ticket information. START: **Hradčanské nám.**

❶ ★ **Main entrance.** The main entry to the castle complex, fronting Hradčanské náměstí, was built to impress. Note the oversized gates and imposing statues of the Battling Titans above. Two guards stand watch and every hour on the hour there's a ritual changing of the guard. Feel free to stand alongside for a photo—the guards are trained not to pay attention but sometimes their eyes stray. ⏱ *15 min.*

❷ **Exterior courtyards.** Proceed through the main gate (entry is free) and walk into the First Castle Courtyard (První hradní nádvoří), passing through another impressive entryway—the Matthias Gate (Matyášova brána)—into the Second Castle Courtyard (Druhé hradní nádvoří). As you go through the Matthias Gate, look to the right to see the offices of the Czech presidency (closed to the public). Both the first and second courtyards, which reflect the formal tastes of the 18th-century Austrian aristocracy, are on the bland side. ⏱ *10 min.*

❸ ★ **Prague Castle Picture Gallery (Obrazárna Pražského hradu).** The entrance to the gallery lies to the left as you enter the second courtyard. We can only imagine

Prague Castle Picture Gallery.

the treasures it once held as the court gallery for Rudolf II. Unfortunately, the holdings were plundered in the Thirty Years' War, and those scattered pictures that survived, more often than not, were carted off to galleries in Vienna. A few masterpieces remain, including works by court favorites Hans von Aachen and Bartholomeus Spranger. ⏱ *30 min.* ☎ *224-373-531. Entry is included in the full-price ticket to the castle complex. Separate admission is 150 Kč. Daily Apr–Oct 9am–6pm; Nov–Mar 9am–4pm.*

❹ ★★★ **St. Vitus Cathedral (Chrám sv. Víta).** Follow the small entryway that leads to the Third Castle Courtyard (Třetí hradní nádvoří) and prepare for a shock— an enormous Gothic cathedral squeezed in among the castle walls. It's hard to exaggerate the importance of St. Vitus Cathedral to the national identity, even if the Czechs are not considered overly religious. Construction began in 1344 on order of Charles IV, but the cathedral was not finished until 1929. In addition to serving as the center of the Catholic Church, the cathedral's crypts hold the remains of the land's most famous rulers, including Charles IV and Rudolf II. Each of the chapels that line the sides of the church seems to hold yet another legend dear to the hearts of Czechs. Leave at least an hour to tour the

St. Vitus Cathedral.

cathedral and the crypts. Entry to the cathedral is free, though you'll need to buy a full castle admission to see the Royal Crypt or climb the South Tower.

The entrance to the cathedral is through the left-hand door at the front and foot traffic moves clockwise once inside. The left side of the front half of the church is lined with small chapels—the most interesting one being the third, with its stained-glass windows painted by the Czech Art Nouveau master Alfons Mucha. Farther along on the left-hand side are the confessionals and, above, an organ loft with an amazing 18th-century organ. As you move deeper into the church, you enter the older section. Here the chapels hold the remains of some of the earliest rulers of the Czech lands, going back nearly 1,000 years. As you proceed around the back, you come to the gaudy, silver sarcophagus of St. John of Nepomuk, a jarring Baroque contrast to the more subdued Gothic of much of the rest of the church. Just beyond this, you'll find the stairs leading underground to the Royal Crypt (Královská krypta), holding the remains of, among others, Charles IV and his four wives, as well as Rudolf II, Wenceslas IV, and King George of Poděbrady. Back up on the main level, you'll see steps— 287 in all—leading up to the South Tower lookout gallery. It's a slow, arduous climb, but well worth it for some amazing views over the Old Town and Malá Strana. Back on ground level in the cathedral, heading toward the exit, you find the most beautiful of all the 22 side chapels, the Chapel of St. Wenceslas (Svatováclavská kaple). Wenceslas—immortalized as a "king" in Christmas carols—was in fact an early Christian prince who was killed by his power-hungry brother Boleslav in A.D. 935. He was canonized soon thereafter. The chapel is considered the spiritual heart of the cathedral and was built over Wenceslas's tomb. Access to the chapel is restricted, but notice the inlaid jewels that cover the walls and altar. A doorway at the back leads to the Crown Chamber and the repository of the Bohemian crown jewels (not open to the public). ⏱ *60 min.*

5 ★★★ **Royal Palace (Královský pálac).** The entrance to the Royal Palace lies to the right of the cathedral facing the front of the church. Until the 16th century this was the main residence of the castle complex. The chief sight here is the enormous Vladislav Hall (Vladislavský sál), noted for its size and its rib-vaulted ceilings—the work of celebrated late Gothic architect Benedikt Ried. At the time it was a tremendous technical feat to have an enclosed room of this size without supporting pillars. Over the centuries, the room has hosted jousting matches, coronations, feasts of all kinds, and in modern

times the inaugurations of Czech presidents. At the end of the Vladislav Hall a door leads to the Ludwig Wing, the site of the infamous 1618 defenestration of two Catholic governors and their secretary that led to the carnage of the Thirty Years' War. Also here is the Old Diet (Stará Sněmovná), the former court where the king would meet with the high representatives of the church on one side and the nobility on the other. ⏱ *45 min. Entry to the Royal Palace is included in both the full- & reduced-price Castle admissions.*

6 ★★ **St. George's Basilica (Kostel sv. Jiří).** Just down from the Royal Palace, you can't miss the simplicity of St. George's Basilica, Prague's oldest surviving Romanesque building dating from the 10th century. After the opulence of St. Vitus Cathedral, St. George's appears positively quaint and welcoming. The main sights here are the building itself and the tomb of St. Ludmila, the grandmother of

The Riding Hall at Royal Palace.

St. George's Basilica.

History 101: Prague Castle

Prague Castle has been at the center of political and religious authority throughout the history of the Czech lands. Archaeological finds indicate there's been a castle on this site since the 9th century, and the complex of royal residences, monasteries, and churches was built up and added to piecemeal over the years. The high point came in the 14th century during the reign of Holy Roman Emperor Charles IV, who made the castle his Imperial residence. He rebuilt the Royal Palace and began work on St. Vitus Cathedral, emulating the best of French Gothic cathedrals of the day. The castle's fortunes waxed and waned with the fate of the Czech lands, falling into ruin during the Hussite wars of the 15th century, then returning to glory during the reign of Holy Roman Emperor Rudolf II at the turn of the 17th century. The defenestration at Prague Castle in 1618—when a group of Protestant noblemen pushed two Catholic governors from a high window and onto a dung heap below—sparked a religious conflagration that spread throughout Europe: the Thirty Years' War. The castle complex languished during the 300 years of Hapsburg occupation until 1918, but once again became the seat of power with the founding of independent Czechoslovakia at the end of World War I. During World War II, the Nazi ruler of Bohemia and Moravia, Reinhard Heydrich, took up residency here. Today the castle serves as the official residence of Czech presidents, though Václav Havel, a modest man, never felt comfortable amid the ostentatious splendor. He preferred his more modest villa in the Prague suburb of Střešovice.

St. Wenceslas. Next to the basilica is the St. George Convent, the oldest convent in the country and now housing a permanent exhibition of Czech Gothic art. ⏱ *30 min. Entry to St. George's Basilica is included in both the full- & reduced-price Castle admissions. Entry to St George's Convent & the museum is included in the full-price ticket only. Separate admission is 100 Kč.*

7 ★★ **Golden Lane (Zlatá ulička).** The ramshackle houses here on this street are impossibly tiny—usually simple one- or two-room abodes, without anything like a kitchen or a bathroom to make them livable. Nonetheless, they housed the castle guards in the 16th century and continued to function as more or less normal dwellings up until the 20th century. Franz Kafka was perhaps the most famous resident, living for a short time at no. 22 (See the tour "Kafka's Prague," above). Now the lane looks like nothing more than a film set. The houses have been converted to gift shops, selling the usual collection of glass, books, and T-shirts. ⏱ *20 min. Entry to Golden Lane is included in both the full- & reduced-price Castle admissions. Separate admission is 50 Kč.*

8 **Dalibor Tower (Daliborka).** Continuing on down toward the end of the complex brings you to a tower that once held the castle's prison. Dalibor, one of the first prisoners here, was a nobleman accused of leading a popular revolt in the 15th century. He apparently learned to play the violin while imprisoned here, and according to legend, the citizens of Prague would gather round to listen to him play. The music stopped in 1498 with his execution. ⏱ *10 min.*

9 **Toy Museum (Muzeum hraček).** Walking through a series of doorways and exit signs takes you to a small courtyard that houses a cafe and this toy museum, housed in what was once the Supreme Burgrave, the seat of the castle administration. Younger children will enjoy this collection of traditional toys, including classic dolls, wooden figures, and trains. The most valuable item is a 2,000-year-old doll from ancient Greece. Note that this is one of the few attractions within the castle complex not included within the general admission price. Nice to know before you've hiked the three flights of stairs to the ticket office. ⏱ *30 min. Jiřská 6.* ☎ *224-372-294. 60 Kč. Daily 9:30am–5pm.*

10 ★★ **Lobkowicz Palace.** Just outside the courtyard, this former 16th-century residence of the noble Lobkowicz family now houses a private exhibition called "The Princely

Lobkowicz Palace and Dalibor Tower.

Prague Castle: Practical Matters

Entry into the Castle grounds and St. Vitus Cathedral is free, but to tour the Royal Palace and to see the other major sights, including the Royal Crypts at St. Vitus, requires a ticket. Buy tickets at the Prague Castle Information Center located in the second court-yard after you pass through the main gates. Two types of tickets are available. Full-price admission (350 Kč adults, 175 Kč children, 500 Kč family) gets you into the Royal Palace, the Royal Crypt and South Tower of St. Vitus Cathedral, St. George's Basilica and Convent, Golden Lane, the Prague Castle Picture Gallery, and a special perma-nent exhibition in the Royal Palace titled "The Story of Prague Cas-tle." A reduced admission (250 Kč adults, 125 Kč children, 300 Kč family) includes only the Royal Palace, the St. Vitus sights, St. George's Basilica, and Golden Lane. The reduced admission is suffi-cient if you have only a couple of hours. English guides are available for 100 Kč per person. If you'd rather explore on your own, rent a small "audioguide," a hand-held recording that takes you to about 50 sights in the Cathedral and the Castle. The commentary, available in several languages, is a little on the long side (you can fast-forward through the slow parts), but adds much-needed context. Audiogu-ides cost 250 Kč for 2 hours, and 300 Kč all day. One or two audiogu-ides is sufficient to share among a small group. Hradčanské náměstí. ☎ **224-372-423.** Open daily April to October from 9am to 6pm, November to March from 9am to 4pm. Metro: Malostranská (plus tram 22 or 23, two stops).

Collections," highlighting the fam-ily's eclectic holdings of paintings, sheet music, rare books, and arms. The paintings include works by Brueghel the Elder and Velázquez, among others. Entry is not included in the castle admission price. 🕐 *60 min. Jiřská 3.* ☎ *602-595-998. 275 Kč (adults), 175 Kč (children 5–15). Daily 10:30am–6pm.*

🔟 **Lobkowicz Palace Cafe.** By this time, you'll be long overdue for coffee or a snack. Even if you don't visit the palace, stop by the court-yard cafe just to the right of the palace entrance. The castle area is not generally known for good or

reasonably priced refreshments. Here, the prices are just as high as elsewhere, but the soups, sand-wiches, and wraps are freshly made, and you may even be serenaded by palace musicians. *Jiřská 3.* ☎ *602-595-998. $$.*

Finish the tour by hiking downhill in the direction of Malá Strana. Steps take you down to near the Mal-ostranská metro station. Or if you've got some daylight left, spend time admiring the beautiful castle gar-dens that surround the complex on both the north and south sides.

German troops marching through the Prague castle gates in 1938, during their invasion of Czechoslovakia.

Modern Art off the Beaten Path

★★ **Veletržní palace,** the National Gallery's collection of modern and contemporary art, is housed on several floors of a restored functionalist building in the outlying district of Holešovice, at Dukelských hrdinů 47 (☎ **224-301-024;** www.ngprague.cz). This was originally hoped to be Prague's version of Paris's Centre Pompidou or New York's MoMA, but it's still a ways off. For one thing, the scruffy Holešovice locale doesn't quite gel. Still, the collection has many high points, including works by Monet, Renoir, Van Gogh, Matisse, Schiele, Klimt, and Picasso, among others. The fascinating 1920s building was designed by architects Josef Fuchs and Oldrich Tyl. When it was done, Swiss Modern master Le Corbusier famously commented it was interesting but not quite "architecture." Partial admissions are available if you're interested in seeing only one floor or one collection. Allow at least an hour for a visit. Full admission is 250 Kč. Open Tuesday to Sunday from 10am to 6pm. The closest Metro stop is Vltavská.

Communist Prague

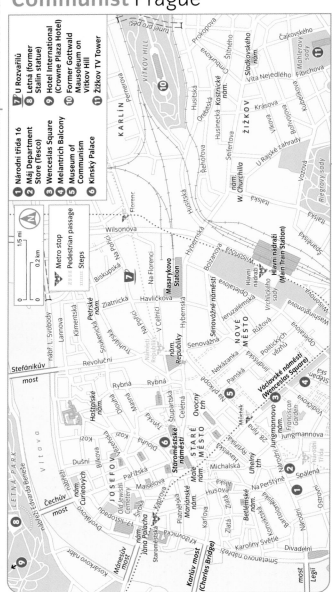

1 Národní třída 16
2 Máj Department Store (Tesco)
3 Wenceslas Square
4 Melantrich Balcony
5 Museum of Communism
6 Kinsky Palace
7 U Rozvařilů
8 Letná (former Stalin statue)
9 Hotel International (Crowne Plaza Hotel)
10 Former Gottwald Mausoleum on Vítkov Hill
11 Žižkov TV Tower

Walking around this colorful and lively city today, it's hard to believe that less than 2 decades ago the Czech Republic was part of the "Eastern Bloc" and the "Warsaw Pact"—as grey and "Soviet" as Leonid Brezhnev's ashen face. Happily, those days are long gone, but a few interesting relics remain scattered around the city as a reminder of those bad old days. This tour begins by following the trail of the moving 1989 student protest known as the Velvet Revolution that peacefully ended 40 years of Communist rule. The start of the tour is easy to walk, and each sight follows closely from the previous one. The last three stops on the tour, though, are more spread out. You may want to choose one or two of the destinations and leave the others for another day. START: **Národní 16, Metro to Národní třída (Line B).**

❶ ★★ Národní třída 16. This address on one of the city's major arteries, Národní třída (National Avenue), near the intersection with Mikulandská ul., marks the spot where the Velvet Revolution began and Czechoslovak Communism was finally defeated. On the night of November 17, 1989, a group of students and activists—encouraged by anti-Communist revolutions elsewhere in Eastern Europe and tired of 40 years of repressive rule here—assembled near the Vltava river and began marching up Národní on their way to Wenceslas Square. The group got as far as this building at no. 16—now memorialized by a simple plaque—before police confronted them and tried to drive them back. It's not clear what really happened that night (there was even a rumor—later disproved—that one of the students, Martin Šmíd, had been killed), but word of the confrontation quickly spread across the country, sparking weeks

of huge demonstrations. By the end of the year, the Communists had capitulated and the revolution's spiritual hero, the dissident playwright Václav Havel, was president. ⏱ *15 min. Národní třída 16, Prague 1. Metro: Národní třída.*

❷ Máj Department Store (Tesco). Walk down Národní třída a couple of blocks toward Wenceslas Square to the intersection with Spalená ul. When this department store was built in the mid-1970s, the building's "love it or loathe it" Brutalist architecture was hailed as a high point of Communist-era design. Brutalism was a popular international style that emphasized exposing a building's inner workings (like pipes and ducts) on the outside. The architects modeled the building on Paris's Centre Georges Pompidou, but there's little resemblance. Critics later derided Brutalism as hideously ugly (the world's most vocal critic was probably Britain's Prince

Velvet revolution marker.

Soviet troops invading Prague in August 1968 to crush the "Prague Spring" reform.

Charles, who famously labeled Brutalist buildings "carbuncles.") A couple of years ago, the current owner, the British retailer Tesco, announced plans to knock the building down and start over. Fans of communist architecture then complained, and now the building—much like the Charles Bridge and the Old Town's Astronomical Clock—is an officially protected cultural landmark. ⏱ *10 min. Národní třída 26, Prague 1. Metro: Národní třída.*

③ ★★ **Wenceslas Square (Václavské nám.).** Continue walking along Národní třída to one of the biggest and best-known squares in Prague. Wenceslas Square has always found itself at the heart of turbulent times. At the end of World War I, thousands gathered here to demand independence from Austria-Hungary; in the run-up to World War II, thousands more came here to protest the Nazi occupation. The tradition continued during the Velvet Revolution. Night after night in those heady days of November 1989, hundreds of thousands of Czechs (and Slovaks) came here to voice their opposition to the Communist regime and to jangle their keys (a way of telling their geriatric overlords it was time to leave).

About three-quarters of the way up the square, just below the statue of the horseman, you'll find a small monument (often strewn with flowers) to the "Victims of Communism." You'll also see plaques marking the memory of two Czech students, Jan Palach and Jan Zajíc, who immolated themselves at separate times in 1969 to protest the Soviet-led invasion of the country a year earlier. That invasion, in August 1968, devastated Czechoslovakia and put a bitter end to a period of hope and political reform known as the "Prague Spring." It ushered in 20 more years of dreary, Soviet-style Communism. ⏱ *45 min. Václavské nám., Prague 1. Metro: Mustek.*

④ ★ **Melantrich Balcony.** Just opposite the memorial to the Victims of Communism, at no. 36 Wenceslas Square (now a branch of the British Marks & Spencer store), you will see a balcony jutting from the Melantrich publishing house. This is where, in late November 1989, the dissident playwright (and soon to be president) Václav Havel made his first historic appearances in front of the hundreds of thousands of people who were clamoring for his leadership. His mumbling yet defiant speeches solidified his position as the popular choice to guide Czechoslovakia out of those dark days. On at least one famous occasion, Alexander Dubček—the popular, ousted leader of the "Prague Spring" reforms—joined Havel on the balcony. By then, Dubček was an old man and had been out of the spotlight for 20 years, but the crowds cheered him on anyway. ⏱ *10 min. Václavské nám. 36, Prague 1. Metro: Mustek.*

⑤ ★★★ **Museum of Communism.** Walk back to the bottom of Wenceslas Square and follow the pedestrian street Na příkopě that leads off to the right. You'll find the "Museum of Communism" a couple of blocks down in a small passageway next to a McDonald's restaurant. Leave it to an American to find a way of making money from Communism. For years after 1989 there was no museum or central focal point to remember the 40 years of Soviet domination here, and in 2001 American entrepreneur Glenn Spicker and his partners decided to fill the gap with this overly commercial effort. The museum is stuffed with kitschy displays of Communist-era apartments and grocery stores, but the entry hall has an excellent series of wall posters explaining the major events of the Communist period, from the 1948 Communist coup, to the stagnation of the 1950s, the 1968 Warsaw Pact invasion, and

finally the 1989 Velvet Revolution. It's a great primer for recent history. The best part is a moving, 15-minute film loop (with English subtitles) mixing images of the Velvet Revolution with Czech folk songs. ⏱ *1 hr. Na příkopě 10.* ☎ *224-212-966. Admission Kč 180. Daily 9am–9pm. Metro: Mustek.*

⑥ ★ **Kinský Palace.** Follow the little street, Havířská, that leads off Na příkopě in the direction of Old Town Square. This lively Baroque palace, at no. 12 on Old Town Square, is normally highlighted in guidebooks as the biggest and pinkest of the square's many palaces (and the site of Franz Kafka's grammar school), but it has another distinction related to the country's Communist past. It was from this balcony in February 1948 that the country's first Communist leader, Klement Gottwald, proclaimed an effective coup d'état by Communist forces. The announcement was greeted with euphoria by the thousands amassed that day on the Old Town Square. Memories of the horrors of World War II were still fresh, and many hoped (naively, in retrospect) that Communism would bring long-desired peace and prosperity. For fans of Czech-born author Milan Kundera, Gottwald's address from this balcony is humorously and ironically recounted in the first chapter of the novel *The Book of Laughter*

Kinský Palace balcony.

and Forgetting. ⏱ *15 min.*
Staroměstské nám. 12, Prague 1.
Metro: Staroměstská.

7 U Rozvařilů. It's getting harder and harder to find communist-era eateries around town. These are usually simple stand-ups, serving classical dishes out of steam tables at prices workers can afford. This is one of the last authentic ones in the center. To find it, walk out toward Náměstí Republiky and continue walking down Na poříčí. *Na poříčí 26. No phone. $.*

8 ★★ Letná (Former Stalin Statue). From the Old Town Square, follow the fashionable street Pařížská to the Vltava river, then cross the bridge and ascend one of the walkways leading up to Letná park. It was here, at the top of the stairs, where a metronome now sways, that the world's largest Stalin statue—a full 50m (164 ft.) tall—once stood. The statue was commissioned in the early '50s at the height of the former Soviet dictator's cult of personality and was finished in 1955. Unfortunately for Czechoslovakia's Communist leaders, by the time the statue was done, Stalin was falling out of favor in the Soviet Union. The statue hovered uneasily over the city for several years, but by the 1960s it was clear it had to go. In 1962, the city dynamited it out of existence with nearly 2,000 pounds of explosives that knocked out windows all around the city. The statue's creator, Otakar Švec, didn't live to see his work demolished—he had committed suicide several years earlier. The Museum of Communism (see above) has several good photographs of the statue and even one of its demolition. The statue's design, depicting Stalin standing at

the head of a line of workers, soldiers, and citizens, was dubbed by local wags at the time as "the world's largest bread line"—a reference to the notorious shortages of food staples. City officials are not quite sure what to do with this area, and for now most of it stands empty, with only the metronome forlornly marking time. ⏱ *15 min. Letná, Prague 1. Metro: Staroměstská.*

9 ★ Hotel International (Crowne Plaza Hotel). This hotel, about 3km (2 miles) northwest of Letná, in the suburb of Dejvice, is the city's best example of 1950s Socialist-Realist architecture. If you've been to Moscow or seen Warsaw's Palace of Science and Culture, you'll recognize this Stalinist skyscraper's signature wedding-cake style. In the years following World War II, Stalin marked his turf in the newly acquired Eastern bloc by offering these skyscrapers as

The world's largest statue of Stalin once stood where this metronome now sways.

"gifts" (that could not be refused). For years, the building operated as a mid-range hotel for party functionaries until it was taken over by the Holiday Inn group in the 1990s and retrofitted into a modern luxury hotel. Today, the building is noteworthy for its overall design and exterior mosaics. Take a look, too, at the lobby, which retains much of its overall 1950s appearance. 🕐 *20 min. Koulová 15, Prague 6.* ☎ *296-537-111. Metro: Hradčanská (plus tram 8).*

🔟 ★ **Former Gottwald Mausoleum on Vítkov Hill.** For more Socialist Realist style and out-and-out Communist kitsch, make a special trip across town to the suburb of Žižkov to a monument that once held the mummified remains of Czechoslovakia's first Communist leader, Klement Gottwald (in much the same way Lenin's remains were preserved at Moscow's Red Square). The complex, which includes the world's largest statue of a horse, was originally designed in the 1920s to honor the legendary 15th-century Hussite general Jan Žižka, but Gottwald co-opted the site in the '50s to function as a kind of Socialist sanctuary for Communist anniversaries and Labor Day celebrations. When Gottwald died in 1953—in keeping with the Communist fashion of the day—his remains were preserved here and put on public display. Unfortunately, the Czech embalmers were not as skilled as their Soviet comrades and it wasn't long before Gottwald's body began to deteriorate. The body had to be re-embalmed every 18 months and was permanently withdrawn from public view in 1961. After 1989, this monument was practically forgotten and only maintains irregulars hours now. If you'd like to see inside, try phoning ahead to arrange a special tour. The monument is now under

Žižkov TV tower.

control of the Czech National Museum, which recently announced plans to develop the site as a museum of modern history. 🕐 *20 min. U památníku, Prague 3.* ☎ *222-781-676. www.nm.cz. Tours by appointment only. Metro: Florenc.*

⓫ ★★ **Žižkov TV Tower.** Prague's multistory TV tower is arguably the ugliest building ever built in the Golden City. At the same time there's something undeniably alluring about its ultrasmooth shape and sheer scale—it dwarfs everything around it. The tower dates from the late 1980s and was built to broadcast TV and radio signals, but there's always been an undercurrent of suspicion that the real purpose was to jam signals coming in from the BBC and Radio Free Europe. The sculptures of babies crawling up and down—by local jokester-artist David Černý—lend a surreal effect. Take the high-speed elevators up to the observation deck for impressive views in the city. 🕐 *30 min. Mahlerovy Sady 1, Vinohrady.* ☎ *242-418-778. 150 Kč (adults), 60 Kč (children). Daily 10am–11:30pm. Metro: Jiřího z Poděbrad.*

Prague with Kids

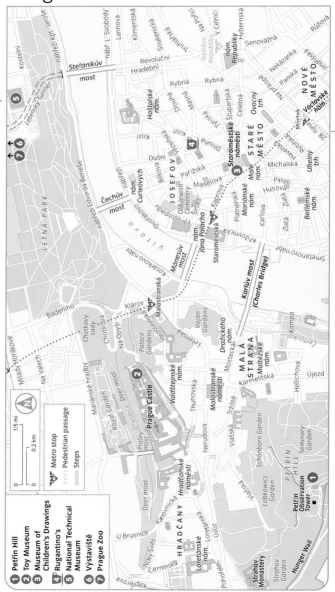

1 Petřín Hill
2 Toy Museum
3 Museum of
  Children's Drawings
4 Rugantino's
5 National Technical
  Museum
6 Výstaviště
7 Prague Zoo

N

```
0 ——————— 1/5 mi
0 ——————— 0.2 km
```

M Metro stop
‡‡‡ Pedestrian passage
⫶⫶⫶ Steps

Prague is not an easy city for kids. Younger children will like the castles, bridges, puppets, and trams, but shuffling the kids around from place to place (over lots of cobblestones) will be a constant challenge. Older kids will probably show only a passing interest in the city's history and architecture and could very well buckle (as anyone would) after an overly long day at Prague Castle. The tourist authorities have been slow to add attractions aimed at younger visitors but fortunately there are a few standbys that have nothing to do with Gothic or Baroque architecture. This is a lot to pack into one day; you may have to choose just one of the last two stops depending on your interest. START: **Žluté lázně (Yellow Beach) or Podolí.**

① ★★ Petřín. The Petřín Hill that rises above Malá Strana is filled with great things for kids. You can follow the Petřín tour on p 84, or take the funicular train (lanová dráha) to the top and just wander around from there. In addition to a mock Eiffel Tower (built to a quarter the size of the original) that you can climb to the top, you'll find an old-fashioned mirror maze ("Bludiště") as well as the Štefánik Observatory, open for stargazing on clear nights. ⏱ *60 min. Petřín. Petřín Tower (Petřínská rozhledna).* ☎ *257-320-112. 60 Kč (20 Kč for children). May–Sept 10am–10pm; Oct–Apr 10am–6pm. Bludiště: 50 Kč (20 Kč for children). May–Aug 10am–10pm; Sept–Apr 10am–6pm. Štefánik Observatory: 50 Kč. Mon–Fri 2–7pm, 9–11pm; Sat–Sun 10am–noon, 2–7pm, 9–11pm. Metro: Malostranská (plus tram 12, 22, or 23 south three stops to Újezd).*

Inside the maze of mirrors on Petřín Hill.

② ★ Toy Museum (Muzeum hraček). When you're 6 or 7 years old, Gothic cathedrals are not very riveting. Fortunately, the Prague castle complex has something for kids as well. This multilevel toy museum is one of the best of its kind in Europe, featuring loads of traditional wooden toys, dolls, construction sets, train sets, and lots of other amusements. It's housed in the offices of the former Supreme Burgrave, the seat of the castle administration (see the tour "A Day at Prague Castle," above). Entry to the museum is not included in the general castle admission. ⏱ *30 min. Jiřská 6, Hradčany.* ☎ *224-372-294. 60 Kč (adults), 30 Kč (children). Daily 9:30am–5pm. Metro: Malostranská (plus tram 22 or 23 north to Pražský hrad).*

TOY ◄ MUSEUM HRAČEK

This sign marks the entrance to the Toy Museum at Prague Castle.

Splish, Splash

As any seasoned parent knows, one of the best way to keep kids occupied and happy is to let them splash around in some water. Fortunately, Prague has a couple of good options.

In good weather, head to **Yellow Beach** (Žluté lázně) for some outdoor fun (Podolské nábřeží, Podolí; ☎ 244-463-777). This popular grassy riverside beach is located south of town on the Old Town side of the Vltava. It has a nice outdoor pool and lots of activities for both big and little kids. A decent on-site restaurant means you can make a day of it. Admission is 80 Kč adults, 30 Kč children. It's open June to September from 8am to 2am.

If it's too cold for Žluté lázně, come to the **Podolí indoor pool** and recreation center situated just across the street (Podolská 74. Podolí; ☎ 241-433-952). There are actually two big outdoor pools here too, making it a good choice in winter or summer. There are a mock beach, solarium, and sauna on the premises. It's open daily from 6am to 9:30pm; admission is 80 Kč Monday to Friday, 110 Kč weekends. To get to either spot, take the Metro to Karlovo náměstí, then tram 3, 16, 17, or 21 to the Dvorce stop.

The whole family can blow off some steam at the Podolí pools.

❸ **Museum of Children's Drawings (Dům U Zelené žáby).** Back in Old Town is a unique family-friendly museum that displays artwork done by children. On weekends, it's a veritable artistic workshop as the kids are invited to come up with their own creations. ⏱ *45 min. U Radnice 13/8.* ☎ *224-234-482. 40 Kč (adults), 20 Kč (children). Tues–Sun 1–6pm. Metro: Staroměstská.*

❹ ★★ **Rugantino's.** Just across Old Town Square from the Museum of Children's Drawings and down a small side street, you'll find the most family-friendly restaurant in the city. Czechs don't often take their children out to restaurants, but here the owners and wait staff welcome kids with open arms. While you're wading through a menu of some of the best pizzas in the city, the staff will be handing out colored pencils and doodling

The fountains at Výstaviště.

paper. Popular venue for children's parties. *Dušní 4.* ☎ *222-318-172. Metro: Staroměstská. $.*

⑤ ★★ National Technical Museum (Národní technické muzeum).

Head north from the city square, across the river, to this fascinating museum stuffed with classic automobiles, historic airplanes, full-sized trains, old bikes, and just about every other mode of transport ever invented. It occasionally hosts special exhibitions for kids, like a highly popular dinosaur show a couple of years back. The museum was closed in 2007 for reconstruction but was scheduled to reopen by 2008. Call for hours and admission prices. ⏱ *1 hr. Kostelní 42, Letná.* ☎ *220-399-111. Metro: Vltavská (plus trams 1, 25, 26 to Kamenická).*

⑥ ★★ Výstaviště.

Beyond the technical museum in the outlying district of Holešovice is another kids' mecca: the Výstaviště fairgrounds complex. Built around the turn of the 20th century in beautiful Art Nouveau architecture, it's got a small amusement park (with a

merry-go-round and a few "Tilt-O-Whirl" type rides), a massive singing fountain (with water and lighting timed to classical and popular music), and a small Sea World–style aquarium called "Mořský svět." Entry to the amusement park is free, but separate admissions are charged for the fountain and Mořský svět. ⏱ *2 hr. Křižík's Fountain (Křižíkova fontána):* ☎ *220-103-224. 180 Kč. Apr–Oct 7–11pm. Seaworld (Mořský svět):* ☎ *220-103-275. 240 Kč (adults), 145 Kč (children 4–15). Daily 10am–7pm. Metro: Nádraží Holešovice (then tram 15 to Výstaviště).*

⑦ ★★ Prague Zoo.

Moving farther north from Výstaviště, Prague's zoo has improved dramatically in recent years. It was nearly totally inundated in the 2002 flood that struck the city, and the authorities have had to invest heavily in new facilities. The collection of giraffes is one of the finest in Central Europe. ⏱ *2 hr. Best on weekdays, when it's less crowded. U Trojského zámku 120.* ☎ *296-112-111. 100 Kč (adults), 70 Kč (children), 300 Kč (families). Apr–Oct 9am–6pm; Nov–Mar 9am–4pm. Metro: Nádraží Holešovice (then bus no. 112).*

Tiger at the Prague Zoo.

Romantic Prague

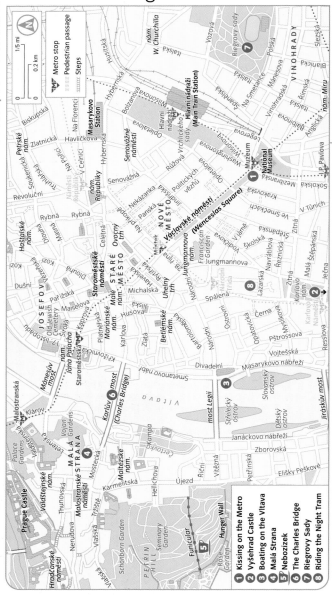

Metro stop
Pedestrian passage
Steps

0   1/5 mi
0   0.2 km

1 Kissing on the Metro
2 Vyšehrad Castle
3 Boating on the Vltava
4 Malá Strana
5 Nebozizek
6 The Charles Bridge
7 Riegrovy Sady
8 Riding the Night Tram

If you've ever read any books by Czech authors Milan Kundera or Ivan Klima, you know that a deep, abiding affection—bordering on obsession—for the opposite sex lies just below the surface here. Prague romance is not the "candlelight and flowers" variety. Czechs, in general, are far too pragmatic. There's no need to waste time on a box of chocolates. Under communism, flirting and drinking beer were practically the only two pleasures left in life, and Czechs made good use of both. Attitudes remain refreshingly relaxed, and you'll see couples holding hands and kissing on park benches, on trams, and in the pubs. It's infectious and there's no point in resisting. So take a walk, hold hands, and do what comes naturally. No one's paying any attention. START: **Metro to Muzeum.**

① **Kissing on the Metro.** Kissing on the metro has a long and honored history in Prague, going back to the days under communism when whole families would live in tiny two- or three-room apartments. Young couples were often at a loss for privacy and had to make do with any space available. Any metro line works, but the C line (Red) between Muzeum and Háje might be the best for this purpose. The gaps between stations seem to stretch on for miles.

② **★★ Vyšehrad Castle.** Prague's "other" castle here at Vyšehrad is far more dignified and in its own way more moving than the admittedly more Disneyesque-style Prague Castle downriver. It's less commercial and there's a feeling of timelessness and place that's increasingly rare in modern-day Prague. Bring a blanket and a bottle of wine and hike up to the castle grounds. If you're lucky

you'll have the place to yourself. *Soběslavová 1.* ☎ *241-410-348. www.praha-vysehrad.cz. Free admission. Metro: Vyšehrad (plus a considerable walk).*

③ **★★ kids Boating on the Vltava.** This is great for kids, but it's not bad for grown-ups either. You can rent little pedal- or rowboats from vendors along the embankment just near the National Theater (Národní divadlo). You can't pedal far, but far enough that no one can see what you're doing in there. *70 Kč an hour. Metro: Národní třída (plus tram 9 or 22).*

④ **★★★ Malá Strana.** It's no accident that all those expensive boutique hotels are situated in the Lesser Quarter (Malá Strana). It's the one neighborhood in Prague that truly gives Paris a run for its money. Just about any walk will do, but try

View from Vyšehrad Castle.

Get cozy in a boat as you drift along the Vltava.

in and around the little streets near Kampa Park. *Metro: Malostranská.*

5 ★ **Nebozizek.** Prague is a city of great views, but there are only a handful of elegant restaurants that can really deliver on this score. Nebozizek stands halfway up Petřín Hill and commands a table view over the sparkling city below. To find it, take the funicular train one stop to Nebozízek station. *Nebozízek.* ☎ *222-318-172. Metro: Malostranská (plus tram 12, 22, or 23 to Újezd & then the funicular). $.*

6 ★★★ **The Charles Bridge at Night.** By day, Prague's signature bridge is thronged with tourists, buskers, sketch artists, touts, and hawkers. The spirit of the place can be totally drowned out. By night, it's a different story. The crowds thin out and the guys selling the cheap jewelry and the old-time photos go home. At the same time, the castle floodlights come on and both the Old Town and Malá Strana sides of the river are caught in the play of light and shadow. Find a spot along the wall of bridge, uncork a bottle of Czech sparking wine, "Bohemia Sekt," and feel the invigorating breeze over the river.

7 ★ **Riegrovy Sady.** Prague has plenty of green spaces to stretch out on a bench or blanket, but Vinohrady's beautiful hillside park combines the best attributes of Lovers' Lanes everywhere: a dreamy castle view in the distance and a row of safe and quiet benches perched along a ridge to give you an excuse to linger. Hike up into the park from Vinohradská třída and follow the path to the edge overlooking the train station below and castle beyond. *Best, of course, after dark. Metro: Muzeum (tram 11 to Vinohradský Pavilon).*

8 **Riding the Night Tram.** Prague's tram system is like Dr. Jekyll and Mr. Hyde. By day, the trams are a paragon of transportation virtue, ferrying carloads of accountants, shop clerks, dentists, workers, and students to their usual destinations. After midnight, the system lets its hair down. Prague's special night trams take over and the trams become veritable parties on wheels. The central night tram junction is at Lazarská ul. in Nové Město. From here cars fan out in all directions until 5am. Do as the locals do and share a seat—guy on the bottom and girl in his lap. *Metro: Národní třída.* ●

Nebozizek is a great place for a romantic dinner.

The Jewish Quarter (Josefov)

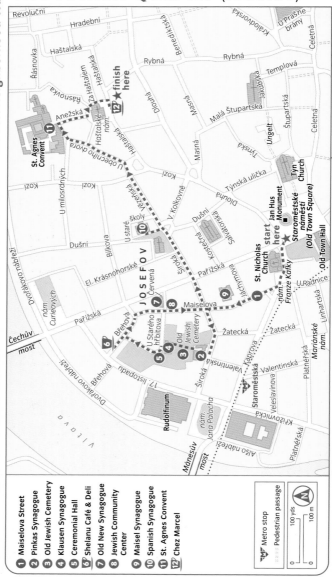

1 Maiselova Street
2 Pinkas Synagogue
3 Old Jewish Cemetery
4 Klausen Synagogue
5 Ceremonial Hall
6 Shelanu Café & Deli
7 Old New Synagogue
8 Jewish Community Center
9 Maisel Synagogue
10 Spanish Synagogue
11 St. Agnes Convent
12 Chez Marcel

Metro stop

Pedestrian passage

0   100 yds
0   100 m

Previous page: A quiet street in Malá Strana.

This tour focuses on the remains of the former Jewish ghetto. The Prague Jewish Museum (Židovské muzeum v Praze) maintains four synagogues as well as the most moving remnant, the Old Jewish Cemetery (Starý židovský hřbitov). Another surviving synagogue, the Old New synagogue (Staronová synagoga), is maintained by the Jewish community of Prague. You can walk the ghetto for free, but to tour the exhibits you need an entry ticket (see the box "The Jewish Quarter: Practical Matters," p 57, for details on admissions charges and hours for Jewish Quarter attractions). The Old New synagogue requires a separate ticket. A combined entry for all of the sights is also available. Note that many of the sights on this tour are closed Saturdays, the Jewish Sabbath, and on Jewish holidays. Try to get an early start; the area gets very crowded in season. START: **Old Town Square.**

① Maiselová Street. From Old Town Square, walk past St. Nicholas Church (Chrám sv. Mikuláše) and then past the birth house of Franz Kafka (p 27, bullet ①). Maiselová begins here and threads its way through the center of the former ghetto. This was "Main Street" when the ghetto was a walled-in community, and here you'll find some of the most important surviving buildings and the former Jewish Town Hall. ⏰ *10 min.*

② ★★ Pinkas Synagogue (Pinkasová synagoga). Continue walking down Maiselová past the Maisel synagogue (we'll return to it later), turning left on Široká. Opposite Široká 4 is the main entrance to the Pinkas synagogue and the Old Jewish

Cemetery. There's a cash desk where you can buy your combined ticket for the Jewish Museum. The Pinkas synagogue is Prague's second-oldest Jewish house of worship, dating from the 1500s. Following World War II, the names of 77,297 Czech Jews who perished in the Nazi concentration camps were painted on the walls. The names include former U.S. Secretary of State Madeleine Albright's paternal grandparents: Arnošt and Olga Koerbel. The synagogue also holds a deeply moving display of pictures drawn by children held at the Terezín concentration camp during World War II. ⏰ *30 min. Entrance opposite Široká 4.*

You'll find this market near Klausen Synagogue and the Ceremonial Hall.

Detail of a tombstone in the Old Jewish Cemetery.

3 ★★★ Old Jewish Cemetery (Starý židovský hřbitov). An absolute must-see on par with Prague Castle. The Old Jewish Cemetery is Prague's oldest surviving Jewish burial ground, dating to the middle of the 15th century. Because local laws at the time prohibited Jews from burying their dead outside the ghetto, this tiny graveyard is crammed with some 12,000 visible tombstones and thousands of more bodies stacked up in 12 to 15 layers below ground. The last grave dates from 1787. The most prominent grave, in the far corner near the Ceremonial Hall, is that of former Jewish scholar Rabbi Loew, the creator of the legendary Golem (he died in 1609). Across from Rabbi Loew's grave is that of Mordechai Maisel, a former leader of the ghetto for whom the Maisel synagogue and Maiselová street are named. Many visitors continue the ancient tradition of placing small pebbles on grave markers or stuffing the graves with small scraps of paper bearing wishes. ⏱ *30 min. Široká 3 (enter through the Pinkas synagogue).*

History 101: The Jewish Quarter

For centuries, Prague harbored one of Central Europe's largest and best-educated Jewish communities. This small area just north of the Old Town Square was the center of Jewish life from the 13th to the late 19th century. Though Jews were restricted from living outside the ghetto for much of that time, the Jewish community enjoyed relative peace and tolerance. The high point came in the late 16th and early 17th centuries during the reign of Emperor Rudolf II. The ghetto began to decline in the 19th century after Jews won the right of abode and could live wherever they wanted. Many chose to leave, and by the end of the 19th century the ghetto had become a slum. In an early version of gentrification, the city knocked down many of the buildings, including several synagogues, and built the luxury turn-of-the-century apartment houses you see today.

The Jewish Quarter is not a Holocaust site per se, but World War II did have a devastating effect on the city's Jews. Tens of thousands were deported and murdered in the concentration camps, leaving behind a small community of just a few thousand. The Nazis originally planned to build a museum here of Europe's extinct race of Jews. Ironically, many of the treasures on display are from Jewish towns and villages that were pillaged by the Germans.

Klausen Synagogue.

4 ★ **Klausen Synagogue (Klausová synagoga).** The Klausen synagogue is situated behind the Old Jewish Cemetery on U Starého hřbitova. It was the biggest synagogue during the ghetto's heyday and today holds a permanent exhibition of everyday Jewish customs and traditions. ⏲ *20 min. U Starého hřbitova 3a.*

5 ★ **Ceremonial Hall (Obřadní síň).** Just down from the Klausen synagogue is the former Ceremonial Hall and mortuary of the Old Jewish Cemetery. Appearances can be deceiving: The Ceremonial Hall looks like the oldest building on the street, but in fact it's one of the youngest, dating to just 1912. The exhibition here describes Jewish customs and traditions relating to illness and death. ⏲ *20 min.*

6 **Shelanu Café & Deli.** Follow U starého hřbitova around until it meets Břehová to find this New York–style kosher deli. They offer a range of classic sandwiches, such as pastrami, egg salad, and smoked salmon. Opens early for breakfast. Closed Saturdays. *Břehová 8.* ☎ *221-665-141.* *$.*

7 ★★ **Old New Synagogue (Staronová synagoga).** From Břehová, find Maiselová again. You can't miss the Old New synagogue, still standing and functioning much as it has for some 800 years. The architectural style is early Gothic and the vaulted interior hall is modeled after a 12th-century synagogue that once stood in the German city of Worms. The synagogue was originally called "New" but took on the name "Old New" in the 16th century when other, newer synagogues were built. The Old New synagogue is not formally part of the Prague Jewish Museum and requires a separate ticket to enter. ⏲ *30 min.*

8 **Jewish Community Center (Židovská radnice).** Next to the Old New synagogue, this was once the Jewish town hall. It now houses an information and cultural center

Old New Synagogue and the Jewish Community Center.

Detail of a house in the Jewish Quarter.

for locals and visitors. On the tower facing the Old New synagogue is an old Hebrew clock that keeps time running counterclockwise. *Maiselová 18.*

❾ ★ Maisel Synagogue.

Retrace your steps back up Maiselová, crossing Široká. This is an original Renaissance synagogue dating from the 16th century that underwent extensive renovation and is now in the neo-Gothic style. It's no longer a functioning synagogue, but it houses the first part of

an exhibition on the history of Jews in Bohemia and Moravia. (The exhibition continues in the Spanish synagogue.) 🕐 *20 min. Maiselová 10.*

❿ ★★ Spanish Synagogue (Španělská synagoga). The

Spanish synagogue is the last stop on a tour of the Jewish museum. It lies just outside the immediate ghetto area, along Široká. The design is Moorish, a popular style for 19th-century synagogues. Arabesque designs fill the stunning interior. The permanent exhibition

Inside the Spanish Synagogue.

continues the history of Jews in Bohemia and Moravia. If you need a quick coffee, there's a small cafe attached to the right of the synagogue. Just outside is a comical statue of the writer Franz Kafka. ⏱ *20 min. Dušní 12.*

⑪ ★★ St. Agnes Convent (Klášter sv. Anežky České).

After all that history, decompress with a short stroll through one of the quietest and loveliest corners of the Old Town. Walk first along Vězeňská, then bear to the left on the small street U obecního dvora until you reach Anežská. You can walk the grounds of this former convent, which is made up of early Gothic buildings dating from the 13th century. The National Museum also maintains a gallery here of Medieval and Gothic art. ⏱ *45 min. U Milosrdných 17.* ☎ *224-810-628. 100 Kč. Tues–Sun 10am–6pm.*

St. Agnes Convent's art gallery.

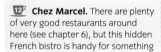

12 **Chez Marcel.** There are plenty of very good restaurants around here (see chapter 6), but this hidden French bistro is handy for something quick and light like a salad or just a glass of good French wine. *Haštalská 12.* ☎ *222-315-676. $$.*

The Jewish Quarter: Practical Matters

A ticket to visit the six Prague Jewish Museum sights (the Pinkas, Klaus, Maisel, and Spanish synagogues; the Old Jewish Cemetery; and the Ceremonial Hall) costs 300 Kč per person (200 Kč children). A separate ticket for entering the Old New synagogue costs another 200 Kč (140 Kč children). A combined admission for all of the sights is available for 480 Kč (320 Kč for children). Tickets are available at cash desks located throughout the former ghetto. All of the major attractions are closed on Saturdays and Jewish holidays, so plan your visit accordingly. For more information, call ☎ **222-317-191** or visit www.jewishmuseum.cz. The museum sights are open Sunday to Friday from 9am to 6pm April through October; from 9am to 4:30pm November through March.

The Lesser Town (Malá Strana)

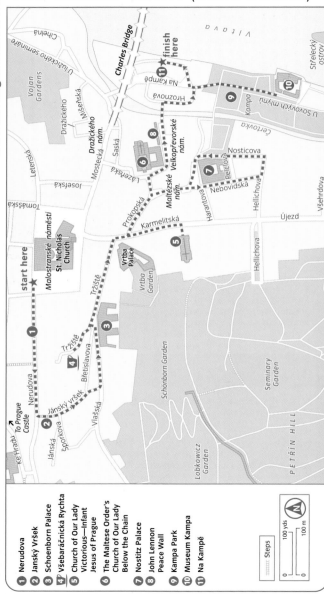

1 Nerudova
2 Jánský Vršek
3 Schoenborn Palace
4 Všebaráčnická Rychta
5 Church of Our Lady Victorious—Infant Jesus of Prague
6 The Maltese Order's Church of Our Lady Below the Chain
7 Nostitz Palace
8 John Lennon Peace Wall
9 Kampa Park
10 Museum Kampa
11 Na Kampě

start here

finish here

To Prague Castle

Charles Bridge

St. Nicholas Church

Malostranské náměstí

Vrtba Palace

Vrtba Garden

Schönborn Garden

Seminary Garden

Lobkowicz Garden

PETŘÍN HILL

Nosticova

Maltézské nám.

Velkopřevorské nám.

Střelecký ostrov

Vltava

Steps

0   100 yds
0   100 m

In contrast to the Old Town, the Lesser Town feels quieter and more refined. It gives Paris a run for its money in terms of romance. Many of the most important sights in the Lesser Town are covered in the "Best in One Day" tour (p 8), and its gardens and parks are covered in the "Gardens of Malá Strana" tour (p 90). This tour covers a little bit of familiar territory but is intended to get you off the main drag and onto the quieter cobblestone streets that define the prettiest part of Prague. Feel free to wander off the recommended course if you see a quiet alley, courtyard, or garden that merits exploring.

START: **Malostranské nám.**

① **Nerudová.** From Malostranské náměstí follow Nerudová up toward the castle. St. Nicholas Church (Kostel sv. Mikuláše, p 15, bullet ⑭) is on your left as you walk uphill. This street takes its name from Czech author Jan Neruda, who was born here in the 19th century. The Nobel prize–winning Chilean poet Pablo Neruda admired Jan Neruda's writings so much that he adopted "Neruda" as a pen name. The street is lined with stunning Baroque palaces, many of which have been given cute descriptive names. Look especially at houses at no. 11 (U červeného beránka/ House of the Red Lamb), no. 12 (U tří housliček/House of the Three Violins), and no. 16 (U zlaté číše/House of the Golden Cup). ⏱ *15 min.*

② **Janský Vršek.** Instead of going all the way to the castle, turn left down these inviting stairs. This takes you into the quiet heart of upper Malá Strana. Many of the streets here still bear traces of the days when Prague was bilingual German-speaking. On the corner with Šporková, the street sign reads JOHANNESBERG GASSE, the German name for Janský Vršek. ⏱ *10 min.*

③ **Schoenborn Palace (Schoenbornský palác).** Continue walking along Janský Vršek, making a left at the intersection with Vlašská. The American flag fluttering in the breeze marks the front of the U.S. embassy, quartered in a 17th-century Baroque palace, the former home of Austro-Hungarian general Count Colloredo-Mansfeld. The U.S. government bought the house in 1925 for the princely sum of $117,000. It has more than 100 rooms and 7 acres of gardens stretching up Petřín Hill. Franz Kafka rented a room here in 1917. The

Nerudová Street.

The "Infant Jesus of Prague."

building is not open to the public. ⏱ *10 min. Tržiště 15.*

4 **Všebaráčnická Rychta.** If you're ready for a cold one or quick bite, this rambling Czech pub has great beer and a wonderful atmosphere. To find it, look for the little part of Tržiště that runs up from the Alchymist Grand Hotel. *Tržiště 23.* ☎ *257-532-461. $.*

5 ★ **Church of Our Lady Victorious—Infant Jesus of Prague.** From the U.S. embassy, walk down Tržiště to the bottom of the street, turning right on Karmelitská. This early-Baroque church of the Carmelite order is famous for the wax statue of baby Jesus displayed on an altar on the right wing of the church. The "Infant Jesus of Prague" was presented to the Carmelites in 1628 and commands an almost cult-like status in some countries. Copies of the "bambino" are sold in the church's small museum and at souvenir shops in the area. ⏱ *15 min. Karmelitská 9.* ☎ *257-533-646. Free admission. Mon–Sat 10am–5:30pm, Sun 1–5pm.*

6 ★★ **The Maltese Order's Church of Our Lady Below the Chain (Kostel Panny Marie pod řetězem).** Cross Karmelitská and walk to the left until you come to Prokopská. Turn down this street and walk into the large Maltézské náměstí, named for this large church off the square belonging to the Knights of Malta. One of the best Romanesque designs in Prague, this church replaced an even older church after it burned in 1420. You can see remnants of the original along the portal and inside the church courtyard. ⏱ *15 min. Lázenská ul. Open during masses.*

7 **Nostitz Palace (Nostický palác).** This palace, now home to the Czech Culture Ministry, is a grand, 17th-century Baroque design attributed to Francesco Caratti. A Prague noble family who strongly supported the arts used to own it, and its ornate halls once housed a famed private art collection. You can sometimes hear chamber concerts through its windows. ⏱ *10 min. Maltézské nám. 1.* ☎ *257-085-111. www.mkcr.cz. Occasionally open to the public; call or visit website (Czech only) for details.*

The Maltese Church.

The graffiti-covered John Lennon peace wall.

⑧ ★ John Lennon Peace Wall.

Before seeing the John Lennon Peace Wall, make a small detour down Nebovidská (to the right of the Nostitz Palace), past the luxurious quarters of the Mandarin Oriental Hotel. Walk to the end of the street and turn left on Hellichová. Make another left onto Nosticová. This is one of the quietest and nicest parts of Malá Strana, fully removed from the city. In a couple of years, this street will be cleaned up like all the rest, but for the moment enjoy the elegant, faded feeling. To find the Lennon Wall, walk down Nosticová, returning to Maltézské náměstí and the Knights of Malta Church. Follow Lázeňská to the right onto another large square: Velkopřevorské náměstí. The French embassy will be to your right and this half-hidden graffiti wall, a Prague original, to your left. The Lennon Peace Wall came into existence shortly after Beatles musician John Lennon was killed in 1980. Under communism it morphed into an impromptu protest space. The secret police tried to stop the graffiti writers, but every day the wall seemed to be covered with new messages extolling the virtues of John Lennon instead of that other "Lenin." Interest in the wall has dropped off in recent years, but in late 2007 the wall was still sporting a large peace sign painted beneath the word IMAGINE. ⏱ *15 min. (20 min. if you plan on writing your own message). Velkopřevorské nám.*

⑨ ★★ Kampa Park.

Continue walking, crossing a small bridge over the Čertovká stream to reach Kampa Island and this park, Malá Strana's biggest stretch of green. There are gorgeous views over the Vltava on one side and the charming footbridges and mills over the Čertovká on the other. The big lawn in the middle is the perfect spot to throw down a blanket and open a book. ⏱ *20 min.*

⑩ ★ Museum Kampa.

Near the Vltava at about the midpoint of the park, you'll find this very good, relatively new museum dedicated to contemporary Central European art. The permanent collection has works by noted Czech sculptor Otto Gutfreund and Czech painter František Kupka. ⏱ *1 hr. U sovových mlýnů 2.* ☎ *257-286-147. 120 Kč. Daily 10am–6pm.*

⑪ ★ Na Kampě.

Return to the center of the city via this small square, lined with hotels and restaurants on both sides. Take the little street that leads off the square to the right of Na Kampě 15 to walk along the edge of the river and get some great photos of the Charles Bridge. ⏱ *15 min.*

The Castle District (Hradčany)

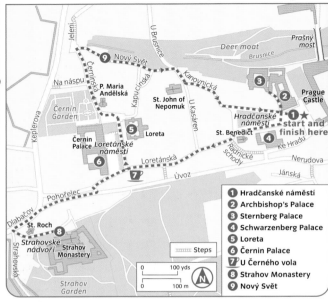

1. Hradčanské náměsti
2. Archbishop's Palace
3. Sternberg Palace
4. Schwarzenberg Palace
5. Loreta
6. Černin Palace
7. U Černého vola
8. Strahov Monastery
9. Nový Svět

The Castle District is quiet and exclusive, populated by embassies, institutes, and ministries. The area was leveled by fire in 1541, and was rebuilt in Renaissance and Baroque styles. It's easy to combine this tour with the longer tour of Prague Castle on p 30.
START: **Hradčanské nám.**

① Hradčanské náměsti One of the most beautiful and tranquil squares in the city, and a nice place to relax on a bench with a book. The plague column in the center was built in 1726 by the Baroque master Ferdinand Brokoff, creator of several statues on Charles Bridge. ⏲ *15 min.*

② Archbishop's Palace (Arcibiskupský palác). The seat of the Prague Archbishop is unfortunately not open to the public, though you can enter the interior chapel once a year, the day before Good Friday. The staid Renaissance

exterior was later remodeled into exuberant late-Baroque Rococo. ⏲ *10 min. Hradčanské nám. 16. No phone. Open 1 day a year.*

③ ★★ Sternberg Palace (Šternberský palác). The real treasure here lies just behind the Archbishop's palace. This is home to the National Gallery's excellent collection of European art from the 14th to the 18th century and includes works by Rembrandt, El Greco, Goya, and Van Dyck. ⏲ *2 hr. Hradčanské nám. 15. ☎ 233-350-068. 100 Kč. Tues–Sun 10am–6pm.*

4 Schwarzenberg Palace.

Across the square, the Renaissance sgraffito on the exterior makes this imposing palace easy to recognize. The Schwarzenberg family acquired the property by marriage in the early 18th century. For years it housed the Military History Museum but in 2008 it was expected to reopen as the National Gallery's Museum of Baroque Art. *Hradčanské nám. 15.*

5 ★★ Loreta.

Follow Loretánská, which leads off the square to the left. This remarkable cloister, church, and Baroque pilgrimage was built in the 17th century. It was modeled on the original Santa Casa (Sacred House) in the Italian town of Loreta. A duplicate Santa Casa stands in the courtyard. Lovers of Baroque will enjoy the ornate interiors and the statuary that lines the outside. The Treasury on the first floor holds a diamond monstrance from 1699 made from some 6,222 diamonds. The carillon of 27 bells is unique in Prague and chimes on the hour. ⏱ *1 hr. Loretánské nám. 7.* ☎ *220-516-740. 110 Kč. Tues–Sun 9am–12:15pm, 1–4:30pm.*

6 Černin Palace (Černinský palác).

Across the street from the Loreta, this forbidding-looking palace is home to the Czech Republic's Foreign Ministry. It was here, in 1948, that Jan Masaryk, the son of the first Czechoslovak president Tomáš G. Masaryk, fell to his death from a high window. He opposed the Communist coup, and it's never been resolved whether he jumped from the window or was pushed. ⏱ *10 min. Loretánské nám. No phone. Closed to the public.*

7 U Černého vola.

This is one of the best traditional Czech pubs still standing. Big wooden tables, decent pub grub, and excellent Kozel beer on tap. *Loretánské nám. 1.* ☎ *220-513-481. $.*

8 ★★ Strahov Monastery (Strahovský Klášter).

From Loretánské náměstí, follow Pohořa elec. This medieval monastery of the Premonstratensian order goes back all the way to the 12th century. It was shut down by the communists but has since reopened. The monks' chambers are off-limits, but visitors can still visit the amazing Strahov Library (Strahovská knihovna), laid out in two immense Baroque halls: the Philosophical Hall and the older Theological Hall. Also worth visiting are ancient printing presses downstairs and the remains of the order's 10th-century founder, St. Norbert. ⏱ *1 hr. Strahovské nádvoří 1.* ☎ *233-107-718. 80 Kč. Daily 9am–noon, 1–5pm.*

9 ★ Nový Svět.

The rest of the tour is simply a stroll through the elegant Castle District. Return to Loretánské náměstí and the Černin Palace, making a left on Černinská. Follow this to the end until you come to the remote and lovely cobblestones of Nový Svět. This little lane is close to town, yet feels far away. Make a right at the end of Nový Svět onto Kanovnická, which will take you back to the start of the tour at Hradčanské náměstí. ⏱ *30 min.*

Loreta Church.

The Old Town (Staré Město)

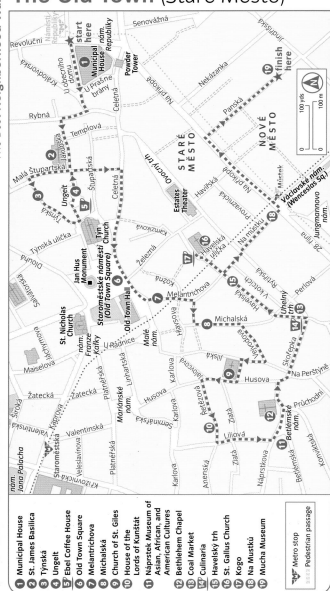

1 Municipal House
2 St. James Basilica
3 Týnská
4 Ungelt
5 Ebel Coffee House
6 Old Town Square
7 Melantrichova
8 Michalská
9 Church of St. Giles
10 House of the Lords of Kunštát
11 Náprstek Museum of Asian, African, and American Cultures
12 Bethlehem Chapel
13 Coal Market
14 Culinaria
15 Havelský trh
16 St. Gallus Church
17 Kogo
18 Na Můstků
19 Mucha Museum

Metro stop
Pedestrian passage

The Old Town is the center of Prague and long the seat of commercial power. The main sights of the Old Town, including the Old Town Square, are covered in the "Best in One Day" tour (p 8). This tour snakes in and around the Old Town Square to see some of the lesser attractions off the beaten path. Feel free to wander at will, but be sure to bring a good map—it's easy to get lost. START: **Náměstí Republiky.**

1 ★★★ Municipal House (Obecní dům). This turn-of-the-20th-century Art Nouveau building has been an important Czech cultural symbol—the document granting independence to Czechoslovakia was signed here in 1918. The Prague Symphony Orchestra performs in Smetana Hall, the most impressive room. ⏱ *15 min. (1.5 hr. if you take a tour). See p 9, bullet* **2**.

2 ★ St. James Basilica (Bazilika sv. Jakuba). Enter the heart of the Old Town along the small street U obecního domu, to the right of the Municipal House. Take a right on Rybná and then a left on Jakubská to the street Malá Štupartská. The Baroque St. James Basilica is Prague's second-longest church, with 21 altars. When you enter, look up just inside the front door. The object dangling above is the shriveled arm of a 16th-century thief. The church's enormous organ has been restored to its original sound, and St. James regularly hosts organ recitals and concerts (see chapter 8). ⏱ *15 min. Malá Štupartská 6.* ☎ *604-208-490. Mon–Sat 9:30am–noon, 2–4pm.*

3 Týnská. As you exit St. James take a right on Malá Štupartská, then follow it to Týnská, a small street on your left. This is a beautiful alleyway of Baroque houses—note the barely discernable relief on the front of no. 10. The area has gotten trendy recently, and amid the junk shops (great for browsing) you'll find some high-end antique dealers and

Art Nouveau fans should be sure to spend some time at the Municipal House.

a couple of good bars and restaurants. ⏱ *15 min.*

4 ★★ Ungelt (Týnský Dvůr). Round the bend at Týnská to see the back of the magnificent Týn Church (kostel Matky Boží před Týnem). Make a left at the church and enter the Ungelt, the fortified area of the former customs house, once the seat of the city's wealth. It's hard to imagine now, but this area was allowed to fall into appalling disrepair and was restored to its present appearance only in the mid-1990s. Now, the Ungelt holds an appealing mix of upscale shops and restaurants. ⏱ *20 min.*

The Ungelt.

5 **Ebel Coffee House.** If you're starting to flag, stop by this excellent coffeehouse for American-style espresso-based drinks and light food items such as bagels and cakes. *Týn 2.* ☎ *224-895-788.* $.

6 ★★★ **Old Town Square (Staroměstské nám.).** Continue walking through the Ungelt, exiting through the gate on the other side. Make a right on Malá Štupartská and follow it to the right, connecting with Celetná and eventually entering Old Town Square on the same road used

Melantrichová.

by Bohemian kings 500 years ago. The "Best in One Day" tour, p 8, covers the square's main sights, so for this tour we'll simply stroll through the square, walking to the left of the Old Town Hall (Staroměstská radnice) and finding Melantrichová, a small street just opposite the Astronomical Clock. ⏲ *15 min.*

7 ★ **Melantrichová.** This tiny lane connects the city's two main squares (Old Town and Wenceslas) and for that reason is clogged night and day. The usual selection of glass and T-shirt shops line this street. Don't miss the "House at the Two Golden Bears" (Dům u dvou zlatých medvědů), on the corner with Kožná. It has one of the city's most beautiful Renaissance portals, dating from 1590. ⏲ *10 min.*

8 **Michalská.** Turn right through an arcade to enter Michalská street, once one of the main arteries of the Old Town. Art galleries, high-end antiques shops, and the luxurious Iron Gate Hotel (p 141) line this picturesque street. ⏲ *15 min.*

9 ★ **Church of St. Giles (Sv. Jiljí).** Follow Michalská nearly to the end, turning right under an archway onto Vejvodová. Turn right again onto Jilská (unmarked) and follow it to the back of this enormous church. St.

Giles was a Hussite church during the 15th-century religious strife, but was given a thorough Baroque makeover after the Austrian Hapsburg occupation. Today, it has perhaps the most opulent interior of any Prague church save St. Nicholas. The Sunday noon mass is popular with the city's growing Polish community. 🕐 *15 min. Husová 8. No phone. Daily 9am–5pm (except during masses).*

Church of St. Giles.

⑩ House of the Lords of Kunštát (Dům Pánů z Kunštátu).

From St. Giles, walk down Husová until you see a small street running to the left called Řetězová. Look for no. 3, one of the oldest houses in Old Town; it dates from 1200 and has some of the city's best-preserved Romanesque chambers. The house was rebuilt in the 15th century in Gothic style and served as an occasional residence for the Hussite King George of Poděbrady. Today it houses occasional exhibitions. 🕐 *10 min. Řetězová 3. No phone.*

⑪ Náprstek Museum of Asian, African and American Cultures (Náprstkovo Muzeum).

Continue along Řetězová, making a left onto Liliová and following that to Bethlehem Square (Betlémské nám.). On the right hand of the square, you'll see the National Museum's collection of primitive, non-European cultures housed in a former brewery. The exhibitions are dry, but the museum has a popular section on North American Indians. 🕐 *30 min. Betlémské nám. 1. ☎ 224-497-500. 80 Kč. Tues–Sun 10am–6pm.*

⑫ ★★ Bethlehem Chapel (Betlémská kaple).

To the left on the square is the real attraction, the Bethlehem Chapel. In the 15th century this was once home to the firebrand Czech Protestant theologian Jan Hus. Hus was burned at the stake as a heretic in 1415 in Constanz in what is now Germany, and became a martyr for the Czech Protestant and later nationalist cause. The chapel was completed in 1394 but thoroughly reconstructed in the 1950s. In the main hall you can see the pulpit from where Hus preached. 🕐 *30 min.*

Bethlehem Chapel.

Betlémské nám. 4. ☎ *224-248-595. 40 Kč. Tues–Sun 10am–6pm.*

⑬ Coal Market (Uhelný trh).
Follow Betlémská out of the square, turning right onto Na Perštýně. Be sure to look up at this point to see Czech artist David Černý's "Hanging Man" statue hanging high above Husová. Cross the street and follow Skořepká into what was once the city's main coal market, marked by a tiny statue in the middle. ⏱ *10 min.*

⑭ Culinaria. If it's lunchtime and a nice day, pick up some sandwiches-to-go at this popular deli situated on the corner of Skořepká and Uhelný trh. The smoothies and coffee drinks are some of the best in town. Eat at tables outside or on benches around the statue at the center of market. *Skořepká 9.* ☎ *224-231-017. $.*

⑮ ★ Havelský trh. From the Coal Market, walk up busy Havelská street. The "Havel Market" was the area's commercial center during the Middle Ages and remains a popular market. The stalls here sell everything from fruits and vegetables to drinks, soap, artwork, and leather goods. Prices here are generally lower than in most shops. ⏱ *20 min.*

St. Gallus Church.

⑯ ★ St. Gallus Church (Kostel sv. Havla). This dignified church, sometimes called St. Havel Church, dominates the end of the square. It dates from the 13th century and is one of the oldest in the Old Town. Jan Hus was an occasional preacher here. The chapel holds the tomb of Bohemian Baroque artist Karel Škréta. It's now undergoing long-term renovation and may not be open when you visit. ⏱ *10 min. Havelská ul. No phone. Daily 10am–5pm.*

⑰ Kogo. This branch of the wildly popular local chain of good pizzas and homemade pastas is perfect for lunch or dinner, or just a glass of good wine. The house specialty is a dry red called Vranac that's imported from Montenegro. *Havelská 27.* ☎ *224-210-259. $$.*

⑱ Na Mustků. From St. Gallus church return in the direction of Havelský trh and turn left on Melantrichová. This brings you back to Mustek metro station and the base of Wenceslas Square. The name "Na Mustků" means "on the little bridge" and refers to the days when this was a small bridge crossing a moat, linking the Old Town (Staré Město) and the New Town (Nové Město). You can still see parts of the original foundation downstairs inside the metro station. ⏱ *10 min.*

⑲ ★★ Mucha Museum. If you've got the time and energy for one last sight (and you're a fan of Art Nouveau), turn left on Na příkopě and walk several blocks until you reach Panská ul. on the right. This museum is dedicated to Czech artist and illustrator Alfons Mucha, who became world famous for his Parisian prints of the actress Sarah Bernhardt. The small collection includes some original paintings, drawings, and poster art. ⏱ *45 min. Panská 7.* ☎ *221-451-333. 120 Kč. Daily 10am–6pm.* ●

Shopping Best Bets

Best for **Philatelists**
Alfafila, *Václavské nám. 28 (Pasáž U Stýblů)* (p 74)

Best Place to **Find Old Maps**
★ **Antikvariát Pařížská,** *Pařížská 8* (p 74)

Best Place to **Buy a Miniature Wooden Rocking Horse**
★ **Hračky,** *Loretánské nám. 3* (p 75)

Best Place to **Buy a Marionette**
★★★ **Truhlář Marionety,** *U Lužického semináře 5* (p 76)

Best **Bohemian Crystal**
★★★ **Moser,** *Na příkopě 12* (p 77)

Best **Contemporary Glass**
★★★ **Artěl,** *Celetná 29* (p 76)

Best **Old-World Shopping Center**
★★★ **Lucerna Pasáž,** *Štěpánská 61* (p 78)

Best **Department Store in a Brutalist Building**
Kotva, *Náměstí Republiky 8* (p 77)

Best Place for **English-Language Books**
★★ **Shakespeare & Sons,** *Krymská 12* (p 79)

Best **Bookstore/Coffeehouse**
★★ **The Globe Bookstore and Coffeehouse,** *Pštrossová 6* (p 79)

Best **Czech Clothing Designers**
★★★ **Timoure et Groupe,** *V kolkovně 6* (p 79)

Best **Deli**
★★ **Culinaria,** *Skořepká 9* (p 80)

Best **Bath Salts & Massage Lotions**
★★ **Botanicus,** *Týn 3* (p 80)

Best Place to **Buy a Cubist Couch**
★★★ **Modernista,** *Celetná 12* (p 81)

Best Place to **Buy a Real Czech Garnet**
★★ **Studio Šperk,** *Dlouhá 19* (p 82)

Colorful wooden toys at Manufaktura.

Malá Strana Area Shopping

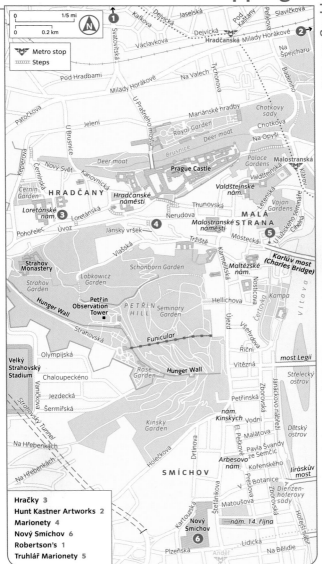

0	1/5 mi
0	0.2 km

M Metro stop

Steps

Hračky **3**
Hunt Kastner Artworks **2**
Marionety **4**
Nový Smíchov **6**
Robertson's **1**
Truhlář Marionety **5**

Photo page 69: Shop window on Golden Lane.

Staré Město Area Shopping

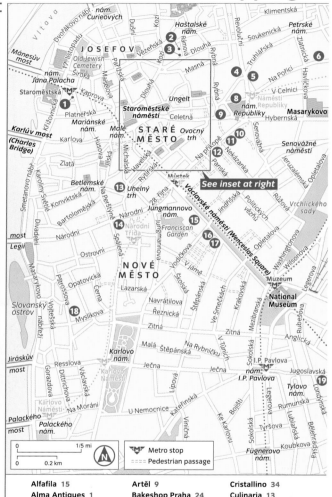

Alfafila 15	**Artěl** 9	**Cristallino** 34
Alma Antiques 1	**Bakeshop Praha** 24	**Culinaria** 13
Anagram 32	**Big Ben Bookshop** 31	**Dorotheum** 43
Antikvariát	**Bílá Labuť'** 6	**Dům Porcelánu** 19
Karel Křenek 8	**Boheme** 26	**Estée Lauder** 39
Antikvariát Pařížská 27	**Botanicus** 30	**Galerie Art Praha** 38
Aromi 20	**Celetná Crystal** 33	**The Globe Bookstore**
Art Deco Galerie 41	**Český Granát** 37	**and Coffeehouse** 18

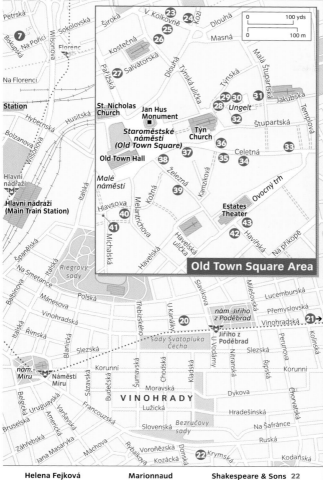

Old Town Square Area

Antikvariát Pařižská.

Antiquarian Books & Maps
Alfafila NOVÉ MĚSTO   A specialist shop in a small passageway off Václavské náměstí catering mainly to stamp collectors, but with an absorbing collection of old postcards, posters, and photographs that should keep noncollectors happy too. *Václavské nám. 28 (Pasáž U Stýblů).* ☎ 224-235-457. *MC, V. Metro: Mustek. Map p 72.*

★★ **Antikvariát Karel Křenek** STARÉ MĚSTO   The Art Nouveau setting of this shop's location in the Obecní dům building brings an elegant, upmarket tone. Especially strong on German-language antiquarian books and Eastern European and Hapsburg-era maps. *U Obecního domu 8.* ☎ 222-314-734. *AE, DC, MC, V. Metro: Náměstí Republiky. Map p 72.*

★ **Antikvariát Pařižská** STARÉ MĚSTO   Small shop on one of the most exclusive streets in the city, with a beautiful selection of older maps and prints. Despite the location, the prices here are not really much higher than elsewhere, and the quality of the goods is among the best you'll find. *Pařižská 8.* ☎ 222-321-442. *AE, DC, MC, V. Metro: Staroměstská. Map p 72.*

Antiques & Collectibles
★ **Alma Antiques** STARÉ MĚSTO Family-owned and fascinating antiques store/junk shop, with an eclectic range of housewares, bric-a-brac, rugs, clothes, accessories, and just about everything else. If you don't see what you're looking for, ask. They have several stores and storage areas around town and can probably find it. *Valentínská 7.* ☎ 222-325-865. *AE, DC, MC, V. Metro: Staroměstská. Map p 72.*

★ **Art Deco Galerie** STARÉ MĚSTO   Cozy shop on a quiet street in Old Town that focuses on signature pieces from the interwar years, when Czechoslovakia, under the First Republic, was one of the world's wealthiest countries. Good collections of glass, personal accessories, small pieces of furniture, and secondhand clothing. *Michalská 21.* ☎ 224-223-076. *MC, V. Metro: Staroměstská. Map p 72.*

★★ **Dorotheum** STARÉ MĚSTO The local branch of the fabled Austrian auction house of the same name. As you can imagine, the goods on offer—jewelry, furniture, and artwork—are some of the best on the market, at prices to match. Excellent 19th-century collections. Good selection of antique jewelry. *Ovocný trh 2.* ☎ 224-216-699. *AE, DC, MC, V. Metro: Mustek. Map p 72.*

★★ **Starožitnosti Ungelt** STARÉ MĚSTO Recognized around Prague as one of the best stores for antique glass, ceramics, and jewelry. Prices here are a little higher than most, but the selection is much better. *Týn 1.* ☎ *224-895-454. MC, V. Metro: Staroměstská. Map p 72.*

Art Galleries

★★ **Galerie Art Praha** STARÉ MĚSTO Impressive gallery on Old Town Square with a focus on 19th- and 20th-century paintings by Czech and Slovak artists. Always something eye-catching in the window. Strong on art during the communist period. *Staroměstské nám. 20.* ☎ *224-211-087. AE, DC, MC, V. Metro: Staroměstská. Map p 72.*

★★ **Hunt Kastner Artworks** LETNÁ This expat-owned contemporary gallery focuses on emerging Czech artists working in a range of visual media. The two small exhibition rooms hold rotating collections. Open in the afternoon Tuesday to Friday or by appointment. *Kamenická 22.* ☎ *233-376-259. AE, DC, MC, V. Metro: Vltavská (plus trams 1, 25, or 26). Map p 71.*

★★ **Jiří Švestka** NOVÉ MESTO Widely considered the leading private gallery in Prague, with a stable of mostly cutting-edge Czech artists

and some internationals. There's also a bookshop here with a good selection of art and architecture titles. *Biskupský dvůr 6.* ☎ *222-311-092. AE, DC, MC, V. Metro: Náměstí Republiky. Map p 72.*

Children: Toys & Puppets

★ **Hračky** HRADČANY Excellent collection of vintage, decidedly low-tech Czech toys, including the signature little wooden rocking horse. It feels like it's from a different age entirely; sure to be a delight for little kids. *Loretánské nám. 3.* ☎ *603-515-745. No credit cards. Metro: Hradčanská. Map p 71.*

★★ **Marionety** MALÁ STRANA Many stores in Prague carry marionettes and puppets, but only a few—such as this place—carry genuine, handmade marionettes from traditional designs. The better ones are not cheap, but the craftsmanship is some of the best you'll find. *Nerudová 51.* ☎ *257-533-035. AE, DC, MC, V. Metro: Malostranská. Map p 71.*

★ **Sparky's** NOVÉ MĚSTO The largest toy store in the city, with a convenient central location. Has a great selection of stuffed animals on the ground floor. Toys for older kids, including lots of model cars, are on the upper floors. Gift-wrapping

Galerie Art Praha.

available. *Havířská 2.* ☎ *224-239-309. AE, DC, MC, V. Metro: Náměstí Republiky. Map p 72.*

★★★ Truhlář Marionety MALÁ STRANA

Well-regarded puppet shop that eschews cheap machine-made marionettes in favor of the handmade, labor-intensive variety. Marionettes have a tradition in Prague going back to the Middle Ages and many of the witch, king, and nobleman motifs here have been in use for centuries. *U Lužického semináře 5.* ☎ *602-689-918. AE, DC, MC, V. Metro: Malostranská. Map p 71.*

China, Crystal & Porcelain
★★★ Artěl STARÉ MĚSTO

American expat Karen Feldman has carved a niche for herself in the high-end glass market by adapting classic Czech designs to modern tastes. Previously, she's sold her designs through department stores like Bloomingdales in New York and Harrods in London. In 2007, she opened up this local flagship on Prague's "glass avenue," Celetná. *Celetná 29.* ☎ *224-815-085. AE, DC, MC, V. Metro: Náměstí Republiky. Map p 72.*

★★ Celetná Crystal STARÉ MĚSTO

Probably the city's largest collection of crystal and cut glass on several floors in a prominent Functionalist-era building from the early 1930s. Several elegant showrooms. The staff is happy to walk you through the collections. *Celetná 15.* ☎ *222-324-022. AE, DC, MC, V. Metro: Náměstí Republiky. Map p 72.*

★ Cristallino STARÉ MĚSTO

Similar to but slightly cheaper than Celetná Crystal (see above) across the street. Has a broad selection of Bohemian lead crystal glasses and vases, as well as more modern-looking pieces and a large collection of glass eggs. *Celetná 12.* ☎ *224-223-027. AE, DC, MC, V. Metro: Náměstí Republiky. Map p 72.*

★ Dům Porcelánu VINOHRADY

In addition to crystal, the Czech Republic is renowned for porcelain—much of it made in or near the spa town of Karlovy Vary. At this large shop in Vinohrady, you'll find designs from all of the leading Czech producers—at prices that haven't been marked up for tourists. *Jugoslávská 16.* ☎ *221-505-320. AE, DC, MC, V. Metro: Náměstí Míru. Map p 72.*

Marionety.

Dům Porcelánu.

★★★ **Moser** NOVÉ MĚSTO   The leading Bohemian producer of luxury cut class, crystal, stemware, and vases for 150 years. The company's gorgeous 1920s showroom on Na příkopě in central Prague is worth a visit on its own, just to see the glass in its proper setting. A perfect gift for someone back home. *Na příkopě 12.* ☎ *224-211-293. AE, DC, MC, V. Metro: Mustek. Map p 72.*

★★ **Swarovski** STARÉ MĚSTO The "Austrian" glassmaker who originally founded this world-famous lead crystal maker, Daniel Swarovski, was actually from a small town in Bohemia. So in a way it's fitting to have such a beautiful store in the center of Prague. The selection here is excellent, but the prices are similar to or higher than what you'll find anywhere else in the world. *Celetná 11.* ☎ *222-315-585. AE, DC, MC, V. Metro: Staroměstská. Map p 72.*

Department Stores & Shopping Centers
Bílá Labut' NOVÉ MĚSTO   Similar to Kotva but even emptier. The lifeless stalls and shoddy merchandise on offer are actually a better display of life under Communism than anything you're likely to see at the Museum of Communism. Worth a stop if only to gauge how far the city

has come in 20 years. *Na poříčí 23.* ☎ *224-811-364. MC, V. Metro: Florenc. Map p 72.*

Kotva STARÉ MĚSTO   This communist-era department store still feels stuck in the 1970s—and might be more interesting because of it. It's adequate for basic purchases, such as housewares, toiletries, and stationery, but give the clothes and shoes a miss. The Brutalist-style building is protected as a cultural monument. *Náměstí Republiky 8.* ☎ *224-801-111. AE, MC, V. Metro: Náměstí Republiky. Map p 72.*

Crystal pieces from Moser.

The unusual upside-down horse sculpture at Lucerna Pasáž.

★★★ Lucerna Pasáž NOVÉ

MĚSTO Funky 1930s-era shopping center stuffed with an absolutely indescribable mix of stores. There are shops selling high Czech fashion, wines, gifts, and even vintage cameras. The main attractions here are the early-modern interior, the elegant Lucerna cinema and cafe, and the wacky David Černý statue of St. Wenceslas riding on an upside-down horse. One of a kind. *Štěpánská 61.* ☎ *224-224-537. Metro: Mustek. Map p 72.*

★ Nový Smíchov SMÍCHOV Big

American-style shopping mall with more than 100 stores. The highlights here are a large Tesco supermarket (one of the best in the city) on the ground floor, a big food court on top, and a multiplex cinema that's heavy on Hollywood blockbusters. *Plzeňská 8.* ☎ *257-284-111. Metro: Anděl. Map p 71.*

★ Palác Flora VINOHRADY Simi-

lar to the Nový Smíchov (see above), with more than 100 stores and a large multiplex cinema. Has the city's—and country's—only 3-D IMAX Theater. Convenient to the metro (A line). *Vinohradská 151.* ☎ *255-741-700. Metro: Flora. Map p 72.*

★★ Palladium NOVÉ MĚSTO

This brand-new high-tech supermall is just off of Náměstí Republiky (across from Kotva). Several floors of high-end stores, with a huge, elaborate—and very expensive—food court on top. *Náměstí Republiky 1.* ☎ *225-770-250. AE, DC, MC, V. Metro: Náměstí Republiky. Map p 72.*

★★ Slovanský dům NOVÉ

MĚSTO Convenient, centrally located shopping center with a number of leading-brand clothing stores, like Mexx, Tommy Hilfiger, and Nautica. The 10-screen multiplex cinema is committed to showing films in English, and is one of the few cinemas in town to regularly carry Czech movies subtitled in English. *Na příkopě 22.* ☎ *221-451-400. Metro: Mustek. Map p 72.*

Tesco NOVÉ MĚSTO Local outlet

of the British retailer that's housed in another noteworthy 1970s building. For anyone familiar with Tesco in the U.K., the goods on offer are a tremendous disappointment. Like Kotva, it's fine for basics, but you'll look high and low for anything of really decent quality. The grocery store in the basement is handy for picnic provisions. *Národní třída 26.* ☎ *222-003-111. MC, V. Metro: Národní třída. Map p 72.*

English Books & Magazines
★★ Anagram STARÉ MĚSTO

Tiny English-language bookshop with an impressive display of art and photography books. Also stocks a nice range of high-end contemporary fiction. Great for browsing. *Týn 4.* ☎ *224-895-737. AE, DC, MC, V. Metro: Staroměstská. Map p 72.*

★★ Big Ben Bookshop STARÉ

MĚSTO Small English-language bookstore with a very good selection of quality fiction, history, and travel guides. Also stocks a small number of hard-to-find magazines like the *New York Review of Books* and the *New Yorker.* Stop by to pick up some reads for the flight back home. *Malá Štupartská 5.* ☎ *224-826-565. AE, DC, MC, V. Metro: Náměstí Republiky. Map p 72.*

★★ The Globe Bookstore and Coffeehouse NOVÉ MĚSTO

New ownership has invigorated the Globe's stock of new books, and it's now arguably the best bookstore in town for English-language fiction and Czech and Eastern European authors in translation. Popular with expats. Computers on-hand for checking e-mail and an excellent cafe-restaurant in the back. *Pštrossová 6.* ☎ *224-934-203. AE, DC, MC, V. Metro: Národní třída. Map p 72.*

★★ Shakespeare & Sons VRŠO-VICE

Wonderfully eclectic used bookstore that's worth a special trip to the outlying district of Vršovice. Thousands of books in all categories and a laid-back atmosphere highly conducive to browsing. Good cafe on the premises. Recommended. *Krymská 12.* ☎ *271-740-839. MC, V. Metro: Náměstí Miru (plus tram). Map p 72.*

Fashion
★★★ Boheme STARÉ MĚSTO
Simple yet fashionable women's clothing designed with younger women in mind. Skirts, tops, jackets, boots, and accessories at decent prices. Friendly, accommodating staff. *Dušní 8.* ☎ *224-813-840. AE, DC, MC, V. Metro: Staroměstská. Map p 72.*

★ Helena Fejková Design
NOVÉ MĚSTO   One of the first Czech female designers to emerge after the 1989 revolution. The quality of the clothing is very good, but the styles and designs are playful to the point of being unwearable. *Štěpánská 61 (inside the Lucerna*

Pasáž). ☎ *224-211-514. AE, DC, MC, V. Metro: Mustek. Map p 72.*

★ Ivana Follová Art and Fashion STARÉ MĚSTO
Highly influential local designer in her 50s. The women's clothes vary from functional to folly, but are well-made. The Týn shop is worth poking around in—not just clothes, but interesting designer jewelry and glass. *Týn 1.* ☎ *224-895-460. AE, DC, MC, V. Metro: Staroměstská. Map p 72.*

★★★ Report's STARÉ MĚSTO
Exclusive well-made Italian clothing for men. Everything from top-of-the-line suits and jackets to shoes, sweaters, belts, and accessories. The showroom is reminiscent of a posh men's club and the service is excellent. *V kolkovně 5.* ☎ *222-329-823. AE, DC, MC, V. Metro: Staroměstská. Map p 72.*

★★★ Timoure et Groupe TEG STARÉ MĚSTO
The name sounds French, but this is the creation of two Czech designers who make sophisticated, wearable women's clothing that's perfect for the office and then for dinner after. *V kolkovně 6.* ☎ *222-327-358. AE, DC, MC, V. Metro: Staroměstská. Map p 72.*

Helena Fejková.

Food

★★★ Aromi VINOHRADY

Brought to you by the folks who run the highly rated Aromi restaurant (p 98) across the street. The spot for perfectly ripened Italian cheeses as well as breads, antipasto, sauces, and lots more. Stop in for a take-away pack before that overnight train and you'll ride away in luxury. *Mánesová 83.* ☎ *222-725-514. AE, DC, MC, V. Metro: Jiřího z Poděbrad. Map p 72.*

★★ Bakeshop Praha NOVÉ MĚSTO

America-inspired bakery featuring freshly prepared sandwiches, soups, and salads, as well as some of the city's best cookies, cakes, and brownies. Good coffee drinks. Eat in or take away. *Kozi 1.* ☎ *222-316-823. MC, V. Metro: Staroměstská. Map p 72.*

★★ Culinaria STARÉ MĚSTO

The most enticing deli case in Prague, filled with goodies like beef Wellington and grilled salmon that you can eat in or take away. Also offers made-to-order sandwiches and salads, as well as fresh smoothies and coffee drinks. There's a small retail business, where homesick Americans can stock up on goodies such as Oreo cookies and Pop-Tarts at about double what they'd pay at home.

Aromi.

Skořepká 9. ☎ *224-231-017. AE, DC, MC, V. Metro: Národní třída. Map p 72.*

★ Robertson's STARÉ MĚSTO

English-style butcher that's evolved into an all-purpose refuge for home-sick Brits and Americans. Excellent steaks and chops cut to suit foreign tastes, but also an excellent range of things like cake mixes, breakfast cereals, hard-to-find baking ingredients, snacks, and beverages. Probably not worth a stop if you're just passing through, but a must if you plan on staying a while. *Jugoslávských partyzánů 38.* ☎ *233-321-142. MC, V. Metro: Dejvická. Map p 71.*

Gifts & Souvenirs

★★ Botanicus STARÉ MĚSTO

A Czech original that's as impressive as it is hard to describe. Sells all-natural products for the bath and kitchen such as bath oils, soaps, shampoos, and cooking oils—all made from ingredients grown locally. Botanicus has several outlets across the city, but this one in Old Town seems to be the best. You'll probably fall in love with everything, and want to stuff your suitcase until it can no longer close. *Týn 3.* ☎ *234-767-446. AE, DC, MC, V. Metro: Staroměstská. Map p 72.*

★★ Manufaktura NOVÉ MĚSTO

This shop is similar to—and probably inspired by—Botanicus, but there's less of a focus here on bath and food items and more on traditional Czech crafts, like lace, wooden toys, coffee mugs, textiles, and even pieces of clothing, like scarves and sweaters. Everything feels all-natural and environmentally friendly. The packaging is so nice, it's like it's been gift-wrapped for you. *Melantrichova 17.* ☎ *221-632-480. AE, DC, MC, V. Metro: Staroměstská. Map p 72.*

Qubus.

Home Furnishings

★★★ Modernista STARÉ MĚSTO
Eye-catching collection of furniture
and accessories extolling the design
virtues of Cubism, functionalism,
and mid-century modern. You'll find
a mix of antiques and reproductions. Many of the items here are
too large to fit in a suitcase, but it's
certainly worth dropping in to take a
look. *Celetná 12.* ☎ *224-241-300.
AE, DC, MC, V. Metro: Náměstí
Republiky. Map p 72.*

★★★ Qubus STARÉ MĚSTO
The epicenter of Prague cool
when it comes to decorative
objects for the home and office.
Arty, arch glassware, plates, vases,
and lots of other one-of-a-kinds.
Also stocks vintage cameras like
the cult classic, all-plastic Holga.
Rámová 3. ☎ *222-313-151. AE,
DC, MC, V. Metro: Staroměstská.
Map p 72.*

All This and a Burberry Too . . .

During the past few years, Prague has become a much more
interesting city for buying clothes and accessories—especially if
you're a woman. Credit for that goes mainly to the international
chains, which have come here to capitalize on both Czechs' rising
personal incomes and—of course—the thousands of tourists.
Pařížská, just off of Old Town Square, is home to the ultra-high-end.
Here you'll find **Hermès** (Pařížská 12, ☎ **224-817-545**), **Burberry**
(Pařížská 11, ☎ **222-317-445**), **Louis Vuitton** (Pařížská 13, ☎ **224-
812-774**), and other similarly vaunted names. If you're looking for
something with a little more street smarts, head to Na příkopě, the
pedestrian zone between Old Town (Staré Město) and New Town
(Nové Město). This is where you'll find **Zara's** big flagship store
(Na příkopě 15, ☎ **224-239-861**), with separate floors for men's,
women's, and children's clothing. **Mango** (Na příkopě 15, ☎ **224-
218-884**)—women only—is right across the street. Europe's current
hottest high-street fashion outlet, **H&M** (Václavské nám. 19, ☎ **234-
656-051**), is just a short walk up Václavské náměstí.

Garnet necklaces from Český Granát.

Jewelry

★ Český Granát STARÉ MĚSTO
You'll see lots of amber outlets in the touristy parts of Prague, but the *echt* Czech gemstone is a deep red garnet, mined in the northern and eastern parts of the country. This centrally located shop focuses almost exclusively on garnets and has an excellent selection of rings, necklaces, bracelets, and broaches. *Celetná 4.* ☎ *224-228-281. AE, DC, MC, V. Metro: Staroměstská. Map p 72.*

★★ Studio Šperk STARÉ MĚSTO
Most of the jewelry stores in town

Contemporary pieces from Studio Šperk.

are unnecessarily conservative, and that's especially true of garnet dealers. This little studio/boutique off of Old Town Square takes chances with more contemporary settings and unique designs. The store takes pride in offering only the highest-quality, genuine Bohemian garnets. *Dlouhá 19.* ☎ *224-815-161. AE, DC, MC, V. Metro: Staroměstská. Map p 72.*

Perfume & Makeup

★★ Estée Lauder STARÉ MĚSTO
This highly rated local beauty salon sells Estée Lauder products and offers services like warm-stones therapy to help customers relax and de-stress. *Železná 18.* ☎ *224-232-023. AE, DC, MC, V. Metro: Mustek. Map p 72.*

★★ Marionnaud Parfumeries
NOVÉ MĚSTO   This welcoming store in the Slovanský dům shopping center carries a full range of international perfumes and cosmetics. The emphasis here is on self-service, meaning you're free to browse and try on scents with minimum staff intrusion. *Na příkopě 22.* ☎ *221-451-243. AE, DC, MC, V. Metro: Mustek. Map p 72.* ●

A Walk across **Petřín Hill**

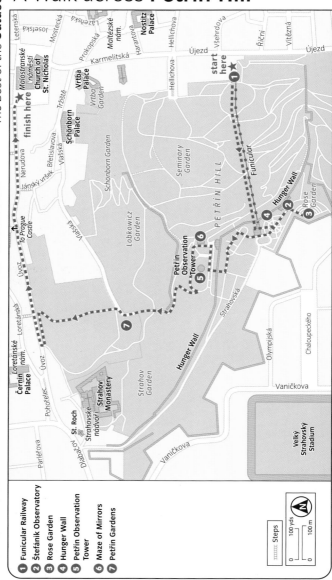

1 Funicular Railway
2 Štefánik Observatory
3 Rose Garden
4 Hunger Wall
5 Petřín Observation Tower
6 Maze of Mirrors
7 Petřín Gardens

Previous page: Petřín Hill peak.

There are lots of lookout spots in this city of a hundred spires that boast of having the best views. Certainly, the beer garden at Letenský zámeček, in Letná (see p 88) has a legitimate claim. But for my money, nothing beats the Prague panorama as seen from the top of the long, sloping valley that runs from the top of Petřín Hill down toward the banks of the Vltava river. This walk begins with a funicular train ride to the top of the hill. The smattering of interesting sights up here include a miniature Eiffel Tower built for the 1891 Prague Jubilee exhibition. After that it's a peaceful stroll through a lovely park and then out across a long meadow, with those vaunted views over Prague Castle and the city below. START: **The funicular station at the Újezd tram stop. From Malostranská metro station, take tram no. 12, 22, or 23 three stops. On exiting the tram, walk back toward Malostranské nám. about 15m (49 ft.).**

① ★ kids Funicular Railway (lanová dráha). This 488m (1,600-ft.) cable railway is part of the city's public transportation system; you'll need a 20 Kč tram ticket to ride it (tram and metro passes work too). The funicular was originally built to ferry passengers to the 1891 exhibition. Now, it's a mainstay of the tourist industry, taking visitors up to the "Eiffel Tower" or hauling concertgoers or sports fans up to an event at giant Strahov Stadium on top of the hill. The line has two

Enjoy the views from a funicular ride to the top of Petřín Hill.

stops; take it to the top, Petřín station. If you'd rather walk up the hill, follow any of the paths leading upward. Figure on a moderately demanding hike of 25 to 30 minutes. ⏱ *15 min. Daily 9am–11:20pm.*

② ★ kids Štefánik Observatory (Štefánikova hvězdárna). As you exit the funicular station, walk to your left to see this still-functioning observatory with a classic Zeiss telescope from the 1920s. In good weather, you can look through the telescope for views of the sun during the day and of the moon, planets, and stars at night. ⏱ *10 min. 1 hr. if you stop to observe. Petřín 205.* ☎ *257-320-540. 50 Kč. Mon–Fri 2–7pm, 9–11pm; Sat–Sun 10am–noon, 2–7pm, 9–11pm.*

③ Rose Garden. This sprawling, very pretty rose garden stands just in front of the Štefánik Observatory and meanders in and around Petřín Hill. Take some time to relax on a bench with a book and people-watch. Popular with seniors on Sunday afternoons. ⏱ *15 min. Free admission. Daily 8am–8pm.*

④ Hunger Wall (Hladová zed'). From the Rose Garden, walk back toward the funicular train

The rose garden.

station and you'll see this tall, snag-gletooth-topped wall running to your left. The wall dates from the mid–14th century and was part of Prague's original medieval defenses—the last thing Prague needed at that time was for Mongol invaders to come pouring in over the hill. The origin of the name "Hunger Wall" is disputed, but the best theory is that the wall was built by the city's poor during a time of famine; workers received food in exchange for their labors. ⏱ *10 min.*

⑤ ★★ kids Petřín Observation Tower (Petřínská rozhledna). Walk along the Hunger Wall for

The mini Eiffel Tower on Petřín Hill.

about 30m (100 ft.) beyond the funicular station, looking for signs to the "Petřínská rozhledna." It's hard to miss this 61m (200-ft.) "Eiffel Tower," which was built in 1891 to resemble the original in Paris. The unbeatable views from the top make the long climb up 299 steps (no lift) worthwhile. On a clear day you can see all the way north to the mountains on the Polish border. ⏱ *30 min. Petřínské sady.* ☎ *257-320-112. 60 Kč (20 Kč for children under 10). May–Sept daily 10am–10pm, Oct–Apr daily 10am–6pm.*

⑥ ★ kids Maze of Mirrors (Bludiště). Another oddity built for the 1891 exhibition, this "House of Mirrors" is just like one you might see at a carnival. To find it, just walk about 30m (100 ft.) to the right of the Petřín Observation Tower. It's great fun for kids (and highly disori-enting for adults!). ⏱ *20 min. 50 Kč (20 Kč for children under 10). May–Aug daily 10am–10pm, Sept–Apr daily 10am–6pm.*

⑦ ★★ Petřín Gardens (Petřín-ské sady). From the Maze of Mir-rors, walk back toward the Petřín Observation Tower and follow the path to the left of the tower running downhill. About 15m (49 ft.) along the path, turn left onto another path and walk toward Prague Castle. Don't worry if you get a little bit lost; all of the paths lead in the same

Seeing Prague by Balloon

Točná Airport (☎ 241-773-454) offers 1-hour flights over Prague and its surroundings in a balloon—weather permitting! The trip costs 6,300Kč per person. Call ☎ **604-320-044** for a reservation and details.

Also, with **Ballooning CZ,** Na Vrcholu 7, Praha 3 (☎ **222-783-995** or 603-337-005; www.ballooning.cz), you can fly like a bird. An hour in a balloon will cost you 4,700Kč Monday to Friday or 5,200Kč on weekends.

general direction. The first 10 minutes of the walk take you through some quiet woods and the last 15–20 minutes through an apple orchid and across a long meadow, with the castle out in the distance and the town spread out in all its glory below. This is a favorite stroll among city residents. Follow the trail across the meadow until you reach the top of Malá Strana on the other side. From here, you can turn right and walk down to Malostranské náměstí.

Take some time to stroll the quiet lanes of Petřín Gardens.

Lounging in Letná

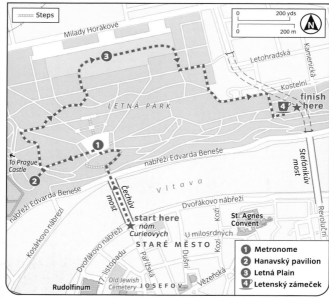

☐☐☐☐☐ Steps

LETNÁ PARK

To Prague Castle

nábřeží Edvarda Beneše

Vltava

Čechův most

Milady Horákové

Letohradská

Kostelní

finish here

Štefánikův most

Dvořákovo nábřeží

Revoluční

St. Agnes Convent

Kozí

start here
nám.
Curieovych
STARÉ MĚSTO

nábřeží Edvarda Beneše

Kosárkovo nábřeží

Dvořákovo nábřeží

17. listopadu

Pařížská

U milosrdných

Dušní

Vězeňská

Rudolfinum

Old Jewish Cemetery

JOSEFOV

kamenická

0   200 yds
0   200 m

N

1 Metronome
2 Hanavský pavilion
3 Letná Plain
4 Letenský zámeček

Whenever I come to Letná, I think of Woody's Allen's movie *Manhattan*. Not the movie so much, but that famous poster of Woody and Diane Keaton sitting on a bench in Brooklyn looking out toward the Manhattan skyline. If they ever came to Prague, this is where they'd sit and look. It's that classic. Letná (Letenské sady) offers something to everyone. Rollerbladers love it for the smooth paths (and you can even rent blades here). Naturally it's a favorite among dog walkers. It's nice, easy jogging terrain, with relatively clean air because of the elevation. It also happens to have the best open-air beer garden in the city. START: **Čechův most (Čechův bridge), which crosses the river from the Intercontinental Hotel in Old Town.**

1 ★ Metronome. Walk across the Čechův most and climb the stairs in either direction up to the top of the hill. In the 1950s, the communist government erected the biggest-ever statue of Soviet dictator Josef Stalin here (see p 42, bullet **8**). Since 1991, the space has been given over to a giant metronome, designed by the Czech Republic's official prankster-in-residence David Černý. It's an interesting concept to have a metronome marking time since the Velvet Revolution but arguably a waste of valuable public space. The area feels neglected, and is appreciated mostly by skateboarders, who gather here to test their skills against the monument's tricky steps and railings. ⏱ *10 min.*

2 Hanavský Pavilon. Facing away from the town below, walk to your left in the general direction of Prague Castle. The path skirting the edge of the hill affords some picture-perfect views over the Vltava River, with Charles Bridge in the background. The Hanavský Pavilon was built for the 1891 Prague Jubilee Exhibition in a neo-Baroque style. Today, it houses a cute cafe and restaurant overlooking the Old Town. ⏱ *10 min. Letenské sady 173.* ☎ *233-323-641. Daily 11am–1am.*

3 ★ Letná Plain. What you do from here depends on your time and interests. If you continue walking in the same direction, you'll eventually come to a footbridge that takes you on toward Prague Castle. If you'd like to see more of Letná, walk toward the interior of the park, choosing any of the trails that strike your fancy. Much of Letná is a giant plain, and in the very earliest years of aviation, this area functioned as Prague's makeshift airport. Much later, the open space was used by the communists to hold their massive May Day rallies on May 1. In more recent times, it's been the site of an open-air mass by Pope John Paul II and in 2003 even hosted the Rolling Stones for a massive alfresco concert. On a typical summer day, it's great for tossing a football or a Frisbee. Note that at press time, much of the plain had turned into a massive construction zone as road workers dig out below the park to build a highway tunnel. ⏱ *20 min.*

4 ★★ Letenský Zámeček. Once you've had your fill of fresh air and sunshine, it's time for liquid refreshment. In the Czech Republic that usually means beer. This complex of restaurants, terraces, and a comfortably down-market beer garden is one of the city's most popular places to meet up after work or on a weekend afternoon. To find it, walk to the extreme eastern end of the park (in the direction away from Prague Castle). The *zámeček* (little castle) houses a decent but expensive restaurant inside and a cheaper pizza-and-barbecue joint on the terrace. Opposite the restaurant and with gorgeous views out over the city are picnic tables where you're free to consume your own food and drinks. Do as the locals do and buy some beers in plastic cups from the little stand out front and relax in the open air. You can also rent balls for lawn bowling (called *pétanque*) and even rollerblades behind the chateau near the public lavatories. ⏱ *1 hr. Letenské sady 341.* ☎ *233-378-200. Daily 11am–11pm.*

Letná Plain.

The **Gardens of Malá Strana**

1. Palace Gardens
2. Wallenstein Gardens
3. Vrtba Garden
4. Kampa
5. Vojan Gardens

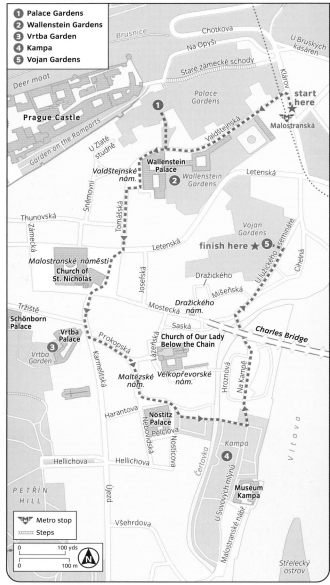

From street level, Malá Strana looks like an impenetrable collection of walls, cobblestones, bricks, and mortar. Beautiful to be sure, but nary a tree or bush in sight. This is only an illusion. Behind every Baroque palais, towering wall, or imposing gate, there lurks a beautifully manicured garden. Many of the mainly Italian masters who laid out these green oases more than 300 years ago were every bit as famous—and meticulous—in their day as the architects and craftsmen who built the lovely residential palaces. Some of the gardens remain closed to the public, but several have been converted to public parks or gardens. Many bear the names of the aristocratic families that once owned them. But be forewarned that most of the parks are open only from April to October. START: **The Malostranská metro station (Line A).**

① ★★ **Palace Gardens (Palácové Zahrady).** Exit the metro station and walk to the left to Valdštejnská ul. At Valdštejnská 12, walk through an iron gate and a small courtyard. This leads you to five beautifully terraced Baroque gardens that front the side of the hill rising up to Prague Castle. One ticket buys entry into all five and you're free to spend as long as you wish walking along the walls and steps from garden to garden. It's confusing keeping track of exactly which garden is which, but you can get a map at the ticket window. The Kolowrat Garden (Kolovratská zahrada) is considered the most

valuable from an architectural point of view, with its lookout garden house. The others include the Ledeburg Garden (Ledeburská zahrada), the Small and Big Palffy Gardens (Malá a Velká Pálffyovská zahrada), and the Furstenberg Garden (Furstenberská zahrada). ⏱ *30 min. Valdštejnská 12.* ☎ *257-010-401. 79 Kč. Apr–Oct daily 10am–8pm. Metro: Malostranská.*

② ★★ **Wallenstein Gardens (Valdštejnská Zahrada).** Continue walking along Valdštejnská ul. until you come to Valdštejnské náměstí (Wallenstein Square). The imposing Baroque Wallenstein

Kolowrat Garden, one of the Palace Gardens.

Palace at no. 4 hides an amazing garden in the back, with an even more amazing limestone drip wall—a grotto—that you have to see to believe. The palais itself was the creation of Albrecht von Wallenstein, a brilliant general during the Thirty Years' War of the 17th century, and was meant to rival Prague Castle in terms of pure shock and awe. Wallenstein's ambitions cost him his life when he was assassinated in 1634 in the western Bohemian town of Cheb (probably on orders of Emperor Ferdinand II). The palais now houses the Czech Senate. The garden follows a formal geometric design and is dotted with ponds and bronze statues. Look closely at the limestone grotto to see animal heads, snakes, and other grotesque figures peeking out. ⏱ *20 min. Valdštejnské nám. 4.* ☎ *257-072-759. Free admission. Daily 10am–7pm.*

③ ★★★ Vrtba Garden (Vrtbovská Zahrada). From Valdštejnské náměstí follow Tomášská ul. to Malostranské náměstí, cross the square diagonally, and walk down Karmelitská ul. to the unassuming door at no. 25. Inside lies a meticulously manicured 18th-century

Vrtba Garden.

terraced garden that truly sets the standard for Baroque gardens. The brilliant statuary, including an eye-catching Atlas as you walk through the door, is the work of Matyáš Bernard Braun. It's a steep hike to the top, but worth it for the views over Malá Strana and the perfect photo op of St. Nicholas Church. ⏱ *30 min. Karmelitská 25.* ☎ *257-531-480. 40 Kč. Apr–Oct daily 10am–6pm.*

④ ★★ Kampa. From the Vrtba Garden walk back a few steps in the direction of Malostranské náměstí, cross the street, and walk down Prokopská ul. Cross Maltézké náměstí and then bear left at the far end of the square onto Nosticová ul. Here you'll find the opening to Kampa Park, the largest expanse of green in Malá Strana. This is my pick for Prague's prettiest park, with gorgeous views over the Vltava on one side and the charming Čertovká stream (with its footbridges and water mills) on the other. The big lawn in the middle is the perfect spot to throw down a blanket and open a book. ⏱ *30 min.*

⑤ Vojan Gardens (Vojanovy Sady). If you have time for one more park, walk through Na Kampě (Kampa Square) in the direction of Charles Bridge. Continue straight, going underneath the bridge, and then bear right on U lužického semináře. The Vojan Gardens is a sprawling series of walkways, benches, lawns, and fountains in the middle of the city, well hidden from the masses behind formidable walls. It began life in the 13th century as a fruit garden, and now mostly functions as an urban idyll for office workers looking to escape modern life for half an hour. ⏱ *20 min. U lužického semináře 17. Free admission. Daily sunrise–sundown.* ●

The Best Dining

Dining Best Bets

Best for Kids
★★★ Rugantino $ *Dušní 4 (p 107)*

Best Vegetarian
★★ Lehká Hlava $ *Boršov 2 (p 105)*

Best View of the Castle
★★★ Bellevue $$$$ *Smetanovo nábř. 18 (p 99)*

Best View of the Bridge
★★★ Hergetova Cihelna $$$ *Cihelna 2b (p 103)*

Best Italian Hideaway
★★★ Aromi $$ *Mánesová 78 (p 98)*

Best When Only Duck Will Do
★★ Perpetuum $$ *Na hutích 9 (p 107)*

Best When for Beer Connoisseurs
★★ Bredovský dvůr $$ *Politických vězňů 13 (p 100)*

Best Thai Food
★★ Arzenal (Siam-I-San) $$$ *Valentinská 11 (p 98)*

Best Czech-Mex
★★ Cantina $$ *Újezd 38 (p 101)*

Best Beer and Burger Joint
★★ Fraktal $ *Šmeralová 1 (p 102)*

Best for Celeb Sightings
★★ Kampa Park $$$$ *Na Kampě 8b (p 103)*

Best Meal for the Money
★★★ Mozaika $$ *Nitranská 13 (p 105)*

Best Czech
★★★ Černý Kohout $$$ *Vojtěšská 9 (p 102)*

Best if Price Is No Object
★★★ Allegro $$$$ *Veleslavínova 2a (p 98)*

Best Meal at the Opera
★★★ Zahrada v Opeře $$$ *Legerová 75 (p 108)*

Best Pork Knuckle
★★★ Kolkovna $$ *V Kolkovně 8 (p 104)*

Cowboys.

Malá Strana Area

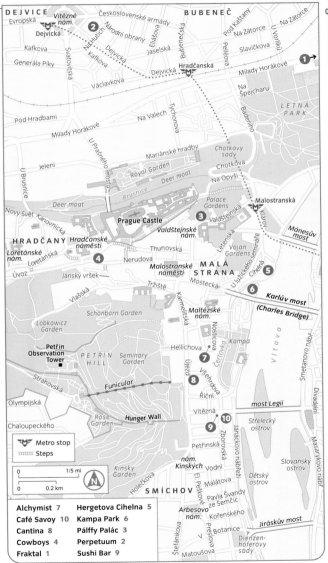

Alchymist 7	Hergetova Cihelna 5
Café Savoy 10	Kampa Park 6
Cantina 8	Pálffy Palác 3
Cowboys 4	Perpetuum 2
Fraktal 1	Sushi Bar 9

Photo p 93: V Zátiši restaurant.

Staré Město Area

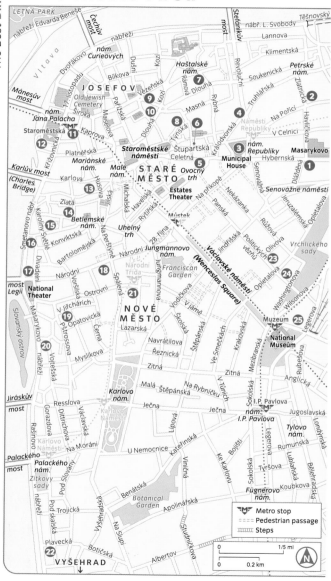

LETNÁ PARK

nábřeží Edvarda Beneše

Čechův most

Stefánikův most

Těšnovský

nábř. L. Svobody

Lannova

nábřeží

Klimentská

Vltava

nám. Curieových

Haštalské nám. ⑦

Revoluční

Soukenická

Petrské nám.

Dvořákovo

Dušní

Kozí

Bilkova

JOSEFOV

Vězeňská ⑨

Ramová

Dlouhá

Rybná

Truhlářská

Zlatnická

❷

17. listopadu

Old Jewish Cemetery

pařížská

Kozi ⑩

Masná

Havlíčkova

Mánesův most

Široká

Maiselova

Na Poříčí

nám. Jana Palacha

⑧ ⑥

Týnská

Náměstí Republiky

V Celnici

Staroměstská

Kaprova

Dlouha

Masarykovo

⑪

Krovnicka

Štupartská

Senovážná

❸

nám. Republiky

Municipal House

Masarykovo

❶

Karlův most (Charles Bridge)

Platnéřská

Mariánské nám.

Celetná

Hybernská

Dlážděná

Křižovnická

Staroměstské náměstí

⑤ Ovocny trh

Senovážné náměstí

⑫

Malé nám.

STARÉ MĚSTO

Karlova

⑬

Michalská

Estates Theater

Na příkopě

Panská

Nekázanka

Jeruzalémská

Opletalova

Karlovy nábř.

Zlatá

Husova

Pštrossova

Betlémské nám. ⑭

Havelská

Rytířská

Můstek

Jindřišská

Růžová

Olivova

Vrchlického sady

Konviktská

Uhelný trh

28. října

Politických vězňů

❷❸

Smetanovo nábř.

Karolíny Světlé

Bartolomějská

Na Perštýně

Jungmannovo nám.

Václavské náměstí (Wenceslas Square)

⑯

Národní

Národní Třída

Jungmannova

Opletalova

❷❹

Washingtonova

most Legií

Divadelní

National Theater

Národní

⑱

Spálená

Franciscan Garden

Vodičkova

Wilsonova

⑰

Ostrovní

NOVÉ MĚSTO

V jámě

Muzeum ❷❺

Slovanský ostrov

V Jirchářích

Opatovická

Lazarská

Štěpánská

Krakovská

Mezibranská

National Museum

⑲

Pštrossova

Černá

Navrátilova

Ve smečkách

Legerova

Masarykovo nábřeží

Voršilská

Myslíkova

Řeznická

Zitná

Sokolská

Anglická

⑳

Vojtěšská

Karlovo nám.

Zitná

V tůních

I.P. Pavlova

Jugoslávská

Jiráskův most

Resslova

Dittrichova

Václavská

Malá Štěpánská

Ječná

Na Rybníčku

Sokolská

nám. I.P. Pavlova

Tylovo nám.

Rumunská

Gorazdova

Ječná

Boišti

Rašínovo nábř.

Karlovo Náměstí

Na Moráni

Lípová

Kateřinská

ke Karlovu

Tyršova

Lublaňská

Bělehradská

Palackého most

Palackého nám.

Zítkovy sady

Pod Slovany

U Nemocnice

Viničná

Fügnerovo nám.

Koubkova

Sokolská

nábř.

Pod Skalská

Na Slupi

Benátská

Botanical Garden

Apolinářská

Studničkova

㉒

VYŠEHRAD

Vyšehradská

Na Slupi

Trojická

Plavecká

Botičská

Albertov

	Metro stop
====	Pedestrian passage
ШШШ	Steps

0   1/5 mi

0   0.2 km

N

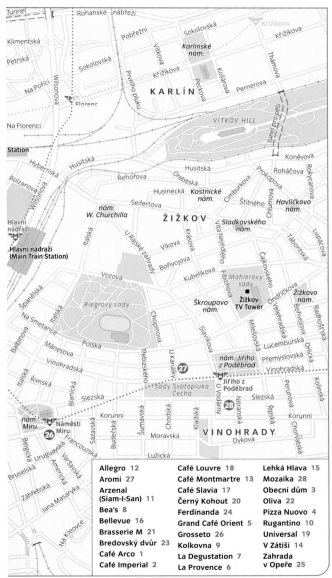

Allegro **12**	Café Louvre **18**	Lehká Hlava **15**
Aromi **27**	Café Montmartre **13**	Mozaika **28**
Arzenal	Café Slavia **17**	Obecní dům **3**
(Siam-I-San) **11**	Černý Kohout **20**	Oliva **22**
Bea's **8**	Ferdinanda **24**	Pizza Nuovo **4**
Bellevue **16**	Grand Café Orient **5**	Rugantino **10**
Brasserie M **21**	Grosseto **26**	Universal **19**
Bredovský dvůr **23**	Kolkovna **9**	V Zátiší **14**
Café Arco **1**	La Degustation **7**	Zahrada
Café Imperial **2**	La Provence **6**	v Opeře **25**

The Best Dining

Prague Restaurants A to Z

★★★ **Alchymist.** MALÁ STRANA *CONTINENTAL* An excellent choice for a special night out, though not everyone will fall in love with the overwrought interior—candelabras, mirrors, and statues. In summer you can dine in a newly opened exotic garden, with a small beach, daybeds, and a Moroccan-style tent; it's really something special. The veal medallions "al Piccata," with lemon sauce, carrots, and eggplant, are very good. *Hellichová 4.* ☎ *257-312-518. Entrees 400 Kč–600 Kč, 3-course set menu 1,150 Kč. AE, DC, MC, V. Lunch & dinner daily. Metro: Malostranská. Map p 95.*

★★★ **Allegro.** STARÉ MĚSTO *ITAL-IAN/CZECH* There aren't many star chefs in Prague, but Allegro's top man in the kitchen, Vito Mollica, is as close as it gets. When the Four Seasons Hotel opened here a few years back, they spared no expense to create Prague's best restaurant for foodies. The menu is eclectic, but leans toward Italian. For starters try the homemade ravioli, stuffed with zucchini and lobster. For mains, you can't go wrong with the light,

delicious seared salmon in a chick-pea purée. In summer, dine on the terrace overlooking the Vltava. *Veleslavínová 2a.* ☎ *221-427-000. Entrees 500 Kč–900 Kč. AE, DC, MC, V. Lunch & dinner daily. Metro: Staroměstská. Map p 96.*

★★★ **Aromi.** VINOHRADY *ITALIAN* This upscale Italian restaurant in residential Vinohrady was the toughest table to book in 2007. The secret: food that approaches the quality of Allegro (see above) at around half the price. The fresh fish may even be better than Allegro's. The menu features simple but trendy choices such as pumpkin risotto and aged balsamic vinegar or salt cod with potato cream and raisin pesto. Owner and head chef Riccardo Lucque has put in time at some of the best restaurants in New York and London. *Mánesová 78.* ☎ *222-713-222. Entrees 250 Kč–500 Kč. AE, DC, MC, V. Lunch & dinner daily. Metro: Jiřího z Poděbrad. Map p 96.*

★★ **Arzenal (Siam-I-San).** STARÉ MĚSTO *THAI* Put this in the "only in Prague" category—a combination

Arzenal (Siam-I-San).

Brasserie M.

upscale Thai restaurant and funky glass shop, featuring the jarring and not-to-everyone's-liking glass designs of Czech artist Borek Šípek. The Thai food is easily the best in Prague. Try the sweet-sharp tofu curry in a sauce of coconut milk, chilies, and sweet basil. The cutlery, glasses, and plates are all for sale. *Valentinská 11.* ☎ *224-814-099. Entrees 240 Kč–400 Kč. AE, DC, MC, V. Lunch & dinner daily. Metro: Staroměstská. Map p 96.*

★ **Bea's.** STARÉ MĚSTO *VEGETARIAN* Vegetarians have it rough in Prague. The practice of eschewing meat has been slow to catch on, and to add insult to injury, even items in the *bez masa* (without meat) section of restaurant menus often contain small bits of ham or bacon (apparently for flavor). This cafeteria-style eatery, just a stone's throw from Old Town Square, serves decent, Indian-inflected, meatless meals such as stewed lentils and curries for possibly the lowest prices in town. Closes early on Sundays. *Týnská 19.* ☎ *777-165-478. Entrees 70 Kč–140 Kč. No credit cards. Lunch & dinner daily (closes at 6pm on Sun). Metro: Staroměstská. Map p 96.*

★★★ **Bellevue.** STARÉ MĚSTO *CONTINENTAL* Until recently, the food here was no match for the dramatic tableside vistas to the castle across the river, but the owners have upped the ante and what's on your plate now vies for at least equal attention. The menu is a bit on the timid side, with items like monkfish and New Zealand lamb, but it's all fresh, and superbly presented. My favorite is the local specialty: Czech pikeperch served in a sauce of Tramín wine. Dress up. *Smetanovo nábř. 18.* ☎ *222-221-443. Entrees 600 Kč–800 Kč. AE, DC, MC, V. Lunch & dinner daily. Metro: Staroměstská. Map p 96.*

★★★ **Brasserie M.** NOVÉ MĚSTO *FRENCH* One of only a handful of Prague restaurants to be accorded Michelin recognition—in this case a "Bib Gourmand," not a star exactly, but something close. The French owner is trying to re-create an authentic Paris bistro in the middle of Prague and has largely succeeded. The menu runs to French classics like coq au vin and beef tournedos seared with foie gras. *Vladislavová 17.* ☎ *224-054-070. Entrees 250 Kč–400 Kč. AE, DC, MC, V. Lunch & dinner daily. Metro: Národní třída. Map p 96.*

The Best Dining

★★ **Bredovský dvůr.** NOVÉ MĚSTO *CZECH* Perhaps only in the Czech Republic does beer deserve such lofty consideration in selecting a restaurant. This Czech tavern serves nonpasteurized Pilsener Urquell from large tanks behind the bar (the equivalent, I suppose, of drinking fine wine right from the barrel). The crowds love it. It's also a great place for the beer's culinary counterpoints—roast pork with bread dumplings and sauerkraut, or roast duck. *Politických vězňů 13.* ☎ *224-215-428. Entrees 150 Kč–250 Kč. No credit cards. Lunch & dinner daily. Metro: Mustek. Map p 96.*

★ **Café Arco.** NOVÉ MĚSTO *TRADI-TIONAL CAFE* This was once the cafe of choice for Prague's German-speaking Jewish writers, including Franz Werfel, Max Brod, and, natu-rally, Franz Kafka. Habitués here were known for a time as "Arco-nauts." Legend has it this was where Kafka met the love of his life, Milena Jesenská. Alas, it's only a shell of its former self, with a lifeless canteen serving bad food on one side and some nondescript offices on the

Café Imperial.

other. A small window exhibition, including an unconvincing portrait of the young Kafka, is the only clue to what once transpired here. *Hybernská 16.* ☎ *974-863-542. Metro: Náměstí Republiky. Map p 96.*

★★★ **Café Imperial.** NOVÉ MĚSTO *TRADITIONAL CAFE* This eclectic, Art Nouveau cafe dates from 1912, but was thoroughly ren-ovated in 2007. The signature tiled pillars and mosaics remain intact, but the renovation brought in nicer tables and chairs and a revamped menu of well-prepared Czech and international dishes. A perfect throwback to the era of the silent screen. Also serves an excellent American breakfast, with eggs, sausage, and bacon. *Na Poříčí 15.* ☎ *246-011-440. Entrees 200 Kč–400 Kč. MC, V. Breakfast, lunch & dinner daily. Metro: Náměstí Republiky. Map p 96.*

★★ **Café Louvre.** NOVÉ MĚSTO *TRADITIONAL CAFE* This former intellectual heavyweight was reput-edly a favorite hangout of German-speaking students in the early years of the 20th century, including—for a time—a visiting professor named Albert Einstein. Even Kafka dropped by for a debate or two. There's nothing remotely cerebral about the place today; it's just a bright, bustling cafe, serving decent coffee drinks and a full menu of Czech and international dishes. *Národní 22.* ☎ *224-930-949. Entrees 100 Kč–300 Kč. MC, V. Breakfast, lunch & dinner daily. Metro: Národní třída. Map p 96.*

★ **Café Montmartre.** STARÉ MĚSTO *TRADITIONAL CAFE* Laid-back student cafe on a quiet, hard-to-find street in the Old Town. The coffee's not that great (you'll get better espresso drinks at the Ebel cafe next door), but the interior

Cantina.

retains the feel of a 1920s cabaret (essentially what it used to be). Good choice for a quiet chat over a glass of wine. Limited food options. *Řetězová 7.* ☎ *222-221-244. No credit cards. Metro: Staroměstská. Map p 96.*

★★ kids **Café Savoy.** MALÁ STRANA *CZECH* A beautiful setting in a restored 19th-century coffee-house, with an eclectic menu running from Czech classics like *svíčková* (marinated beef tenderloin served in a cream sauce with bread dumplings) to full-on English and American breakfasts. Ideal for lunch or for coffee and cakes between meals. At meal times, reservations are recommended. *Vitězná 1.* ☎ *257-311-562. Entrees 150 Kč–300 Kč. AE, DC, MC, V. Lunch & dinner daily. Metro: Malostranská. Map p 95.*

★ **Café Slavia.** STARÉ MĚSTO *TRADITIONAL CAFE* This legendary dissident cafe has the added advantage of a perfect view out over the river toward Prague Castle. The Slavia was once a meeting point for Václav Havel and other dissident

intellectuals from the theater and film worlds; it was remodeled in the 1990s and never fully recaptured its cachet. Now, it's mostly filled with tourists perched at the window admiring the castle. Both the coffee and the food are hit-and-miss, but it's still a must visit for Havel fans. *Smetanovo náb. 2.* ☎ *224-218-493. Entrees 150 Kč–300 Kč. MC, V. Lunch & dinner daily. Metro: Národní třída. Map p 96.*

★★ **Cantina.** MALÁ STRANA *MEXI-CAN* Czechs line up out the door for a chance at a chicken or beef burrito or a plate of sizzling fajitas. Mexican food has had a rough ride in Prague—it's considered too spicy for local tastes. Cantina has mellowed it just enough to make it palatable, but not so much as to make it bland. Tequila keeps the atmosphere more than festive, but book in advance or be prepared for a long wait for a table. *Újezd 38.* ☎ *257-317-173. Entrees 120 Kč–250 Kč. No credit cards. Lunch & dinner daily. Metro: Malostranská. Map p 95.*

Černý Kohout.

★★★ **Černý Kohout.** NOVÉ MĚSTO *CZECH*

One of the few places in town that's capable of elevating Czech food to the best of international cuisines. Game is a staple of Czech cooking, and here you can try both wild boar and wild duck in one entree, served on red cabbage with apples. Offers an amazing-value set business lunch for 199 Kč, with simpler Czech dishes like venison served with homemade bacon dumplings. *Vojtěšská 9.* ☎ *251-681-191. Entrees 400 Kč–500 Kč. AE, DC, MC, V. Lunch & dinner daily. Metro: Karlovo nám. Map p 96.*

★★ **Cowboys.** MALÁ STRANA *STEAKHOUSE*

This is a leading destination for steak lovers—with the top draw the highly recommended rib-eye (served with baked potato in a red-wine sauce). Cowboys is run by the same team that owns Kampa Park, but the atmosphere here is festive, not snooty. In nice weather, keep climbing to the top to the open-air terrace, just below Prague castle. Chocolate cheesecake is the perfect way to end the meal. *Nerudová 40.* ☎ *800-157-626. Entrees 300 Kč–600 Kč. AE, DC, MC, V. Lunch & dinner daily. Metro: Malostranská. Map p 95.*

★ **Ferdinanda.** NOVÉ MĚSTO *CZECH*

Popular Czech pub right off of Wenceslas Square, serving decent local fare and beers brought in from the small Ferdinand brewery located in Benešov, about 48km (30 miles) south of Prague. Goulash gets top billing here, served Czech-style, cooked with cumin and sweet paprika and served with fresh grated onions on top. The beers are excellent. Try the sweetish dark beer *(tmavé)*, or a stronger semidark, Sedml kuli. *Opletalová 24.* ☎ *222-244-302. Entrees 100 Kč–160 Kč. MC, V. Lunch & dinner daily. Metro: Muzeum. Map p 96.*

★★ **Fraktal.** LETNÁ *SANDWICHES*

Not long ago, this used to be the smokiest beer-swilling dive this side of the river. The owners decided to clean up their act and offer arguably the best burgers and bar-style Mexican food (burritos and quesadillas) in Prague. Try the goat-cheese burger with pistachio nuts. The perfect choice if you're looking for a great bite and want to tie one on later: You won't have to move from your seat all night. In nice weather, sit on the streetside terrace, but call in advance to reserve. Good brunches on weekends from 11am until 3pm. *Šmeralová 1.* ☎ *777-794-094. Entrees 100 Kč–200 Kč. No credit cards. Lunch & dinner daily. Metro: Vltavska, plus tram 1 or 25. Map p 95.*

★★★ **Grand Café Orient.** STARÉ MĚSTO *TRADITIONAL CAFE* Beautifully refurbished Flapper-era cafe that lays claim to being the only Cubist cafe in the world. It's delightfully free from the tour-bus crowd and an excellent spot for a quiet coffee and cake or a glass of wine during the day. *Ovocný trh 19 (at the corner of Celetná).* ☎ *224-224-220. Entrees 100 Kč–200 Kč. MC, V. Breakfast, lunch & light dinner daily. Metro: Národní třida. Map p 96.*

★ **Grosseto.** VINOHRADY *ITALIAN* This popular pizzeria at the Náměstí Miru metro stop is a good choice for lunch or a casual dinner. Grosseto's "Moderni"—a white pizza topped with sun-dried tomatoes, rocket (arugula), and pine nuts—won the Prague Post's annual "Best Pizza" award in 2007. The deal breaker is the lovely, secluded garden in the back—one of the nicest spots in leafy Vinohrady to while away the hours. *Francouzská 2.* ☎ *224-252-778. Entrees 100 Kč–240 Kč. No credit cards. Lunch & dinner daily. Metro: Náměstí Miru. Map p 96.*

★★★ **Hergetova Cihelna.** MALÁ STRANA *CONTINENTAL* This restaurant boasts what just might be Prague's best riverside dining, with a view to the Charles Bridge that even Charles IV would appreciate. The dining concept here is high-end casual: pastas, sandwiches, and burgers, but the menu also has a nice range of salads and grilled meats. The cheeseburger vies for the best in Prague, but I'm partial to the Wiener schnitzel, served here, oddly, with mashed potatoes. The dessert pancakes come topped with blueberries and maple-syrup ice cream. Part of the Kampa Park group's stable of very good restaurants. *Cihelna 2b.* ☎ *296-826-103. Entrees 300 Kč–500 Kč. AE, DC, MC, V. Lunch & dinner daily. Metro: Malostranská. Map p 95.*

★★ **Kampa Park.** MALÁ STRANA *CONTINENTAL* Year after year, a table here is widely considered the best in town, even if the cooking has slipped a notch and the prices have gone through the roof. The list of

Hergetova Cihelna.

who's dined here reads like the Hollywood Walk of Fame: Johnny Depp, Matt Damon, Bruce Willis, Brad Pitt, Bruce Springsteen, and Bill and Hillary Clinton (to name a few). For something a little different, try the venison with mushrooms, parsnips, and figs, served in a cardamom reduction. *Na Kampě 8b.* ☎ *296-826-102. Entrees 600 Kč–900 Kč. AE, DC, MC, V. Lunch & dinner daily. Metro: Malostranská. Map p 95.*

★★★ **Kolkovna.** STARÉ MĚSTO *CZECH* This classic Czech pub is part of a chain owned by the Pilsener Urquell brewery, but don't let that deter you. The standards for food and service are high, and it's even worth stopping in for the beer alone. This is a good place to sample a massive pork knee *(koleno),* served on a wooden board with slices of bread, plus mustard and horseradish. You won't eat again for 2 days. Gets crowded at mealtimes, so book in advance. *V Kolkovně 8.* ☎ *224-819-701. Entrees 140 Kč–280 Kč. MC, V. Lunch & dinner daily. Metro: Staroměstská. Map p 96.*

★★★ **La Degustation.** STARÉ MĚSTO *CZECH/CONTINENTAL*

A veritable orgy of fine food. Diners are offered a choice of three elaborate, 12-course set menus, featuring either Czech or Continental classics. The meal unfolds over 3 hours, and sommeliers are on hand to suggest the wines to match the dishes. Not cheap, but a one-of-a-kind culinary adventure. Reservations essential. *Haštalská 18.* ☎ *222-311-234. Set menu 2,000 Kč. AE, DC, MC, V. Lunch & dinner Mon–Sat. Metro: Staroměstská. Map p 96.*

★★★ **La Provence.** STARÉ MĚSTO *FRENCH* This relaxed French restaurant has long been a mainstay in Prague's fine-dining firmament, and with the arrival of chef Jerome Lorieux in 2006, it's only gotten better. It's actually two restaurants—an informal "brasserie" upstairs and more intimate space below ground. Both menus are similar and feature classic French cooking like beef bourguignon and rabbit Provençal. They do a very good duck here, served in a red-wine and ginger sauce with mustard-flavored mashed potatoes. *Štupartská 9.* ☎ *296-826-155. Entrees 400 Kč–600 Kč. AE, DC, MC, V. Lunch & dinner daily. Metro: Staroměstská. Map p 96.*

Kolkovna.

La Provence.

★★ **Lehká Hlava.** STARÉ MĚSTO
VEGETARIAN Arguably the best
vegetarian restaurant in Prague,
and one of the few places that manage to make a virtue of tofu. The
eclectic menu borrows from Spanish,
Mexican, Middle Eastern, and Asian
cooking. Try the veggie tofu stir-fry
with fresh ginger or the baked quesadillas with cheddar cheese and
jalapeños. The whole place is nonsmoking, and the casual, funky interior makes it a fun place to hang
out. *Boršov 2.* ☎ *222-220-665.*
*Entrees 100 Kč–200 Kč. No credit
cards. Lunch & dinner daily. Metro:
Staroměstská. Map p 96.*

★★★ **Mozaika.** VINOHRADY
CZECH/ECLECTIC This popular
neighborhood place draws an even
mix of Czechs, visitors, and expats.
The food is excellent, and the
muted modern decor perfect for
a quiet evening for two or a business meal. The food is essentially
Czech, with noticeable French and
Asian influences. Excellent and
reasonably priced wine list. Try
the fish lasagna, stuffed with tuna,
salmon, and ricotta cheese. Not
on the menu anymore but worth
asking for is the seared salmon
with wasabi mashed potatoes.

Nitranská 13. ☎ *224-253-011.*
*Entrees 200 Kč–400 Kč. MC, V. Lunch
& dinner daily. Metro: Jiřího z
Poděbrad. Map p 96.*

★★★ **Obecní dům.** STARÉ MĚSTO
TRADITIONAL CAFE It's a pity this
incredible place seems frequented
only by tourists; I'd consider it a
serious contender for the list of
world's top 10 most beautiful cafes.
The Art Nouveau details, such as
the ornamented chandeliers and
tiled mosaics, the evening piano

Obecní dům.

A dish at Perpetuum: Confit of duck, smoked bacon, potato and cheese soufflé, and cranberries.

music, and even the beautiful lavatories overwhelm the comparatively humdrum business of serving coffees and cakes. You can sit on the terrace in nice weather, but who would want to when it's this nice inside? Also serves a full range of wines, beer, and mixed drinks. *Náměstí Republiky 5.*

☎ *222-002-763. Entrees 100 Kč–300 Kč. Breakfast, lunch & light dinner daily. Metro: Náměstí Republiky. Map p 96.*

★★★ **Oliva.** NOVÉ MĚSTO
FRENCH/ECLECTIC Similar to Mozaika in that it's a neighborhood place with lofty culinary ambitions that mostly delivers. Here, the emphasis is more on French cooking, but there are some surprises on the menu, like a grilled octopus starter served on potato salad or a delicious Moroccan chicken tagine with tomato couscous. The perfectly seared crème brûlée is a Prague institution among those in the know. *Plavecká 4.* ☎ *222-520-288. Entrees 220 Kč–400 Kč. MC, V. Lunch & dinner Mon–Sat. Metro: Karlovo nám. Map p 96.*

★★ **Pálffy Palác.** MALÁ STRANA
CONTINENTAL If nothing less than an über-elegant Baroque salon, complete with candles and flowers, will do, then this is your place. In summer, they open a terrace with a jaw-dropping view of the castle. The yellowfin tuna with pumpkin purée entree is highly recommended and something you don't see everyday on Prague menus. *Valdštejnská 14.* ☎ *257-530-522. Entrees 500 Kč–700*

Some Dining Warnings

Some Czech restaurants are notorious for placing seemingly free bowls of nuts or olives on the table or offering platters of appetizers or aperitifs that appear to be compliments of the house. They're not. When the bill comes, you might find that you're paying the equivalent of $5 for a bowl of stale cashews. Always ask before nibbling.

Many places, especially in the evening, tack on an extra 30 Kč or 50 Kč per person as a cover charge, even if they don't offer live entertainment. If this charge is mentioned at all, it will be written discreetly on the menu as *couvert*.

Kč. AE, DC, MC, V. Lunch & dinner daily. Metro: Malostranská. Map p 95.

★★ **Perpetuum.** DEJVICE *CZECH* Duck rarely gets the attention it deserves. Even in Prague, where it's a local staple, most restaurants pre-cook their birds and warm them to order, leaving the meat dry and tasteless. Here they do duck right. The specialty is roast duck with cumin, served with bread and potato dumplings as sides. The grilled Barberie duck with purple potato purée and duck reduction is excellent. The setting is refined but casual. Perfect for a quiet dinner. *Na hutich 9.* ☎ *233-323-429. Entrees 220 Kč–340 Kč. AE, DC, MC, V. Lunch & dinner Mon–Sat. Metro: Dejvice. Map p 95.*

★★★ **kids Pizza Nuovo.** STARÉ MĚSTO *PIZZA* Vies with Rugantino (see below) for the best pizza in Prague. Not only are the ingredients imported from Italy, but so is the pizza chef (in this case from Naples). Pizza Diavolo—spicy pepperonis and mozzarella—is worth going out of your way for. The only drawback is a complicated ordering system where you're given a form to fill out, which you hand to the waitress. Don't ask me to explain it, I don't get it either. Just ask for the menu and point to what you want. Casual and fun with a large nonsmoking section. *Revoluční 1.* ☎ *221-803-308. Entrees 160 Kč–250 Kč. AE, DC, MC, V. Lunch & dinner daily. Metro: Náměstí Republiky. Map p 96.*

★★★ **kids Rugantino.** STARÉ MĚSTO *PIZZA* Easily the most family-friendly restaurant in all of Prague, with highchairs at the ready and staff who seem oblivious to hordes of little tykes scurrying between the tables. It also happens to have the best thin-crust pizza in town, with Italian-imported olive oils

and mozzarella. Pizza Calabrese, a spicier version of American-style pepperoni pizza, is a local classic. *Dušní 4.* ☎ *222-318-172. Entrees 120 Kč–200 Kč. No credit cards. Lunch & dinner daily. Metro: Staroměstská. Map p 96.*

★★ **Sushi Bar.** MALÁ STRANA *JAPANESE* Sushi restaurants in Prague tend to be sterile and a little lifeless. This Czech-run place is tiny, intimate, and always hopping. Prices have climbed in recent years, but the fish is the freshest in Prague. Standard sushi and maki sets. The eight-piece "Dragon Roll" is made from grilled eel, avocado, and sesame. *Zborovská 49.* ☎ *603-244-882. Entrees 400 Kč–600 Kč. No credit cards. Lunch & dinner daily. Metro: Malostranská plus tram 22, 12. Map p 95.*

★ **Universal.** NOVÉ MĚSTO *FRENCH/CZECH* A Czech pub that fancies itself a French bistro,

Sushi Bar.

V Zátiší.

with excellent salads and comfort food at affordable prices. The big-bowl salads include a very good Caesar. For a main course, try the lamb cutlets, priced at about half what you'd pay elsewhere. It's very popular, so call in advance and be prepared to wait in the bar (even if you've reserved). *V Jirchářích 6.* ☎ *224-918-182. Entrees 120 Kč–280 Kč. No credit cards. Lunch & dinner daily. Metro: Národní třída. Map p 96.*

★★ **V Zátiší.** STARÉ MĚSTO *CONTI-NENTAL* The "Still Life" restaurant is the jewel in local restaurateur San-jiv Suri's crown of high-end restaurants (which also includes Bellevue, above). The quiet location, just off Betlémské náměstí, makes it a favorite for intimate dinners or important business engagements. Like Suri's other restaurants, the menu holds few surprises (standards such as grilled salmon, pork tender-loin, and roast lamb), but the quality of the ingredients and presentation

is flawless. My favorite: the roast lamb shank, with hazelnut flavored potato purée. *Liliová 1.* ☎ *222-221-155. Entrees 400 Kč–700 Kč. AE, DC, MC, V. Lunch & dinner daily. Metro: Staroměstská. Map p 96.*

★★★ **Zahrada v Opeře.** VINOHRADY *CONTINENTAL* Pity that the "Garden at the Opera" is so close to Radio Free Europe. Security concerns mean you have to skirt a concrete bunker and cross a busy road to find the entrance. But rest assured, this is one of the best meals in Prague for the money. The menu is eclectic. Chicken and pork dishes mix it up with more exotic fare like Nasi Goreng (spicy fried rice with shrimps, calamari, and chicken). The atmosphere is dressy-casual, and the opera location makes it a convenient spot for a pre- or post-performance bite. *Legerová 75.* ☎ *224-239-685. Entrees 280 Kč–500 Kč. AE, DC, MC, V. Lunch & dinner daily. Metro: Muzeum. Map p 96.* ●

Staré Město Area

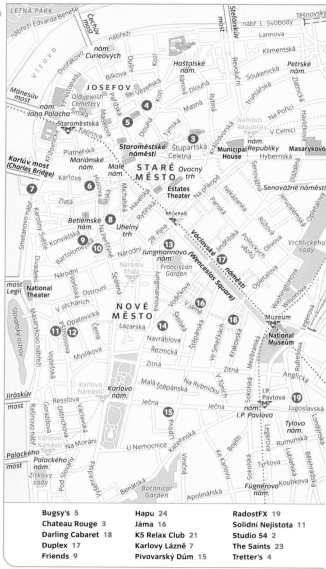

Bugsy's 5
Chateau Rouge 3
Darling Cabaret 18
Duplex 17
Friends 9

Hapu 24
Jáma 16
K5 Relax Club 21
Karlovy Lázně 7
Pivovarský Dům 15

RadostFX 19
Solidní Nejistota 11
Studio 54 2
The Saints 23
Tretter's 4

Previous page: Karlovy Lázně dance club.

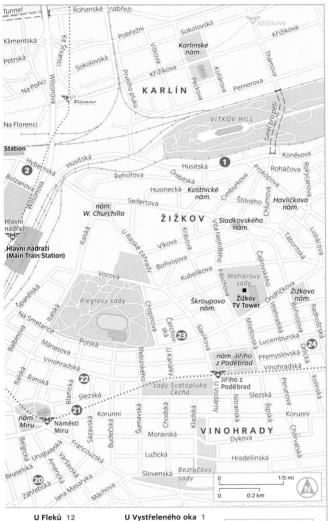

U Fleků 12
U Medvídků 10
U Pinkasů 13
U Sudu 14
U Vejvodů 8
U Vystřeleného oka 1
U Zlatého tygra 6
Valentino 22
Žlutá Pumpa 20

◥M F Metro stop
==== Pedestrian passage
ⅢⅢⅢ Steps

Malá Strana Area

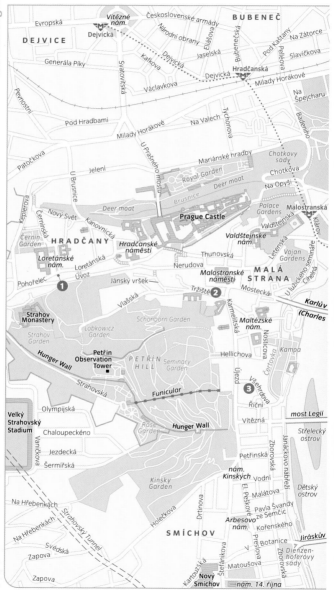

Evropská

Vitězné nám.

Československé armády

BUBENEČ

Dejvická

DEJVICE

Národní obrany

Eliášova

Bubenečská

Pod Kaštany

Na Zátorce

Pelléova

Slavíčkova

Generála Piky

Kafkova

Dejvická

Jaselská

Svatovítská

Dejvická

Hradčanská

Václavkova

Milady Horákové

Na Špejcharu

Pevnostní

Badeniho

Pod Hradbami

Na Valech

Tychonova

Patočkova

Milady Horákové

U Prašného mostu

Jeleni

Mariánské hradby

Chotkovy sady

U Brusnice

Royal Garden

Chotkova

Keplerova

Černínská

Nový Svět

Kanovnická

Deer moat

Brusnice

Deer moat

Na Opyši

Palace Gardens

Malostranská

Černín Garden

HRADČANY

Hradčanské náměstí

Prague Castle

Valdštejnská

Valdštejnská nám.

Klárov

Loretánské nám.

Loretánská

Úvoz

Thunovská

Letenská

Vojan Gardens

U lužického semináře

Cihelná

Pohořelec

Jánský vršek

Nerudova

Malostranské náměstí

MALÁ STRANA

❶

Vlašská

Tržiště ❷

Mostecká

Karlův (Charles

Strahov Monastery

Lobkowicz Garden

Schönborn Garden

Karmelitská

Maltézské nám.

Nosticova

Čertovka

Kampa

Strahov Garden

Petřín Observation Tower

PETŘÍN HILL

Seminary Garden

Hellichova

Újezd

Všehrdova

Hunger Wall

Strahovská

Funicular

❸

Říční

Velký Strahovský Stadium

Olympijská

Rose Garden

Hunger Wall

Vitězná

most Legii

Vaníčkova

Chaloupeckého

Petřínská

Zborovská

Janáčkovo nábřeží

Střelecký ostrov

Jezdecká

Šermířská

Kinský Garden

Drtinova

Vodni

El. Peškové

Malátova

Pavla Švandy ze Semčíc

Dětský ostrov

Na Hřebenkách

Strahovský Tunnel

Holečkova

SMÍCHOV

nám. Kinských

Arbesovo nám.

Kořenského

Botanice

Jiráskův

Na Hřebenkách

Švédská

Zapova

Štefánikova

Kartouzská

V Preslova

Zborovská

Dienzen-hoferovy sady

Zapova

Matoušova

Nový Smíchov

nám. 14. října

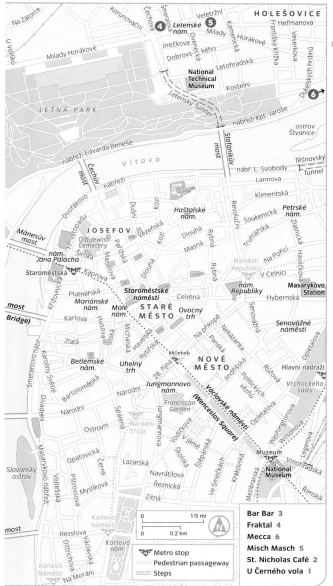

Bar Bar 3
Fraktal 4
Mecca 6
Misch Masch 5
St. Nicholas Café 2
U Černého vola 1

Nightlife Best Bets

Best Martini
★★★ Hapu, *Orlická 8 (p 117)*

Best 15th-Century Beer
★ U Fleků, *Křemencová 11 (p 115)*

Best Modern Beer
★★★ Pivovarský Dům, *Lípová 15 (p 116)*

Best Czech Hospoda
★★★ U Zlatého tygra, *Husová 17 (p 116)*

Best Wine Bar
★★★ U Sudu, *Vodičková 10 (p 118)*

Best for Celeb Spotting
★★ Tretter's, *V kolkovně 3 (p 118)*

Best Dance Club
★★★ Mecca, *U pruhonu 3 (p 119)*

Best for Vegetarians
★★ RadostFX, *B lehradská 120 (p 119)*

Best for Stag Parties
★ Darling Cabaret, *Vc Smeckach 32 (p 120)*

Best Microbrewery
★★★ Pivovarský Dům, *Lípová 15 (p 116)*

Best for Those Over 30
★★ Bugsy's, *Pařižská 10 (p 116)*

Best for Those Under 20
★ Karlovy Lázně, *Smetanovo náb. 198 (p 118)*

Best if You Are Mick Jagger
★★ Duplex, *Václavské nám. 21 (p 118)*

Best at 5am
★★ Studio 54, *Hybernská 38 (p 119)*

Best Gay Bar
★★★ The Saints, *Polská 32 (p 120)*

Best Steam Bath
★★ K5 Relax Club, *Korunní 5 (p 120)*

Karlovy Lázně.

Prague Nightlife A to Z

Traditional Czech Pubs (Hospody)

★★★ U Černého vola HRAD-ČANY One of the few remaining traditional pubs in the immediate area of Prague castle. This a gem. Big wooden tables, unfazed regulars who've seen and done it all, and excellent and increasingly hard-to-find Kozel beer on tap. Worth going out of your way for. *Loretánské nám. 1.* ☎ *220-513-481. Metro: Hradčanská. Map p 112.*

★ U Fleků NOVÉ MĚSTO This 15th-century brewpub falls somewhere between "tourist trap" and "must visit." It's certainly no stranger to the many tour buses that stop here nightly at the front door, and the waiters have been known to pad the bill of unsuspecting visitors. On the other hand, U Fleků might well be the most famous watering hole in the city. Its strong house lager is made from a recipe that's more

than 500 years old. And the Czech food is decent and not too expensive (given the clientele). Still, you're unlikely to see a Czech in the room (besides the waiter). *Křemencová 11.* ☎ *224-934-019. Metro: Národní třída. Map p 110.*

★★ U Medvídků STARÉ MĚSTO Most pubs in Prague serve either Pilsener Urquell or Staropramen beers (both great beers, but sometimes you need a little variety). The "Little Bear" is one of a seemingly dwindling number of places in the city that serves original Budweiser, Budvar, from the southern Bohemian city of České Budějovice. Like U Fleků, this place is a storied, centuries-old pub that's become immensely popular with visitors. Try to time your arrival to avoid mealtimes or call in advance to reserve a seat. *Na Perštýně 7.* ☎ *224-211-916. Metro: Národní třída. Map p 110.*

U Medvídků.

★★ U Pinkasů NOVÉ MĚSTO A standard in nearly every guidebook on Prague, but still worth recommending for the excellent Pilsener Urquell beer, passable Czech food, and wonderfully old-fashioned pub feel. In cold weather, settle back at your table and just let the waiters bring round after round. In summer, tables in the back become an impromptu inner-city beer garden. *Jungmannovo nám. 16.* ☎ *221-111-150. Metro: Mustek. Map p 110.*

★★★ Pivovarský Dům NOVÉ MĚSTO A relative rarity in this beer-soaked town: a microbrewery. Purists will likely turn their noses up at oddities like sour-cherry beer and banana beer, but the fact remains that this is one of the most popular pubs in town. They must be doing something right. Also serves a full menu of very good Czech classics, like the ever-present *vepřo-knedlo-zelo* (roast pork, dumplings, and sauerkraut). Reservations highly recommended. *Lípová 15.* ☎ *296-216-666. Metro: Staroměstská. Map p 110.*

★ U Vejvodů STARÉ MĚSTO Back in the early '90s, this was a classic Czech pub: smoky, dirty, and filled with drunken old codgers, yet it always had great beer and tons of atmosphere. Now it's been remodeled into one of the slickest, biggest, and busiest taverns in the center of town, serving beer by the keg-load to hundreds and hundreds of customers—mostly tourists—each night. On the plus side, the beer (Pilsener Urquell) is still pretty good and the place is so big you'll never be turned away for a lack of seats. *Jilská 4.* ☎ *224-219-999. Metro: Národní třída. Map p 110.*

★★ U Vystřeleného oka ŽIŽKOV The "Shot-Out Eye" is a legendary Žižkov pub that's contributed immensely to this working-class

Almond cigar cocktail at Bugsy's.

neighborhood's "bad-boy" image. Not particularly tourist-friendly, but certainly the real deal if it's a Czech pub you're after. The name refers to 15th-century Hussite general Jan Žižka, who, although blind, rarely lost a battle. The district of Žižkov is also named for him. Nice beer garden in summer. Serves excellent Radegast and Kozel beers. *U Božích bojovníků 3.* ☎ *222-540-465. Metro: Hlavní nádraží (plus tram 5, 9, or 26). Map p 110.*

★★★ U Zlatého tygra STARÉ MĚSTO The "Golden Tiger" is one of the very few true-blue Czech pubs in the center that hasn't sold its soul to the tourist trade. The regulars still line up for the 3pm opening, much as they always have. The Pilsener Urquell served here is reputed to be some of the best in the city. Former U.S. President Bill Clinton once raised a glass here with Václav Havel and fabled Czech writer Bohumil Hrabal. The photo of that strange night is still on the wall. *Husová 17.* ☎ *222-221-111. Metro: Staroměstská. Map p 110.*

Bars

★★ Bar Bar MALÁ STRANA This cozy, student-oriented bar and small restaurant is convenient to Kampa park. In addition to the usual beer and wine offerings, they make a great mulled wine in winter and have a full menu of sweet and savory crepes. The back room is a nice place to while away a rainy afternoon. *Všehrdová 17.* ☎ *257-312-246. Metro: Malostranská. Map p 112.*

★★ Bugsy's STARÉ MĚSTO This calm and cool cocktail and cigar bar lies just off of fashionable Pařížská. A perfectly refined spot to get the evening rolling or to say goodnight over a nightcap. The bartenders know their drinks, and will gladly make one to order if you want something that's not on the menu. *Pařížská 10.* ☎ *224-810-287. Metro: Staroměstská. Map p 110.*

★ Chateau Rouge STARÉ MĚSTO Whatever international reputation Prague has as a party town owes a lot to this raucous bar not far from Old Town Square. The two big ground-floor bars—and several rooms downstairs—fill up fast in the evening, and the festivities usually last well into the

night. Highly popular with revelers from around the world. *Jakubská 2.* ☎ *222-316-328. Metro: Náměstí Republiky. Map p 110.*

★★ Fraktal LETNÁ Not long ago this was a scruffy basement joint reserved exclusively for hard-core partiers. The owners cleaned up their act and took Fraktal slightly more up-market. The result is the friendliest and most enjoyable pub in this part of town. Decent Mexican food and an English-speaking staff round out the charms. *Šmeralová 1.* ☎ *777-794-094. Metro: Hradčanská (plus tram 1, 8, 25, or 26). Map p 112.*

★★★ Hapu ŽIŽKOV This modest neighborhood speak-easy–type place is perfect for people who enjoy well-made cocktails, but don't like the pretension that's sometimes associated with "cocktail bars." Comfortably down-market surroundings, such as amiably frayed rugs and thrift-store couches, contribute to the relaxed vibe. The drinks are the best in town. *Orlická 8.* ☎ *222-720-158. Metro: Flora. Map p 110.*

★★ Jáma NOVÉ MĚSTO This fun, college-town-bar type of place draws an eclectic crowd of Czechs, expats,

St. Nicholas Cafe.

and tourists from all walks of life. The "Cheers"-type bar—with English-speaking bartenders (usually female)—is great for solo travelers. After a few drinks, you'll have a roomful of new friends. *V jámě 7.* ☎ *224-222-383. Metro: Mustek. Map p 110.*

★ **St. Nicholas Cafe** MALÁ STRANA The inviting downstairs drinking room at this cafe is perfect for a quiet conversation, with low light, funky tables and chairs, and a relaxed vibe. The bar stocks the usual selection of beer and wine, and some mixed drinks. Resist the temptation to order the sub-par pizza. Instead, make this a pre- or post-dinner stop. *Tržiště 10. No phone. Metro: Malostranská. Map p 112.*

★★ **Tretter's** STARÉ MĚSTO This elegant Old Town cocktail bar attracts the glamour set as well as a fair number of Hollywood celebrities in town for a movie shoot. Arrive before 9pm to snag a coveted table along the wall opposite the bar. Dress up after 11pm in order to get past the doorman out front. Good gimlets. *V kolkovně 3.* ☎ *224-811-165. Metro: Staroměstská. Map p 110.*

U Sudu.

★★★ **U Sudu** NOVÉ MĚSTO You'll find this labyrinthine wine bar just a short walk from Václavské náměstí. People come here not for the fine wines—the drink card contains mostly ordinary Czech whites and reds—but for the all-important social and party aspect of drinking. If at first you don't find a seat, keep on walking down and down. In the fall, look out for *burčák*, a cloudy young wine with a sour-sweet taste and deceptively high potency. *Vodičková 10.* ☎ *222-232-207. Metro: Mustek. Map p 110.*

★★ **Žlutá Pumpa** VINOHRADY Students flock to this informal watering hole in Vinohrady. Impossibly crowded after midnight, so come early or content yourself with standing at the bar. They serve passably good Mexican food, but truth be told, most people are here for the beer and the party vibe. *Belgická 12.* ☎ *608-184-360. Metro: Náměstí Miru. Map p 110.*

Dance Clubs

★★ **Duplex** NOVÉ MĚSTO The main advantage of this crowded rooftop dance club is location—right in the middle of Václavské náměstí. A bit more sophisticated than Karlovy Lázně (see below), with a slightly older, more established clientele. Mick Jagger thought so much of the place that he picked Duplex for his 60th birthday party a few years ago (though most of the customers are well south of 60). *Václavské nám. 21.* ☎ *732-221-111. Cover 150 Kč. Metro: Mustek. Map p 110.*

★ **Karlovy Lázně** STARÉ MĚSTO Karlovy Lázně advertises itself as Central Europe's biggest dance club, and that may well be true. Each of the several floors of dancing has a different sound and theme: techno, metal, pop, oldies, funk, depending on the night. Popular with students and 20-somethings, who line up at the door at midnight and stay until dawn. *Smetanovo náb. 198.* ☎ *222-220-502. Cover 100 Kč–200 Kč. Metro: Staroměstská. Map p 110.*

★★★ **Mecca** HOLEŠOVICE This cool, designer disco tends to draw a successful, trendier-than-thou crowd in their 20s to 40s. Great DJs. Wear your best clubbing duds and take a map—you'll need it to find this place, in a still-scruffy part of Holešovice. Free admission on Wednesdays. *U průhonu 3.* ☎ *283-870-522. Cover 100 Kč–200 Kč. Metro: Nádraží Holešovice. Map p 112.*

★★ **Misch Masch** LETNÁ The latest incarnation of a famed club from the 1990s of the same name— a wide-open, no-holds-barred dance club that gets going only after midnight. Separate rooms for funk and oldies. Most revelers are in their student years and 20s, but you'll see all ages here. ☎ *603-222-227. Cover 100 Kč–200 Kč. Metro: Vltavská (plus tram 1 or 25). Map p 112.*

★★ **RadostFX** NOVÉ MĚSTO This sophisticated music club, vegetarian restaurant, and cafe broke new ground when it first opened in the early 1990s and is still going strong. Every few years the interior gets a makeover and it looks as fresh as the day it opened. Draws a well-heeled crowd in their 20s and 30s, mixed straight and gay. *Bělehradská 120.* ☎ *603-181-500. Cover 100 Kč–200 Kč. Metro: I.P. Pavlova. Map p 110.*

★ **Solidní Nejistota** NOVÉ MĚSTO A bar/restaurant combo that after 8pm or so transforms itself into a classic disco meat market. Get there early to get a table.

Solidní Nejistota.

The place to go on those nights when nothing less than Abba, the soundtrack from *Grease,* and Gloria Gaynor's classic "I Will Survive" will do. Inexplicably popular from the day it opened. *Pštrossová 21. Cover 150 Kč.* ☎ *605-000-500. Metro: I.P. Pavlova. Map p 110.*

★★ **Studio 54** NOVÉ MĚSTO One of the few genuine after-party clubs in Prague. It's kind of down at heel, and in a dicey part of town not far from Masarykovo nádraži; nevertheless, it's the center of the action after everything else closes down. The club opens around 5am on Saturday and Sunday mornings and you can dance into the afternoon. The music is loud, thumping techno that's guaranteed to keep you awake no matter how many you've had. *Hybernská 38. No phone. Cover 150 Kč. Metro: Náměstí Republiky. Map p 110.*

Gay & Lesbian Bars & Clubs

★★ **Friends** STARÉ MĚSTO A centrally located bar and club that's popular with both locals and tourists. Runs a weekly lesbian night on Fridays. *Bartolomějská 11.*

☎ 224-236-772. Metro: Národní třída. Map p 110.

★★★ The Saints VINOHRADY

This welcoming, British-owned pub hosts regular theme parties and pub quiz nights in a relaxed, informal atmosphere. Thursday night is ladies' night. The website has a good overview of other bars and Prague's gay scene. *Polská 32.* ☎ *222-250-326. www.praguesaints.cz. Metro: Jiřího z Poděbrad. Map p 110.*

★★ Valentino VINOHRADY

Prague's biggest gay dance club functions more or less as the unofficial ground zero of the city's gay life. Operates on three floors, with two full-sized dance floors. Can get crowded on Fridays and Saturdays after midnight. The owners also run the adjacent Celebrity cafe. *Vinohradská 40.* ☎ *222-513-491. Metro: Muzeum. Map p 110.*

Cabarets & Adult Entertainment

★ Darling Cabaret NOVÉ MĚSTO

Probably the biggest and best-known of Prague's many "cabarets"—in this instance, a polite word for strip club. It advertises more than 150 girls nightly, with all kinds of dances and entertainment. Highly popular with the many British guys who come to Prague for a relatively cheap bachelor-party stag. *Ve Smečkach 32.* ☎ *777-099-997. Metro: Muzeum. Map p 110.*

★★ K5 Relax Club VINOHRADY

This high-end gentlemen's club caters to a mostly corporate clientele. It occupies three floors of a Vinohrady townhouse, with a restaurant, a cocktail bar, and a large area for sauna, massage, and steam baths. Also offers an escort service. *Korunní 5.* ☎ *224-250-505. Metro: Náměstí Miru. Map p 110.* ●

Friends.

Arts & Entertainment Best Bets

Best **Opera House**
★★★ Státní Opera, *Wilsonová 4*
(p 128)

Best Place **to Hear Classical Music**
★★★ Rudolfinum, *Náměstí Jana Palacha (p 128)*

Best Place **to See Classical Music**
★★★ Obecní dům's Smetana Hall, *Náměstí Republiky 5 (p 127)*

Best **Theater**
★★★ Švandovo Divadlo na Smíchově, *Stefaniková 57 (p 126)*

Best for **Don Giovanni**
★★ Stavovské Divadlo, *Ovocní trh 1 (p 126)*

Best for **"Donnie" Giovanni**
★★★ Národní Divadlo Marionet (National Puppet Theater), *Žatecká 1 (p 126)*

Best **Black Light Theater**
★★★ Divadlo Image, *Pařížská 4 (p 126)*

Best **Jazz Club**
★★★ AghaRTA, *Železná 16 (p 129)*

Best **Club for 20-Somethings**
★★ Roxy, *Dlouhá 33 (p 131)*

Best **Club for 30-Somethings**
★★ Palac Akropolis, *Kubelikova 27 (p 131)*

Best Place **to See a Ballet**
★★★ Národní Divadlo, *Národí třida 2 (p 126)*

Best for **Experimental Theater**
★★★ Švandovo Divadlo na Smíchově, *Stefaniková 57, (p 126)*

Best **Organ Concerts**
★★★ St. James Basilica (Bazilika sv. Jakuba), *Malá Stupartská 6 (p 128)*

A performance of Candide at the Státní Opera.

Malá Strana Area

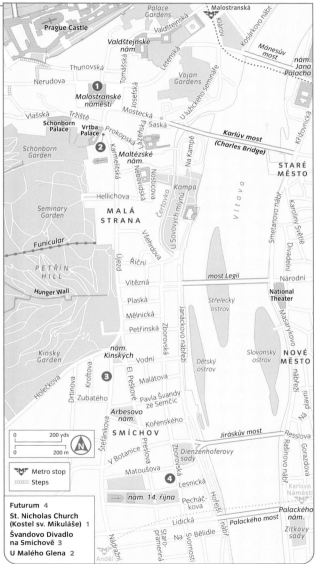

Prague Castle

Valdštejnské nám.

Palace Gardens

Malostranská

❶ Malostranské náměstí

Schönborn Palace

Vrtba Palace **❷**

Schönborn Garden

Seminary Garden

MALÁ STRANA

Kampa

Maltézské nám.

Vltava

STARÉ MĚSTO

Funicular

PETŘÍN HILL

Hunger Wall

Kinsky Garden

nám. Kinských

❸

SMÍCHOV

most Legii

Střelecký ostrov

National Theater

Slovanský ostrov

Dětský ostrov

NOVÉ MĚSTO

Jiráskův most

Dienzenhoferovy sady

❹

nám. 14. října

| 0 | 200 yds |
| 0 | 200 m |

🚇 Metro stop

⊡⊡⊡ Steps

Futurum 4

St. Nicholas Church (Kostel sv. Mikuláše) 1

Švandovo Divadlo na Smíchově 3

U Malého Glena 2

Photo p 121: Prague Symphony Orchestra performing at Obecní dům's Smetana Hall.

Staré Mešto Area

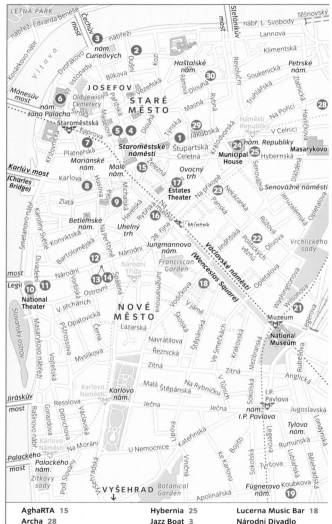

LETNÁ PARK
nábřeží Edvarda Beneše
Čechův most
Štefánikův most
nábř. L. Svobody
Těšnovský
nábřeží
Lannova
Klimentská
Petrské nám.
nám. Curieových
Dušní
Kozí
Haštalské nám.
Revoluční
Soukenická
Zlatnická
Na Poříčí
Havlíčkova
Masarykovo
Dvořákovo
17. listopadu
Bilkova
Ramova
Dlouhá
Masná
Rybná
Truhlářská
V Celnici
Náměstí Republiky
JOSEFOV
Old Jewish Cemetery
Vězeňská
Pařížská
STARÉ MĚSTO
Týnská
Jakubská
Králodvorská
nám. Republiky
Hybernská
Dlážděná
Senovážná
Senovážné náměstí
Jeruzalémská
Opletalova
Mánesův most
nám. Jana Palacha
Staroměstská
Kaprova
Maiselova
Široká
Staroměstské náměstí
Štupartská
Celetná
Municipal House
Křížovnická
Platnéřská
Mariánské nám.
Malé nám.
Michalská
Železná
Ovocný trh
Nekázanka
Panská
Karlův most (Charles Bridge)
Karlova
Husova
Pštrossova
Zlatá
Betlémské nám.
Na Perštýně
Havelská
Rytířská
Uhelný trh
Estates Theater
Na příkopě
Jindřišská
Politických vězňů
Růžová
Olivova
Vrchlického sady
Smetanovo nábř.
Karoliny Světlé
Konviktská
Bartolomějská
28. října
Jungmannovo nám.
Můstek
Václavské náměstí (Wenceslas Square)
Opletalova
Washingtonova
most
Divadelní
Národní
Voršilská
Ostrovní
Spálená
Národní Třída
Franciscan Garden
Jungmannova
Muzeum
National Museum
Wilsonova
Legii
National Theater
V Jirchárích
Pštrossova
NOVÉ MĚSTO
Lazarská
Vodičkova
V Jámě
Školská
Ve Smečkách
Krakovská
Mezibranská
Slovanský ostrov
Masarykovo nábřeží
Vojtěšská
Opatovická
Černá
Myslíkova
Navrátilova
Řeznická
Štěpánská
Sokolská
Anglická
Jiráskův most
Rašínovo nábř.
Gorazdova
Dittrichova
Václavská
Karlovo Náměstí
Karlovo nám.
Malá Štěpánská
Ječná
Na Rybníčku
V Tůních
Ječná
Zitná
Zitná
I.P. Pavlova
nám. I.P. Pavlova
Jugoslávská
Palackého most
Karlovo Náměstí
Na Moráni
Palackého nám.
Zítkovy sady
Resslova
Na Slupi
Vyšehradská
U Nemocnice
Kateřinská
Viničná
Ke Karlovu
Bojiště
Sokolská
Legerova
Tyršova
Tylovo nám.
Rumunská
Lublaňská
Bělehradská
Koubkova
Londýnská
VYŠEHRAD
Botanical Garden
Apolinářská
Fügnerovo nám.

AghaRTA 15	Hybernia 25	Lucerna Music Bar 18
Archa 28	Jazz Boat 3	Národní Divadlo
Bohemia Ticket International 23	Jiří Srnec Black Light Theatre 13	Marionet (National Puppet Theater) 7
Church of Saints Simon and Jude (Kostel sv. Šimona a Judy) 2	Laterna Magika 11	Národní Divadlo (National Theater) 10
Divadlo Image 4		

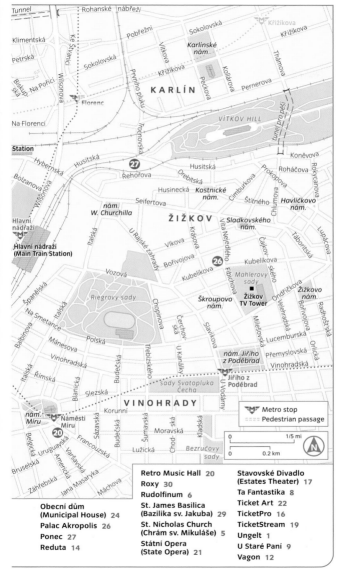

Retro Music Hall 20
Roxy 30
Rudolfinum 6
St. James Basilica
(Bazilika sv. Jakuba) 29
St. Nicholas Church
(Chrám sv. Mikuláše) 5
Státní Opera
(State Opera) 21

Stavovské Divadlo
(Estates Theater) 17
Ta Fantastika 8
Ticket Art 22
TicketPro 16
TicketStream 19
Ungelt 1
U Staré Paní 9
Vagon 12

Obecní dům
(Municipal House) 24
Palac Akropolis 26
Ponec 27
Reduta 14

Prague A&E A to Z

Theater

★ **Hybernia** NOVÉ MĚSTO This glitzy, tourist-friendly theater focuses on big-budget musicals and theater spectacles. In 2007, the theater put on a musical version of *The Golem*, available in seven languages, including Hebrew. *Náměstí Republiky 4.* ☎ *221-419-419. www.divadlo-hybernia.cz. Tickets 200 Kč–800 Kč. Metro: Náměstí Republiky. Map p 124.*

★★★ **Národní Divadlo (National Theater)** NOVÉ MĚSTO For more than a century, the leading stage in the Czech Republic has offered an alternating program of high-end theater, ballet, and opera. For non-Czech speakers, the ballet and opera performances will be of most interest (many of the operas are supertitled in English and German). The program has become more innovative in recent years, breaking away from bread-and-butter Czech classics in favor of more international offerings. Dress up.

Foyer of the National Theater.

Národní třída 2. www.narodni-divadlo.cz. ☎ *224-901-668. Tickets 100 Kč–1,000 Kč. Metro: Národní třída. Map p 124.*

★★ **Stavovské Divadlo (Estates Theater)** STARÉ MĚSTO An offshoot of the National Theater with a similar repertoire. The theater's main claim to fame is that it hosted the premier of Mozart's *Don Giovanni* in 1787—with none other than Wolfgang himself in the conductor's role. In summer, a private company offers nightly performances of the opera for tourists. In season, a more demanding, experimental version of Don Giovanni is performed here as part of the National Theater. *Ovocní trh 1.* ☎ *224-228-503. www.narodni-divadlo.cz. Tickets 30 Kč–1,000 Kč. Metro: Mustek. Map p 124.*

★★★ **Švandovo Divadlo na Smíchově** SMÍCHOV Experimental space offering an eclectic and often high-quality program of theater, dance, and live music. The repertoire leans toward modern and alternative works, with a commitment to international artists. Many of the theater performances are subtitled in English. *Stefaniková 57.* ☎ *257-318-666. www.svandovodivadlo.cz. Tickets 140 Kč–400 Kč. Metro: Anděl. Map p 123.*

Puppet & Black Light Theater

★★★ **Divadlo Image** STARÉ MĚSTO Highly popular black light theater in Old Town. The nearly nightly production, "Black Box," mixes traditional black light techniques with high-tech imagery, dance, and music. Entertaining. *Pařížská 4.* ☎ *222-314-458. www.imagetheatre.cz. Tickets 480 Kč. Metro: Staroměstská. Map p 124.*

Národní Divadlo Marionet.

★★ Jiří Srnec Black Light Theatre

NOVÉ MĚSTO   Well-respected black light theater from one of the innovators of the concept back in the 1960s. In summer, they offer daily performances of "The Best of Black Light Theater," essentially a montage of great scenes from the past 40 years. *Národní třída 20.* ☎ 721-589-244. *www. blacktheatresrnec.cz. Tickets 520 Kč. Metro: Národní třída. Map p 124.*

★★ Laterna Magika

NOVÉ MĚSTO   The original Black Light theater troupe that traces its roots back to the 1958 Brussels World Expo, where this peculiarly Czech form of drama first hit the international stage. *Národní 4.* ☎ 224-931-482. *Tickets 540 Kč–680 Kč. Metro: Národní třída. Map p 123.*

★★★ kids Národní Divadlo Marionet (National Puppet Theater)

STARÉ MĚSTO   Puppets are big in Prague, and this theater in Old Town is the big time in puppet land. Offers a daily performance of Mozart's *Don Giovanni* that's great for kids and in many ways more entertaining than the serious productions at the Stavovské Divadlo (see above). *Žatecká 1.* ☎ 224-819-322. *www.mozart.cz. Tickets 490 Kč–590 Kč. Metro: Staroměstská. Map p 124.*

★★ Ta Fantastika

STARÉ MĚSTO   Another highly regarded black light theater. This one's marquee feature is "Aspects of Alice," an adaptation of Lewis Carroll's *Alice and Wonderland* and highly suitable for kids. *Karlová 8.* ☎ 222-221-366. *www. tafantastika.cz. Tickets 200 Kč–600 Kč. Metro: Staroměstská. Map p 124.*

Opera, Dance & Classical

★★★ Obecní dům (Municipal House)

STARÉ MĚSTO   Home to one of the leading orchestras, the Prague Symphony Orchestra (abbreviated "fok"), and housing probably the country's most beautiful room for listening to classical music, the Bedřich Smetana Hall. In summer, the Obecní dům is also rented out by private musicians, who hold concerts of varying quality aimed at tourists. *Náměstí Republiky 5.*

St. Nicholas Church.

☎ *222-002-121. www.obecni-dum.cz. Tickets 200 Kč–1,100 Kč. Metro: Náměstí Republiky. Map p 124.*

★★ **Ponec** ŽIŽKOV   A beacon of civility in an otherwise dreary part of town, Ponec is Prague's center for contemporary dance and movement theater. Home to the annual Tanec Praha dance festival. *Husitská 24.* ☎ *222-721-531. www.divadlo ponec.cz. Tickets 200 Kč–300 Kč. Metro: Florenc. Map p 124.*

★★★ **Rudolfinum** STARÉ MĚSTO This beautiful neo-Renaissance concert hall hosts the Czech Philharmonic Orchestra and arguably boasts the best sound quality of any classical venue in the country. Attracts some big-name musicians. Most concerts take place in the main Dvořák hall. The smaller Suk hall toward the back is used for chamber concerts. Another chance to dress up. *Náměstí Jana Palacha.* ☎ *227-059-227. www.czechphil harmonic.cz. Tickets 200 Kč–1,000 Kč. Metro: Staroměstská. Map p 124.*

★★★ **Státní Opera (State Opera)** NOVÉ MĚSTO   The leading opera house in Prague, offering a highly polished repertoire of classics like *Carmen, Rigoletto, Madame Butterfly,* and *The Magic Flute.* Operas are sung in the original language, with Czech and occasionally English captions. Also hosts regular performances of ballet and modern dance. The location is less than ideal, across a busy highway and sandwiched between the main train station and the headquarters of Radio Free Europe. *Wilsonová 4.* ☎ *224-227-266. www.opera.cz. Tickets 400 Kč–1,150 Kč. Metro: Muzeum. Map p 124.*

Church Concerts

★★★ **Church of Saints Simon and Jude (Kostel sv. Šimona a Judy)** STARÉ MĚSTO   For a real treat, try to catch one of the Prague Symphony Orchestra's chamber concerts here. *Dušní.* ☎ *222-002-336. www.fok.cz. Tickets 770 Kč–980 Kč. Metro: Staroměstská. Map p 124.*

★★★ **St. James Basilica (Bazilika sv. Jakuba)** STARÉ MĚSTO A good place to catch organ recitals and concerts, particularly during the Easter and Christmas holidays. The church's enormous 18th-century organ has been restored to its original sound. *Malá Štupartská 6.* ☎ *604-208-490.* *www.audite organum.cz. Tickets 300 Kč–500 Kč. Metro: Staroměstská. Map p 124.*

★ St. Nicholas Church (Chrám sv. Mikuláše) STARÉ MĚSTO

A popular venue for afternoon and early-evening concerts done by private outfits looking to make a little cash on the side. Quality is uneven, but the Baroque church makes for a lovely place to sit and listen. *Staroměstské nám.* ☎ *224-190-994. Tickets 400 Kč–600 Kč. Metro: Staroměstská. Map p 124.*

★★ St. Nicholas Church (Kostel sv. Mikuláše) MALÁ STRANA

The interior of this church is one of the great treasures of Prague Baroque. The concerts here are of high quality and the organizers are determined to vary the program, which like everywhere else seems top-heavy on Mozart, Brahms, and Vivaldi. *Malostranské nám.* ☎ *257-534-215. www.psalterium.cz. Tickets 300 Kč–450 Kč. Metro: Malostranská. Map p 123.*

Jazz
★★★ AghaRTA STARÉ MĚSTO
This atmospheric cellar from the

Middle Ages is a wonderful place to catch a jazz concert. The hitch is that seating is very limited. The only way to get a chair is to arrive by 7pm and camp out until showtime at 9pm. *Železná 16.* ☎ *222-211-275. www.agharta.cz. Tickets 200 Kč. Metro: Staroměstská. Map p 124.*

★★ Jazz Boat STARÉ MĚSTO

This passenger boat, the *Kotva,* cruises up and down the Vltava River nightly in season. They also serve decent food and drinks, including munchies like nachos to have as you groove. *Leaves at 8:30pm from pier no. 5 just below Čechův bridge.* ☎ *731-183-180. www.jazzboat.cz. Tickets 590 Kč. Metro: Staroměstská. Map p 124.*

★★ Reduta NOVÉ MĚSTO Thirty

years ago this was Prague's preeminent venue for live music, and the interior hasn't changed a jot since then. If you'd like to see Fusion jazz played in an authentic '70s-style room, this is your place. *Národní třída 20.* ☎ *224-933-487. www. redutajazzclub.cz. Tickets 200 Kč–300 Kč. Metro: Národní třída. Map p 124.*

★★ U Malého Glena MALÁ

STRANA The name ("At Little Glen's") refers to the owner, a short

AghaRTA.

American guy named Glen, but it could also apply to the microscopic size of this cellar club. That's a shame, because on good nights you can't get anywhere near the music. Go early or try to reserve a table. *Karmelitská 23.* ☎ *257-531-717. www.malyglen.cz. Tickets 200 Kč–300 Kč. Metro: Malostranská. Map p 123.*

★ **Ungelt** STARÉ MĚSTO This cozy cellar club, just a short walk from the Old Town Square, is one of the more recent jazz clubs to open and seems to cater more to tourists than locals. The program is big on blues and fusion. *Týnská 2.* ☎ *224-895-748. www.jazzblues.cz. No admission charge. Metro: Staroměstská. Map p 124.*

★★★ **U Staré Paní** STARÉ MĚSTO One of the few jazz clubs in town where you can also eat dinner. Good for when a big name is on the card and you have to get there early to get a table. Features mostly Czech players doing '70s- and '80s-style fusion and Latin mixes. Limited seating, so if you arrive after 9pm you're going to be standing up. *Michalská 9.* ☎ *603-551-680. www.jazzlounge.cz.*

Tickets 200 Kč. Metro: Staroměstská. Map p 124.

Rock & Live Music

★★★ **Archa** NOVÉ MĚSTO This experimental stage hosts everything from visiting bands like The Talking Heads and Sonic Youth to local groups, and alternative dance and theater troupes. Check the website to see what's on. It's invariably good. *Na Poříčí 26.* ☎ *221-716-333. www.archatheatre.cz. Tickets 200 Kč–600 Kč. Metro: Florenc. Map p 124.*

★ **Futurum** SMÍCHOV This legendary Prague metal club has smoothed over its rough edges and now mostly hosts popular "best of the '80s and '90s" dance nights. But the program still includes an occasional group of headbangers from the U.S. or Western Europe. *Zborovská 7.* ☎ *257-328-571. www.musicbar.cz. Tickets 100 Kč–200 Kč. Metro: Anděl. Map p 123.*

★★★ **Lucerna Music Bar** NOVÉ MĚSTO A great underground bar and stage located below the Lucerna Pasáž shopping center just off Wenceslas Square. The weekday

U Malého Glena.

Palac Akropolis.

live acts tend toward medium-sized Czech bands, with a few international musicians thrown in. Weekends are given over to a wildly popular (and fun) retro '80s and '90s disco extravaganza. *Vodičková 36. ☎ 224-217-108. www.musicbar.cz. Tickets 100 Kč–200 Kč. Metro: Mustek. Map p 124.*

★★★ **Palac Akropolis** ŽIŽKOV This former theater was rescued from demolition in the '90s and has now morphed into the most interesting performance venue in the city. The Akropolis regularly hosts visiting fringe bands from the U.S. like the Flaming Lips, as well as great Czech acts and groups from around the world. There's usually something cool going on. On off nights, DJs spin for dancing and drinking in the smaller rooms off the main hall. *Kubelíková 27. ☎ 296-330-911. www.palac akropolis.cz. Tickets 50 Kč–500 Kč. Metro: Jiřího z Poděbrad. Map p 124.*

★ **Retro Music Hall** VINOHRADY This is the new kid on the block in suburban Vinohrady. As the name suggests, the club appears to be capitalizing on Praguers' insatiable interest in retro acts and rock dinosaurs. In 2007, Retro hosted aging British rockers the Yardbirds and Sweet, among others. *Francouzská 4. ☎ 222-510-592. www. roxy.cz. Tickets 180 Kč–500 Kč. Metro: Náměstí Miru. Map p 124.*

★★ **Roxy** STARÉ MĚSTO Like the Akropolis, another former theater that's carved a niche as the city's leading venue for live performances of techno, electronic music, Asian dub, and other new sounds. The Old Town location has put a crimp on late-night noise, so concerts here tend to start and finish early. *Dlouhá 33. ☎ 224-826-296. www.roxy.cz. Tickets 200 Kč–600 Kč. Metro: Staroměstská. Map p 124.*

★ **Vagon** NOVÉ MĚSTO Informal rock venue with live acts most days of the week. The card is heavy on Czech and local revival bands. A recent month featured no less than revival bands for Led Zeppelin, Guns 'n' Roses, and Black Sabbath. Some of these guys are pretty good. *Národní třída 25. ☎ 221-085-599. www.vagon.cz. Tickets 100 Kč–200 Kč. Metro: Národní třída. Map p 124.*

Vagon.

Buying Tickets

The cheapest tickets are at theater box offices, which are generally open daily until a few minutes before the start of a performance. Hotel reception desks and concierges are also usually able to secure tickets, the latter probably charging a service fee. If you're not sure exactly what you want to see or haven't worked out a schedule, drop by one of the following ticketing agencies. Most of the agencies generally sell tickets to the same events, though some may have

exclusive arrangements. All charge a booking fee (usually around 60 Kč).

Bohemia Ticket International NOVÉ MĚSTO   Good source for performances at the Národní Divadlo, Státní Opera, and the Stavovské Divadlo. Offers hotel delivery for 200 Kč. *Na Příkopě 16.* ☎ *224-215-031. www.ticketsbti.cz. Metro: Mustek. Map p 124.*

Ticket Art NOVÉ MĚSTO   Decent ticket agency oriented toward concerts and musical theater productions. *Politických vězňů 9.* ☎ *222-897-552. www.ticket-art.cz. Metro: Mustek. Map p 124.*

TicketPro NOVÉ MĚSTO   Probably the best all-around agency, with an easy-to-use website and helpful staff. The main office near the Mustek metro station is a good place to check for special events and big concerts that might be on while you're here. *Rytířská 12.* ☎ *296-329-999. www.ticketpro.cz. Metro: Mustek. Map p 124.*

TicketStream NOVÉ MĚSTO General ticketing agency is a good source for church concerts, shows at the Retro Music Hall (see above), and sporting events. Also sells tickets to the nightly performances of Don Giovanni in summer at the Stavovské Divadlo. *Koubková 8.* ☎ *224-263-049. www.ticketstream.cz. Metro: I.P. Pavlova. Map p 124.* ●

Lodging Best Bets

Best **Views**
★★★ Domus Henrici $$
Loretánská 11 (p 140)

Best **Hot Stones**
★★★ Hotel Le Palais $$$$
U Zvonařky 1 (p 141)

Best for **Honeymooners**
★★★ U Zlaté Studně $$$ *U Zlaté Studně 166/4 (p 145)*

Best for **Fashionistas**
★★ Josef $$$ *Rybná 20 (p 143)*

Best **Budget Hotel**
★★★ Castle Steps $ *Nerudová 7 (p 139)*

Best for **Minimalists**
★★★ Anděl's $$$ *Stroupežnického 21 (p 138)*

Best for **Music Lovers**
★★★ Aria $$$$ *Tržiště 9 (p 139)*

Best **if You Miss the 1960s**
★★ Yasmin $$$ *Politických vězňů 12 (p 146)*

Best **Socialist Realist Architecture**
★ Crowne Plaza $$$$ *Koulová 15 (p 139)*

Best **Luxury Chain Hotel**
★★★ Mandarin Oriental $$$$
Nebovidská 1 (p 143)

Best **Art Nouveau**
★★ Paříž $$$ *U Obecního Domu 1 (p 144)*

Best **Hideaway**
★★★ U Raka $$$ *Černinská 10 (p 145)*

Best for **Incurable Romantics**
★★★ Alchymist Grand Hotel and Spa $$$$ *Tržiště 19 (p 138)*

Best **Business Hotel**
★★ Marriott $$$ *V Celnici 8 (p 143)*

Alchymist Grand Hotel and Spa.

Malá Strana Area Lodging

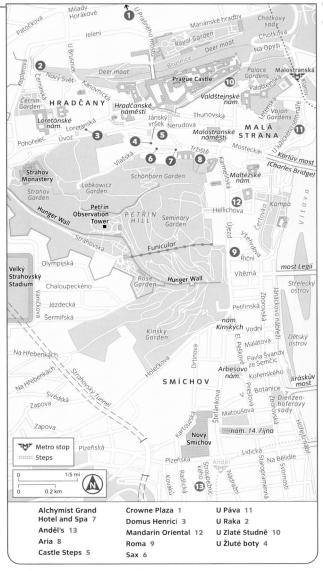

Alchymist Grand Hotel and Spa 7	**Crowne Plaza** 1	**U Páva** 11
Anděl's 13	**Domus Henrici** 3	**U Raka** 2
Aria 8	**Mandarin Oriental** 12	**U Zlaté Studně** 10
Castle Steps 5	**Roma** 9	**U Žluté boty** 4
	Sax 6	

Photo p 133: The Royal Tower Suite at Paříž.

Staré Město Area Lodging

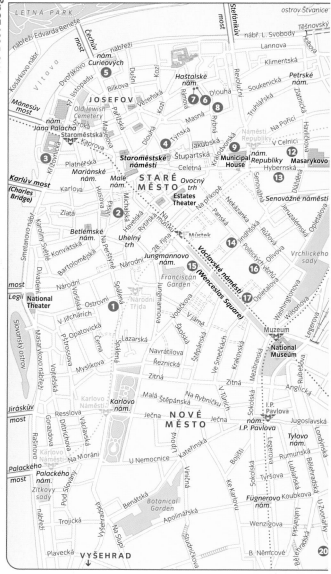

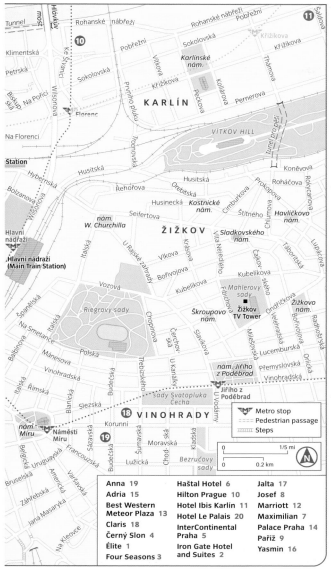

Map Key

- Metro stop
- ===== Pedestrian passage
- ▮▮▮▮▮ Steps

	1/5 mi
0	0.2 km

Anna 19	Haštal Hotel 6	Jalta 17
Adria 15	Hilton Prague 10	Josef 8
Best Western	Hotel Ibis Karlin 11	Marriott 12
Meteor Plaza 13	Hotel Le Palais 20	Maximilian 7
Claris 18	InterContinental	Palace Praha 14
Černý Slon 4	Praha 5	Pařiž 9
Élite 1	Iron Gate Hotel	Yasmin 16
Four Seasons 3	and Suites 2	

Prague Hotels A to Z

★★ **Adria** NOVÉ MĚSTO   An 18th-century burgher's house on Wenceslas Square houses this newly renovated hotel. Good value if you want to be close to the action. The rooms are small but tasteful in a contemporary chain-hotel style. The Adria cuts rates during summer and offers discounts if you book over the Web. *Václavské nám. 26.* ☎ *221-081-111. www.adria.cz. 88 units. Doubles 3,300 Kč–5,500 Kč. AE, DC, MC, V. Metro: Mustek. Map p 136.*

★★★ **Alchymist Grand Hotel and Spa** MALÁ STRANA   Portions of this extravagantly restored Baroque townhouse date back to the 15th century. The owners spared no expense in creating arguably the most opulent, luxurious lodging in Prague, with canopy beds, hardwood floors, beautifully tiled bathrooms, and statues of cherubs peering from every pedestal. The website often offers weekend packages, with prices shaved by as much as a third off the rack rates. *Tržiště 19.* ☎ *257-286-011. www.alchymisthotel.com. 46*

units. *Doubles 8,200 Kč. AE, DC, MC, V. Metro: Malostranská. Map p 135.*

★★★ **Anděl's** SMÍCHOV   You'll find this arty design hotel in up-and-coming Smíchov, 10 minutes by metro from the center. The aesthetic here could be described as hard-core minimalist, with the spare decor relieved by colorful pillows and spreads. The hotel's 2-day "Golden Prague" package includes a complimentary dinner, tour of the city, and airport transfers at about 80% of the standard room rate. *Stroupežnického 21.* ☎ *296-889-688. www.andelshotel.cz. 230 units. Doubles 6,900 Kč–8,300 Kč. AE, DC, MC, V. Metro: Anděl. Map p 135.*

★★★ **Anna** VINOHRADY   This elegant, family-run hotel occupies a 19th-century neoclassical townhouse in residential Vinohrady. There's not much in the way of services, but you'll get a warm welcome at the reception and satisfaction from knowing you're getting good value. Check the website for special offers. *Budečská 17.* ☎ *222-513-111.*

Hotel Anna.

www.hotelanna.cz. *24 units. Doubles 2,500 Kč. AE, DC, MC, V. Metro: Náměstí Miru. Map p 136.*

★★★ **Aria** MALÁ STRANA   Aria compares favorably to the nearby Alchymist Grand in terms of jaw-dropping luxury and room prices to match, but it's less showy. In keeping with the music theme, each of the 52 rooms and suites is named after a different composer or performer. Each has a different decor, ranging from tasteful contemporary to 19th-century period piece. The rooftop terrace commands an incredible view. *Tržiště 9.* ☎ *225-334-111.* www.ariahotel.net. *52 units. Doubles 8,800 Kč. AE, DC, MC, V. Metro: Malostranská. Map p 135.*

★★ **Best Western Meteor Plaza** NOVÉ MĚSTO   Rates have risen recently, but the Meteor Plaza remains a decent option. The Best Western standards are evident in the comfortable if uninspiring rooms. The location, down from the Powder Tower and 5 minutes from the Old Town, is excellent. *Hybernská 6.* ☎ *224-192-559.* www.hotel-meteor.cz. *73 units. Doubles 3,300 Kč–4,400 Kč. AE, DC, MC, V. Metro: Náměstí Republiky. Map p 136.*

★★★ **Castle Steps** MALÁ STRANA   Simple rooms, some with lovely views out the back, in a beautifully remodeled Baroque palais. Each one shares a bathroom and common kitchen. The best choice in town if you're looking for historic 17th-century Malá Strana atmosphere at a fraction of the Alchymist rates. *Nerudová 7.* ☎ *257-531-941.* www.castlesteps.com. *35 units. Doubles 1,200 Kč–2,000 Kč. AE, DC, MC, V. Metro: Malostranská. Map p 135.*

★★ **Claris** VINOHRADY   Similar to the Anna (see above)—a small, family-run hotel that's an excellent value. The hotel dates from the '30s and the exterior reflects some of that

The Willow Room at Castle Steps.

stripped-down, functionalist style. The rooms are plain but clean. Ask for one away from busy Slezská street. *Slezská 26.* ☎ *242-446-111.* www.hotel-claris.cz. *24 units. Doubles 2,500 Kč–3,000 Kč. AE, DC, MC, V. Metro: Náměstí Miru. Map p 136.*

★★ **Černý Slon** STARÉ MĚSTO   This small hotel's ancient, atmospheric wine cellar sets it apart, as does its location—in a perfect part of the Old Town, a block away from Old Town Square. An excellent out-of-season choice, as rates drop by more than a quarter and the crowds that invariably stream past the hotel's doorstep thin to a mere trickle. The rooms are old-style charming, with creaky wooden floors and clean linens. *Týnská 1.* ☎ *222-321-521.* www.hotelcernyslon.cz. *16 units. Doubles 3,500 Kč–4,500 Kč. AE, DC, MC, V. Metro: Staroměstská. Map p 136.*

★ **Crowne Plaza** DEJVICE   Given its location in suburban Dejvice, 20 minutes by tram from the center, the Crowne Plaza is overpriced. But fans of Socialist Realist architecture may want to stay here anyway. The hotel is Prague's best example of the early 1950s Stalinist "wedding cake" style and a real period piece. When the Holiday Inn group bought

Domus Henrici.

the property in the 1990s, they fittingly replaced the communist red star on the top with their own corporate green one. The interior has been thoroughly renovated, but many of the older Socialist murals and decorative elements remain. *Koulová 15.* ☎ *296-537-111. www. crowneplaza.cz. 254 units. Doubles 8,200 Kč. AE, DC, MC, V. Metro: Dejvická. Map p 135.*

★★★ **Domus Henrici** HRADČANY A sleek, upmarket bed-and-breakfast, a stone's throw from Prague Castle. Emperor Rudolf II was a former ownerand that feeling of exclusiveness lingers in the well-proportioned rooms, tasteful contemporary furnishings, and gorgeous views out the back toward Petřín Hill and Strahov Monastery. Check the website for specials. Rates generally drop in midsummer. *Loretánská 11.* ☎ *220-511-369. www.domus-henrici.cz. 8 units. Doubles 3,000 Kč–5,000 Kč. AE, DC, MC, V. Metro: Hradčanská. Map p 135.*

★★ **Élite** NOVÉ MĚSTO Another nicely renovated 14th-century townhouse, this one on a quiet side street in one of the busiest parts of town. Night revelers will appreciate that the main stop on the city's nighttime tram service is right around the corner. The rooms are a pleasing mix of period and contemporary, with some authentic antiques tossed in. Ask to see the suite, with its 17th-century Renaissance frescoes. *Ostrovní 32.* ☎ *224-932-250. www. hotelelite.cz. 78 units. Doubles 3,000 Kč–5,000 Kč. AE, DC, MC, V. Metro: Národní třída. Map p 136.*

★★★ **Four Seasons** STARÉ MĚSTO When the Four Seasons opened a few years ago, it set new standards for Prague hotels. Everything—from the heart-stopping views toward the Charles Bridge to the seamless service to the award-winning Allegro restaurant (p 98)—is what you'd expect from the Four Seasons name. Oddly, at these prices, breakfast is not included in the rate. Check the Web for seasonal "4th night free" deals. *Veleslavínová 2a.* ☎ *221-427-000. www.four seasons.com/prague. 161 units. Doubles 8,200 Kč–16,500 Kč. AE, DC, MC, V. Metro: Staroměstská. Map p 136.*

★ **Haštal Hotel** STARÉ MĚSTO The location, a beautiful and quiet part of the Old Town not far from the St. Agnes cloister, is the major draw at this smaller, locally owned hotel. The rooms are plain to the point of drab, but the prices, particularly off-season, are reasonable.

You'll get a 20% discount if you book online. *Haštalská 6. ☎ 222-314-335. www.hastal.com. 24 units. Doubles 2,400 Kč–3,800 Kč. AE, DC, MC, V. Metro: Staroměstská. Map p 136.*

★★ **Hilton Prague** NOVÉ MĚSTO This is where President George W. Bush stays when he comes to Prague. It's easy to see why: The isolated location by a freeway is easy to protect. Inside, the hotel is all modern atriums and see-through elevators. It's the kind of hotel that always seems to be hosting five business conferences at once. Service is top-notch, but watch the add-ons—for example, parking costs another 800 Kč a night. *Pobřezní 1. ☎ 224-841-111. www.prague.hilton.com. 775 units. Doubles 4,400 Kč–8,200 Kč. AE, DC, MC, V. Metro: Florenc. Map p 136.*

★★ **Hotel Ibis Karlin** KARLÍN Karlín is a gentrifying neighborhood outside the center of Prague (east of Old Town, along the river), but with excellent metro connections. It was hit hard by the 2002 floods, but has come back and is now home to a lively pub and theater scene. Like all Ibises, this is no-frills contemporary—a decent room at a decent price. *Šaldová 54. ☎ 222-332-800. www.ibis.com. 226 units. Doubles 2,700 Kč. AE, DC, MC, V. Metro: Křižikova. Map p 136.*

★★★ **Hotel Le Palais** VINOHRADY A special luxury boutique in a 19th-century Belle Epoque townhouse. With all the little reading rooms, hidden nooks, and places to cozy up to the fire with a glass of brandy, you won't want to leave the hotel. The fitness room is one of the nicest in the city, complete with aromatherapy, hot stones, and all the rest. The location in leafy Vinohrady is a plus. *U Zvonařky 1. ☎ 234-634-635. www.palaishotel.cz. 60 units. Doubles 8,000 Kč. AE, DC, MC, V. Metro: Náměstí Miru. Map p 136.*

★ **InterContinental Praha** STARÉ MĚSTO The hotel's 1970s Brutalist architecture was actually intended to mesh with the surrounding Jewish quarter in a style dubbed "ghetto moderne." Inside, it's easier on the eyes, with sleek sofas and silky fabrics. The rooms are clean and quiet, but small for the money. The fitness club downstairs, with an indoor pool, has great equipment. Popular with package tours. *Náměsti Curieových 5. ☎ 296-631-111. www.ichotelsgroup.com. 372 units. Doubles 4,100 Kč–6,800 Kč. AE, DC, MC, V. Metro: Staroměstská. Map p 136.*

★★★ **Iron Gate Hotel and Suites** STARÉ MĚSTO Another beautiful boutique carved out of a series of Baroque burghers' houses, with many of the facade reliefs still intact. The rooms are different, so look at a couple before deciding. Many have the original wood-beamed ceilings. The tasteful contemporary decor toes the line between high style and comfort. *Michalská 19. ☎ 225-777-777. www.irongate.cz. 44 units. Doubles 8,200 Kč. AE, DC, MC, V. Metro: Staroměstská. Map p 136.*

The Four Seasons.

Surviving Sticker Shock

It wasn't that long ago that the price of a decent hotel room in Prague, while not quite as good a deal as the beer, was at least affordable. Alas, with the strengthening Czech crown, prices have risen through the roof. Don't be surprised to find yourself paying more here than in Paris or Amsterdam for comparable accommodation. Of course, there's a silver lining. As prices have risen, so have standards, and smaller hotels in Malá Strana and parts of Old Town are some of the best you'll find in this part of the world.

There are some steps you can take to minimize the pain. Always check the hotel's website beforehand. Hotel owners are adept at adjusting rates according to demand, and impromptu cuts of 10% to 20% posted on the Web are not uncommon. Even if you arrive at the hotel with a fixed price in hand, it never hurts to ask if that's the best offer available. Also, consider traveling out of season if possible. January, February, November, and most of December are considered "low" season, and prices fall as much as 50% from spring and fall rates. Midsummer (July and Aug) is "shoulder" season, and a prime time to wheel and deal. The flip side of this is to avoid Prague over the New Year's and Easter holidays. Not only are there no deals to be had, but there are no beds either.

If hotels are just not in the budget, there are other options. Several agencies offer short-term apartment rentals for as short as a few days or as long as a month. These are often very nice apartments, with great central locations, at around half the price of comparable hotels (without the services, of course). **Apartments in Prague** (Petřínská 4, Malá Strana; ☎ **251-512-502;** http://apartments-in-prague.org) offers several units in Malá Strana, Old Town, and around the Charles Bridge. Another popular agency, **Prague Mary's Apartments** (Italská 31, Vinohrady; ☎ **222-254-007;** www.marys.cz), has properties all around the city at nearly every price point. Check the website to see photos.

As for hostels, Prague is filled with them, but most are seasonal affairs timed to open just as college classes are letting out. A few are more permanent and even offer the option of a private double at near-hostel prices. Try the **Clown and Bard** (Bořivojová 102, Žižkov; ☎ **222-716-453;** www.clownandbard.com), a longtime fixture on the hostel scene, and one of the easiest places in town to meet fellow travelers or expats who like to hang out at the hostel's pub.

★★ **Jalta** NOVÉ MĚSTO   Even under communism, the Jalta was one of the better hotels in Prague. The Socialist Realist facade from the 1950s was thoroughly renovated in 2007 and has UNESCO protection as a world heritage site. The hotel's location, on the upper reaches of Wenceslas Square, is ideal for sightseeing. During the Velvet Revolution, it was the

Hotel Le Palais.

favored hotel of Western journalists, who could cover the anticommunist demonstrations from the hotel balcony without ever leaving their rooms. *Václavské nám. 45.* ☎ *222-822-111. www.jalta.cz. 94 units. Doubles 4,400 Kč–6,000 Kč. AE, DC, MC, V. Metro: Muzeum. Map p 136.*

★★ **Josef** STARÉ MĚSTO   The Josef was one of the first minimalist boutiques to open up shop, and fans of updated mid-century modern—chrome and white—will find a second home here. The high style extends to the lobby and the all-white cocktail bar. The gorgeous chrome-and-glass rooms receive splashes of color from bedspreads or pillowcases. *Rybná 20.* ☎ *221-700-111. www.hoteljosef.com. 110 units. Doubles 4,700 Kč–7,400 Kč. AE, DC, MC, V. Metro: Náměstí Republiky. Map p 136.*

★★★ **Mandarin Oriental** MALÁ STRANA   My favorite of the five-star international chains. The Mandarin opened in 2006 in a restored 14th-century monastery, and has used the quirks and character of the building to strong advantage. There are no cookie-cutter corporate rooms here. The rooms feel fresh and clean, with white walls, parquet flooring, and big bouquets of flowers. The spa, in a former

Renaissance chapel, defines minimalist chic. *Nebovidská 1.* ☎ *233-088-888. www.mandarinoriental.com. 99 units. Doubles 7,000 Kč–15,000 Kč. AE, DC, MC, V. Metro: Malostranská. Map p 135.*

★★ **Marriott** NOVÉ MĚSTO   This upmarket chain, which emphasizes comfort and business amenities over style, is a solid corporate choice. The location, just down from central Náměstí Republiky, is excellent. Easy-in, easy-out if you happen to be arriving by car. *V Celnici 8.* ☎ *222-888-888. www.marriott.com.*

Iron Gate Hotel and Suites.

290 units. Doubles 4,100 Kč–8,200 Kč. AE, DC, MC, V. Metro: Náměstí Republiky. Map p 136.

★★ Maximilian STARÉ MĚSTO The Maximilian goes for the same light, modern, minimalist aesthetic as the Josef (see above), but it's not quite as chic. It does have a superb location, however, in an overlooked and beautiful part of the Old Town. Ask for a room with a view toward the nearby St. Agnes cloister. The rooms are spare, in keeping with the overall look, but comfortable. The hotel is short on amenities, but the location makes up for it. *Haštalská 14. ☎ 225-303-111. www.maximilian hotel.cz. 71 units. Doubles 3,800 Kč–7,700 Kč. AE, DC, MC, V. Metro: Staroměstská. Map p 136.*

★★ Palace Praha NOVÉ MĚSTO This was one of the first luxury properties to open in the early '90s and for a time was the best in town. Now it's starting to show its age. That said, the hotel has a great location, a couple blocks off Wenceslas Square, and the professional service, complete with concierge and doorman, is fully in keeping with the high expectations. *Panská 12. ☎ 224-093-111. www. palacehotel.cz. 124 units. Doubles*

Josef.

4,400 Kč–8,200 Kč. AE, DC, MC, V. Metro: Mustek. Map p 136.

★★ Pařiž STARÉ MĚSTO This beautiful Art Nouveau hotel recalls much of the glory of turn-of-the-century Prague and the interwar period under the First Republic. The "Paris" is a local landmark, and was immortalized in Hrabal's *I Served the King of England.* The public areas, restaurant, and cafe are pure Art Nouveau museum pieces. The rooms are plainer but comfortable. *U Obecního Domu 1. ☎ 222-195-195. www.hotel-paris.cz. 86 units. Doubles 4,400 Kč–8,200 Kč. AE, DC, MC, V. Metro: Náměstí Republiky. Map p 136.*

★ Roma MALÁ STRANA At this price point, you can probably do better at some of the other hotels in Malá Strana. The rooms are small and the stripped-down modern aesthetic is more plain than trendsetting. Nevertheless, it's a nice fallback with a great location, not far from the funicular to Petřín Hill. *Újezd 24. ☎ 222-500-222. www.hotel-roma-prague.com. 87 units. Doubles 3,300 Kč–4,400 Kč. AE, DC, MC, V. Metro: Malostranská. Map p 135.*

★ Sax MALÁ STRANA You'll find this small, family-run hotel in a quiet

Marriott.

corner of Malá Strana. The hotel's 22 rooms are clean but spartan, with a bed, a desk, and a couple of chairs. This hotel's website is clunky and hard to navigate. But once you settle in, the friendliness of the staff will win you over. *Jánský Vršek 3.* ☎ *257-531-268. www.sax.cz. 22 units. Doubles 3,000 Kč–4,000 Kč. AE, DC, MC, V. Metro: Malostranská. Map p 135.*

★★ **U Páva** MALÁ STRANA A member of the Czech chain of Romantic Hotels, which specializes in small, special properties. "At the Peacock" is situated on Kampa Island, with views both toward the river and up to the castle. Many rooms have the original wooden ceilings and antique furnishings. Ask for a castle view. *U Lužického Semináře 32.* ☎ *257-533-360. www. romantichotels.cz. 27 units. Doubles 4,100 Kč–6,600 Kč. AE, DC, MC, V. Metro: Malostranská. Map p 135.*

★★★ **U Raka** HRADČANY   Relax in the garden courtyard of this secluded luxury log cabin, and imagine you're at a country cottage. Stroll Nový Svět, the timeless lane on the far side of Prague Castle that leads up to U Raka, and feel like you have the entire city to yourself.

Enjoy royal treatment at the Japanese spa. And by all means, book far in advance; the five rooms fill up fast. Special. *Černínská 10.* ☎ *220-511-100. www.romantikhotel-uraka. cz. 5 units. Doubles 5,000 Kč–6,000 Kč. AE, DC, MC, V. Metro: Hradčanská. Map p 135.*

★★★ **U Zlaté Studně** MALÁ STRANA   An all-round perfect boutique, with drop-dead views of Malá Strana, gorgeous rooms with parquet flooring and period furnishings, and a renowned chef turning out gourmet meals for a bite on the

Paříž.

U Páva.

★★ U Žluté boty MALÁ STRANA
This cute, historic inn occupies one
of the most picturesque areas of
Malá Strana. Some rooms are still
sided in original dark-wood beams.
The room furnishings are simple;
some rooms seem almost empty.
During midsummer, the hotel runs a
"stay 4 nights, pay for 3" special.
Jánský Vršek 11. ☎ *257-532-269.*
*www.zlutabota.cz. 9 units. Doubles
2,500 Kč–3,300 Kč. AE, DC, MC, V.
Metro: Malostranská. Map p 135.*

★★ Yasmin NOVÉ MĚSTO
Another modern boutique, a la
Hotel Josef (see above), but more
fun, and less pretentious. Here, too
the rooms are uncluttered variations
of white and beige, but warm and
inviting. The lobby's loopy, organic-
shaped chairs and tables—think
1960s Goldie Hawn—are a welcome
antidote to design aesthetics that
take themselves too seriously. *Politických vězňů 12.* ☎ *234-100-100.
www.hotel-yasmin.cz. 200 units.
Doubles 6,000 Kč. AE, DC, MC, V.
Metro: Muzeum. Map p 136.* ●

terrace. The Renaissance house
once belonged to Emperor Rudolf II
and for a time housed the Danish
astronomer Tycho de Brahe. *U Zlaté
Studně 166/4.* ☎ *257-011-213. www.
zlatastudna.cz. 24 units. Doubles
4,400 Kč–5,500 Kč. AE, DC, MC, V.
Metro: Malostranská. Map p 135.*

U Raka.

Fairy Tale **Karlštejn**

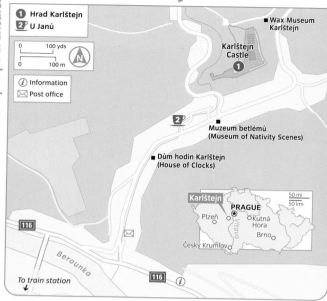

1 Hrad Karlštejn
2 U Janů

■ Wax Museum Karlštejn

Karlštejn Castle 1

0 ── 100 yds
0 ── 100 m

(i) Information
✉ Post office

2 ■ Muzeum betlémů (Museum of Nativity Scenes)

■ Dům hodin Karlštejn (House of Clocks)

Karlštejn
PRAGUE
Plzeň ○   ○ Kutná Hora
Vltava
Brno ○
Český Krumlov ○
50 mi
50 km

116

✉

Berounka

To train station
↓

116 *(i)*

Karlštejn is far and away the most popular Prague day trip—for both city residents and visitors. It's an easy 40-minute ride out on the train, and the quaint village, with its gingerbread-style houses guarded over by an enchanted-kingdom castle, is a welcome antidote to the city. The surrounding countryside is lovely and unspoiled. Plan on a leisurely day of strolling along the town's main road, popping in at the numerous gift shops and pubs as you make your way slowly up to the castle.

1 ★ **Hrad Karlštejn.** They don't come much more majestic than Karlštejn Castle, a high-Gothic beauty that dates from the middle of the 14th century (though much of the exterior was restored and embellished in the 19th century). The castle was built on orders of Charles IV to protect what were then the coronation jewels of the Holy Roman Empire. The jewels

Previous page: Český Krumlov.

were later moved to Prague Castle during the turbulent 17th century (where they sit today under lock and key), leaving Karlštejn Castle pretty much empty. Even if you're not that much into castles, it's still fun to make the climb up here for the fabulous views. There are two tours on offer. Tour 1 is quicker and cheaper, and includes a nice overview of highlights like the Imperial Palace

Karlštejn Castle.

and Royal Bedroom. But it omits the real treasure: the jewel-studded Chapel of the Holy Rood, with its 2,000 precious and semiprecious inlaid stones. The chapel visit comes only with Tour 2, but the catch is you have to book that one in advance. If you have the time and interest, it's worth the effort. ⏱ *2 hr. with tour, 1 hr. without. Karlštejn.* ☎ *311-681-617, 274-008-154 (for reserving Tour 2). 220 Kč (Tour 1, includes guide), 300 Kč (Tour 2, includes guide). May–Sept Tues–Sun 9am–5pm; Oct–Jan Tues–Sun 9am–3pm; Mar–Apr 9am–3pm. (Closed Feb.)*

2 **U Janů** Let's face it. None of the restaurants in Karlštejn is going to win a Michelin star anytime soon. This little tavern at the top of the village, not far from the castle, at least has the advantage of a terrace in summer and a cozy fireplace inside during the colder months. The menu includes Czech standards like fried cheese, roast pork and dumplings, and even a decent trout. Excellent prices. *Karlštejn 90.* ☎ *311-681-210. $.*

Karlštejn: Practical Matters

There are no buses to Karlštejn from Prague, so trains are the only public transportation option. Trains leave approximately once an hour during the day from Prague's main station (Hlavní nadráží). If you don't see Karlštejn on the timetable, look for trains heading in the direction of Beroun. The trip costs about 40 Kč each way and takes about 40 minutes. The walk into the village from the train station takes about 20 minutes. If you'd like to drive, head west along the D5 motorway out of the city in the direction of Plzeň and then follow the signs to Karlštejn. Depending on traffic, you can make the drive in about 30 minutes.

Charming Český Krumlov

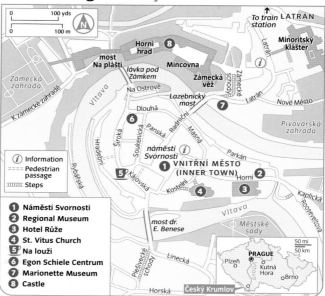

1. Náměstí Svornosti
2. Regional Museum
3. Hotel Růže
4. St. Vitus Church
5. Na louži
6. Egon Schiele Centrum
7. Marionette Museum
8. Castle

After Prague, it's hard to imagine being totally wowed by yet another riverside town in the Czech Republic. Well, prepare to be wowed. Český Krumlov's location, south of České Budějovice, feels impossibly remote. But back in the heyday of the landed aristocracy—in the 14th and 15th centuries—this was the seat of the powerful Rožmberk (Rosenberg) family, whose influence once spread far and wide in these parts. The family insignia—a five-petal rose—adorns castles and houses throughout southern Bohemia. The town's startling castle is second only to Prague Castle in terms of sheer moment. Český Krumlov is relatively compact and can easily be walked in a day. As you take the tour outlined below, feel free to meander at will, crossing the various bridges and poking down little alleyways and behind gates. There are surprises at every turn.

1 Náměstí Svornosti. Český Krumlov's main square is surprisingly quiet, but a good place to get your bearings. The Town Hall at no. 1—easily identified by the Renaissance arcades—houses the highly proficient tourist information office (a great source for learning about special events or exhibits that might be going on). The buildings on this square are some of the oldest in town, with cellars dating from the 13th century. ⏱ *15 min. Náměstí Svornosti.*

2 Regional Museum (Okresní Muzeum). From Náměstí Svornosti, follow picturesque Horní ul., with some great panoramas over the city. This small museum and picture gallery offers an informative overview of the history of the town; it's worth the 30 minutes or so it takes to familiarize yourself with the basics. The very realistic miniature town model will help you get your bearings. ⏲ *30 min. Horní 152.* ☎ *380-711-674. 50 Kč. May–Sept 10am–5pm; Oct–Apr Tues–Fri 10am–4pm, Sat–Sun 1–4pm.*

3 Hotel Růže. Just across the street from the museum, this former Jesuit residence (and later army barracks) from the 16th century is now a privately owned luxury hotel. It's worth a peek inside to see how the Renaissance and Baroque touches have been restored. ⏲ *15 min. Horní 154.* ☎ *380-772-100.*

4 ★ St. Vitus Church (Kostel sv. Víta). Walk back toward the center of town and turn off on Kostelní. This enormous church was intended as an ecclesiastical counterweight to the secular authority of the castle. The church's steeple can

Allow some time to wander Český Krumlov's cobblestone streets.

be seen for miles around—and the view from on high is impressive. Construction of the church began in the late 14th century and was completed about 50 years later. It underwent the typical transformation into a more ornate Baroque church in the 17th century with the rise of Austrian influence. In the 19th century many of these Baroque elements, including an onion dome on top, were stripped away to restore its original Gothic appearance. ⏲ *20 min. Kostelní. No phone. Daily 9am–5pm.*

Český Krumlov's town square.

Krumlov Castle.

5 **Na louži.** Continue walking along Kostelní, which then becomes Kájovská street (don't worry if you get lost—all roads eventually lead back to the center). Na louži is a classic Czech pub that's been spruced up to accommodate visitors. They serve delicious home-cooked meals and some of the best fruit dumplings (*ovocné knedlíky*) in the Czech Republic. It can get crowded, so try to visit slightly before or after traditional meal hours. *Kájovská 66.* ☎ *380-711-280. $.*

6 ★★★ **Egon Schiele Centrum.** Walk left out the door from Na louži to find Široká street. Český Krumlov has always had a love-hate relationship with the controversial Austrian portraitist Egon Schiele. Schiele's mother was born here, and the painter had a fondness for the place. But when he moved here in the early years of the 20th century to paint his now-prized portraits of scantily clad girls, he was run out of town as a pornographer. Today, the Egon Schiele Centrum is one of the most innovative and outward-looking art museums in the Czech Republic. In addition to displaying a small but important collection of Schiele's own portraits and graphics, it hosts often-fascinating visiting exhibitions—for example, in 2007, the museum brought Keith Haring's comic illustrations to the Czech Republic for the first time. ⏱ *1 hr. Široká 70.* ☎ *380-704-011. 120 Kč. Daily 10am–6pm.*

7 ★ **kids** **Marionette Museum.** Continue walking along Široká, then follow painfully

A fountain on the castle grounds.

Český Krumlov: Practical Matters

From Prague, you can take either the bus or the train to Český Krumlov. Buses are quicker and cheaper, and drop you off at Český Krumlov's convenient bus station, just a 5- to 10-minute walk from the main sites. Buses depart from Prague's Florenc bus station and the trip takes a little over 3 hours. Try to arrive well before departure time to get a seat; the buses tend to fill to capacity, especially on weekends. Trains leave from Prague's Hlavní nadráží and require a change in České Budějovice. Figure on about 4 hours in total. Český Krumlov's train station is a good 25-minute walk into town. If you're driving, follow the D1 motorway out of Prague, heading south toward Brno. Follow the signs first to České Budějovice and then once there to Český Krumlov. Depending on traffic, the trip takes about 3 hours.

picturesque Dlouhá (leaving time to pop in at shops along the way). Turn left at the main street, Radniční, and cross the bridge over the Vltava for an awesome photo op. At Latrán 6, you'll find this excellent collection of historical puppets, most dating from the 19th century, as well as sets from puppet theater. This museum is a local offshoot of the National Puppet Theater in Prague (p 127). ⏱ 30 min. Latrán 6. ☎ 380-711-175. 70 Kč. Daily 10am–5pm.

⑧ ★★★ Castle (Hrad). Just up from the museum on Latrán is the main entrance to the castle. This was the residence of the powerful Rožmberk family until the line died out at the beginning of the 17th century. It later fell into the hands of the Eggenberg family and then the Schwarzenberg family, the largest noble landholders in the Czech Republic. The castle was built up in stages, with the oldest part being the 13th-century observation tower,

which was given its Renaissance appearance in the 16th century. The gardens are open year-round, but the interiors are accessible only from April to October, and by guided tour only. The tour possibilities are confusing, but most visitors will be content with Tour 1 (focusing on the Renaissance and Baroque interiors) and perhaps a scramble up the 162 steps to the top of the observation tower. Tour 2 focuses on the Schwarzenberg family. It's also possible to visit the lapidary (if you have a special interest in statues) and the Baroque theater. The tours take around an hour each. Be sure to leave yourself at least another hour to wander around and take in the upper gardens. ⏱ 2 hr. Zámek 59. ☎ 380-704-711. Tour 1 160 Kč (includes guide), Tour 2 140 Kč (includes guide), theater tour 180 Kč, lapidary 20 Kč, tower 35 Kč. Apr–Oct Tues–Sun 9am–5pm (last tours start an hour before closing).

Bone-Chilling Kutná Hora

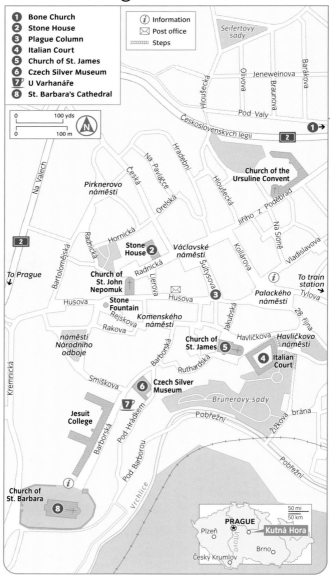

1. Bone Church
2. Stone House
3. Plague Column
4. Italian Court
5. Church of St. James
6. Czech Silver Museum
7. U Varhanáře
8. St. Barbara's Cathedral

ⓘ Information
✉ Post office
⸺ Steps

0   100 yds
0   100 m

Seifertovy sady

Jeneweinova

Hloušecká   Olivova   Braunova   Barákova

Pod Valy

Československých legii   1 →   2

Na Valech

Pirknerovo náměstí

Na Pavláčce

Česká

Hradební

Hloušecká

Church of the Ursuline Convent

Jiřího z Poděbrad

Na Sioně

Vladislavova

2

To Prague ↓

Bartolomějská   Radnická

Hornická

Orelská

Stone House 2

Václavské náměstí

Šultysova

Kollárova

ⓘ

To train station   Tylova →

Church of St. John Nepomuk

Radnická

Lierova

Husova

3   ✉

Palackého náměstí

28. října

Stone Fountain

Husova

Rejskova

Komenského náměstí

Jakubská

Rakova

náměstí Národního odboje

Barborská

Church of St. James 5

Havličkova

Havličkovo náměstí

4 Italian Court

Kremnická

Smíškova

Ruthardská

Czech Silver Museum 6

Bruneovy sady

Žižkova brána

Jesuit College

Pod Hrádkem

7

Pobřežní

Barborská

Pod Barborou

Vrchlice

ⓘ

Church of St. Barbara 8

Pobřežní

50 mi
50 km

PRAGUE ★   Kutná Hora

Plzeň

Brno

Český Krumlov

Back in the early years of the Bohemian kingdom, in the 13th and 14th centuries, Kutná Hora was Prague's main rival for power and influence. The town grew rich on the back of the silver mines, and became a major financial center and even a secondary royal residence. Decline began to set in around the 16th century and what you see today is a smallish Czech town overshadowed by its splendiferous medieval past. That makes it all the more fun for a trip back into time. Kutná Hora is easily reachable from Prague by bus or rail. As an added bonus, you can visit possibly the most ghoulishly fascinating church in Central Europe.

1 ★★★ kids **Bone Church (Kostnice).** The interior of this small church is made up entirely of human bones. Altars, chalices, chandeliers . . . it simply must be seen to be believed. For centuries, the area was used as a mass burial ground. In the 19th century, a Czech woodcarver named František Rint came up with this unique solution for using the bones. ◷ *45 min. Zámecká 127 (Sedlec).* ☎ *728-125-488. 40 Kč. Apr–Sept 8am–6pm; Oct–Mar 9am–noon, 1–4pm.*

2 ★ **Stone House (Kamenný dům).** The triangular gable on the front of the house is widely considered one of the high points of late Czech Gothic architecture. Now it holds a small offshoot of the Czech Silver Museum that focuses on life in the 18th century; it's worth the admission price for a look around inside. ◷ *20 min. Václavské nám.* ☎ *327-512-821. 40 Kč. May–Sept 10am–6pm; Apr 10am–5pm; Oct–Nov 10am–4pm. (Closed Nov–Dec.)*

3 **Plague Column (Morový sloup).** The "Black Death" swept through Kutná Hora in 1713. This Baroque column dates from the period immediately after and was meant to ward off the plague. *Šultysová.*

4 ★ **Italian Court (Vlašský dvůr).** During the Middle Ages, this was the seat of considerable wealth and influence. It was here where the

Fascinating, creepy Bone Church.

main workshops were housed for reworking the silver and minting coins. Operations were halted toward the end of the 16th century and the building fell into ruin. It was "rediscovered" in the 19th century and given a thorough neo-Gothic makeover, essentially what you see today. ◷ *30 min. Havlíčkovo nám.* ☎ *327-512-873. 80 Kč. Apr–Sept 9am–6pm; Oct–Mar 10am–4pm.*

5 **Church of St. James (Kostel sv. Jakuba).** This stately, somber Gothic church is visible for miles around. The interior was reworked as Baroque in keeping with the fashion of the 17h century.

Kutná Hora: Practical Matters

Kutná Hora lies about 80km (50 miles) to the east of Prague, with regular connections during the day by train or bus. The hitch is that the train station is in Sedlec—close to the Bone Church—while the bus station is much closer to the center of town. The tour above assumes that you take the train into Kutná Hora, walk to the Bone Church from there, and then proceed into town. The return trip to Prague is by bus. Figure on about 90 minutes of travel each way and a cost of 60 Kč (by bus) or 90 Kč (by train) per trip. If you're driving, head east out of Prague along Vinohradská třída, continuing straight, picking up local highway no. 2 until you see signs to Kutná Hora. Figure on about an hour's drive.

Unfortunately, it's seldom open to the public, but you may be able to catch a Sunday service for a peek inside. *Havlíčkovo nám. No phone. Sometimes open for Sun mass.*

⑥ ★★★ kids Czech Silver Museum (České Muzeum Stříbra/Hrádek). This 15th-century residence houses the main branch of the Czech Silver Museum and its collection of coins from the Middle Ages. The Renaissance-style painted ceilings are also valuable. But the real highlight of a visit here is the chance to descend into an abandoned silver mine. Great for kids, but not recommended for claustrophobics. ⏱ *1 hr. Barborská 28.* ☎ *327-512-159. 110 Kč. Apr–Oct 9am–5pm.*

⑦ U Varhanáře. Delightful terrace restaurant connected to a small inn along the main walkway to St. Barbara's. The draw here is the commanding view out over the valley and the Czech specialties are well done. Service can be uneven. *Barborská 578.* ☎ *327-512-769. $$.*

⑧ ★★★ St Barbara's Cathedral. (Chrám sv. Barbory). This is widely considered the second-most-impressive Gothic cathedral in the country after St. Vitus at Prague Castle. Over the years, the masters who worked on the church read like a who's who of Czech Gothic and late-Gothic architecture. St. Barbara is considered the patron saint of miners, and the miner motifs are seen throughout the church. You'll need an hour to see the frescoes and chapels. ⏱ *1 hr. Barborská. No phone. 40 Kč. May–Sept Tues–Sun 9am–6pm; Oct–Apr Tues–Sun 9am–noon, 2–4pm.* ●

St. Barbara's Cathedral.

The
Savvy Traveler

Before You Go

Government Tourist Offices

In the US: CzechTourism, 1109–1111 Madison Ave., New York, NY 10028 (☎ 212/288-0830, ext. 101). **In Canada:** Czech-Tourism, 401 Bay St., Suite 1510, Toronto, M5H 2Y4 (☎ 416/363-9928). **In the U.K. & Ireland:** CzechTourism UK, Scotland, and Ireland, 13 Harley St., London W1G 9QG (☎ 020/7631-0427).

The Best Times to Go

Prague is gorgeous in **spring,** when the trees blossom and the city shrugs off a long winter. **Fall** can be equally pleasant, with long, warm days and usually reliably sunny weather. Avoid travel over **Christmas, New Year's,** and **Easter,** when the city fills to brimming with tour groups from Germany and Italy. Midsummer is considered "in-between" season, with slightly lower hotel prices; but it can be stiflingly hot and many hotels lack air-conditioning. You might consider coming in low season, February and November, when the crowds thin and you finally feel you have this beautiful city to yourself.

Festivals & Special Events

SPRING. The **Prague Spring Music Festival** (www.festival.cz), held in late spring, is a world-famous, 3-week series of symphony, opera, and chamber performances. **Prague Khamoro** (www.khamoro.cz), usually held at the end of May, is a celebration of Roma (gypsy) culture. **Febiofest** (www.febiofest.cz), in March, is one of the largest non-competitive film and video festivals in Central Europe. Many of the films are shown in English or with English subtitles. The **One World** film festival (www.jedensvet.cz), also in March, brings together the best human rights and documentary films of the past year. Many of the screenings are in English.

SUMMER. The summer kicks off with the **Prague Writers' Festival** (www.pwf.cz) in June. A handful of contemporary writers from around Europe and the United States, including usually a couple big names, hold readings, book signings, lectures, and happenings. **Tanec Praha** (Dance Prague; www.tanecpraha.cz) is an international dance festival in June that focuses on contemporary dance and movement theater. **United Islands** (www.unitedislands.cz) festival, usually a long weekend in June, is a carnival of jazz, rock, folk, and house music spread out over several islands in the Vltava River.

FALL. The **Prague Autumn Music Festival** (www.pragueautumn.cz), in late September and October, is similar to the spring festival but the focus is more on orchestral music, bringing some of Europe's best ensembles to play at Prague's Rudolfinum. The weeklong **Prague International Jazz Festival** (www.jazzfestivalpraha.cz), each October, attracts some of the world's best jazz musicians. Performances are usually held in the Lucerna Music Hall and the city's oldest jazz venue, Reduta.

WINTER. The Christmas season begins on **St. Nicholas Eve** (Dec. 5), when children traditionally dress as St. Nicholas, the devil, or an angel. The annual Prague Christmas Market in Old Town Square gets going about then. Stalls hawk all manner of food, mulled wine,

MONTHLY AVERAGE TEMPERATURE						
	JAN	FEB	MAR	APR	MAY	JUNE
Daily Temp (°F)	30	33	40	48	57	63
Daily Temp (°C)	0.9	0.8	4.6	9.2	14.2	17.5
	JULY	AUG	SEPT	OCT	NOV	DEC
Daily Temp (°F)	66	65	58	49	39	33
Daily Temp (°C)	19.1	18.5	14.7	9.7	4.4	0.9

ornaments, and cheap gifts in a festive atmosphere that toes a fine line between traditional and tacky. **New Year's Eve** is literally a blowout—and the entire town comes out to light firecrackers on Old Town Square, Wenceslas Square, and Charles Bridge. Watch your head, as every year hundreds of people are injured by errant bottle rockets.

The Weather

Spring and **fall** generally bring the best weather for touring, with warm days and cool nights. **Summers** can be hit or miss, with some years bringing lots of rain and others weeklong stretches of hot sunshine. **Winters** can be cold and unusually long, sometimes lasting into April. Rain is a possibility at any time of year, so be sure to pack an umbrella.

Useful Websites

- **www.pis.cz/en:** The city's main tourist information portal. Good source for general information and cultural calendars. Includes an excellent "ABC Listing" for tourists on everything from accommodations to weather.

- **www.mapy.cz:** Online maps and journey planner; covers Prague and the entire Czech Republic. Simply type in an address and a map shows you exactly where it is.

- **www.dp-praha.cz:** The ins and outs of Prague's public

transportation system, including system maps and info on tickets and travel passes.

- **www.idos.cz:** Online timetable for trains and buses, including international destinations. Just type in the city (using the Czech spellings, for example, "Praha" for Prague) and you'll get a complete listing of train and bus connections.

- **www.praguemonitor.com:** Excellent online English magazine about all things Prague and Czech. Good sections on politics and economics, and a lifestyle section that includes cultural listings and restaurant reviews.

Cellphones (Mobile Phones)

Czech cellphones operate on a GSM band of 900/1800MHz. This is the same standard in use throughout Europe but different from the one used in the U.S. **U.S. mobiles** will work here provided that they are triband phones (not all phones are triband) and that you've contacted your service provider to allow for international roaming. Keep calls to a minimum, however, since roaming charges can be steep. **U.K. mobiles** should work without any problem provided that you've contacted your service provider to activate international roaming (the same precautions about steep prices apply to U.K. mobiles.) One way of avoiding international roaming charges is to

purchase a pay-as-you-go SIM card for your cellphone and a pre-paid calling card. This provides you with a local number and allows you to make calls and send text messages at local rates. All of the major local telephone operators offer this service. Vodaphone (www. vodafone.cz) offers a visiting SIM card, including 200 Kč of phone credit, for 200 Kč.

Car Rentals
There's very little need to rent a car in Prague, but if you're determined to do so, it's usually cheapest to book a car online before you leave home. All of the major rental agencies offer cars in Prague (with pickup either in town or at the airport). Try Hertz (www.hertz.com), Avis (www.avis.com), or Budget (www.budget.com).

Getting **There**

By Plane
Prague's busy international airport, known as Ruzyně (☎ 220-113-314; www.prg.aero), lies about 18km (11 miles) west of the center of town. The airport has two main passenger terminals, North 1 and North 2 (in Czech: Severin 1 and Severin 2). North 1 handles destinations outside the European Union, including most overseas flights, as well as flights from the U.K. North 2 handles what are considered "internal" flights, within the European Union. Prague is well served by European and international carriers, including several budget airlines. The Czech national carrier, CSA (www.csa. com), operates regular direct service to New York's JFK airport, as well as Toronto and Montreal. Delta Airlines (www.delta.com) offers direct service between Prague and Atlanta.

From Ruzyně to town: Taxis are the quickest but most expensive option. Two cab companies are licensed to operate at the airport. The more reliable of the two is "AAA" (☎ 222-333-222; www.aaa-taxi.cz), which maintains stands outside both main terminals. Fares with AAA average about 600 Kč to the center. The trip takes about 25 minutes. If you're staying in the immediate center of town, a cheaper alternative is the minibus operated by CEDAZ (☎ 220-114-296). Minibuses run regularly between the airport and central Náměstí Republiky for 90 Kč per person. The most affordable alternative is public transportation. City bus no. 119 stops at both terminals and runs regularly from the airport to Dejvická metro station (on Line A). Bus no. 100 runs south from the airport to the area of Zličín, and connects to metro Line B. Travel on both requires a 20 Kč ticket purchased from the driver or from yellow ticket machines. Buy two tickets if you're carrying large luggage. A special Airport Express (designated "AE" on buses) runs from Ruzyně to Prague's Holešovice train station and costs 45 Kč per person. This is convenient if you are connecting directly to an international train leaving from Holešovice station.

By Car
The main highways into Prague are the D-1 motorway from the east (Brno, Bratislava, and connections to Kraków and Budapest); the D-5 from the south and west (Plzeň, Nürnberg, and Munich, with connections to Italy and points in Western Europe); the D-8 from the north (Dresden, Berlin).

By Train

The Czech Republic is not a member of the Eurail network and the Global Eurailpass is not valid here, though there are a number of other options. The **European East Pass** and the **Austria-Czech Republic** pass (www.railpass.com) are both accepted. The European East pass, including Austria, Slovakia, Poland, and Hungary, for example, offers 5 days of unlimited rail travel within a calendar month for $187 (second-class). **RailEurope** (www.raileurope.com) offers a couple of passes valid only within the Czech Republic, including a Czech Flexipass giving 3 days of unlimited travel within 15 calendar days for $86 (second-class). The passes must be purchased in North America before you leave on your trip.

Many rail passes are available in Great Britain for travel to the Czech Republic, including the popular **InterRail** and **InterRail Youthpass** (www.internationalrail.com). It's also possible to purchase an InterRail–Czech Republic pass offering 3 days of unlimited travel in the Czech Republic within 1 month for £36. To purchase an InterRail pass you must be a permanent resident of one of the participating countries (residents of the U.S. and Canada are prohibited).

International trains arrive at either the main station, Hlavní nádraží (Wilsonova 80, Prague 1; ☎ 224-614-071; metro stop: Hlavní nádraží, Line C), or the northern suburban station, Holešovice (Vrbenského ul., Prague 7; ☎ 224-615-865; metro stop: Nádraží Holešovice, Line C). This is a source of endless confusion, so look carefully at the tickets or ask if in doubt. The website www.idos.cz has an online timetable for train departures.

Prague lies on major east–west and north–south rail lines, with good connections to Dresden and Berlin to the north, and Brno, Vienna, Bratislava, and Budapest to the south and east. **New high-speed rail service,** the Pendolino, was recently introduced on the Prague–Vienna run, shortening the travel time to Vienna to a little over 4 hours.

By Bus

The main European international bus line, **Eurolines** (www.eurolines.com), maintains regular service to Prague from around Europe. International buses arrive and depart from Prague's Florenc bus station (Křižíkova 5, Prague 8; ☎ 900-144-444; metro stop: Florenc, Line C).

Getting **Around**

On Foot

Prepare to do plenty of walking. Most of the center of the city is closed to vehicles, including taxis, meaning you'll have to walk pretty much everywhere. Distances are relatively close, but be sure to wear comfortable shoes, since many of the streets are paved (if that's the right word . . .) with cobblestones.

By Public Transportation

Prague's public transportation system (www.dp-praha.cz) of metros, trams, and buses is excellent. A 20 Kč ticket, which you can buy at tobacco kiosks or from yellow ticket machines, gives you 75 minutes (90 min. on weekends) of unlimited travel on any metro, tram, or bus. For shorter journeys, a 14 Kč ticket gives you 20 minutes of travel (30 min. on the metro) but prohibits transfers. For longer stays, you can buy a 24-hour ticket for Kč 80, or 3-day (Kč 220), 7-day (Kč 280), or 15-day (Kč 320) passes. On metros, validate tickets in punching machines located at the top of the escalators. On trams and buses, these machines are located in the vehicle. Hold on to your ticket until the end of the journey. Spot-checks are infrequent, but fines are steep.

By Taxi

Taxis rates are reasonable, but watch for dishonest drivers. In an honest cab, the meter will start at around 40 Kč and rise 28 Kč per kilometer after that. Fares for destinations within the center should not be higher than 150–200 Kč. Refrain from hailing cabs on the street; instead order cabs by phone. AAA (☎ 222-333-222; www.aaa-taxi.cz) employs honest drivers, and operators speak English. Rates are also cheaper if ordered by phone.

By Car

Driving is not recommended as traffic is heavy and many areas of the central city are closed to motor vehicles. Parking can be difficult. You'll need a special sticker to park in the center (available only to residents) or pay very high short-term rates. If you arrive by car, the cheapest option is to find a spot in one of the neighborhoods well outside of the center, where parking is free.

Prague's **Architectural Mix**

Look up. That's maybe the best advice we can give you. Prague's majestic mix of medieval, Renaissance, and Art Nouveau architecture shares one fairly universal element—the most elegant and well-appointed facades and fixtures aren't at eye level or even street level, but are on top floors and roofs. Hundreds of buildings are decorated with intricately carved cornices or ornamental balconies and friezes depicting mythical, religious, or heroic figures.

The grime of Prague pollution has been gradually stripped away, and each restored building reveals previously obscured details. What's interesting, though, is how visitors react to the grime. When people visit Paris or Venice and see dirty, crumbling buildings, they consider them quaint. When they see the same old, dirty, crumbling buildings in Prague, however, they point to the failure of Communism—not entirely fair. If you look at photos of Prague taken in 1900, you'll also see dirty, crumbling buildings.

The city's earliest extant forms are Romanesque, dating from 1100 to 1250. The long Gothic period followed from 1250 to 1530. You'll find many Gothic buildings in Staré Město. Plus Prague Castle's most visible superstructure, St. Vitus Cathedral, is a Gothic masterpiece—that is, its older east-facing half (the cathedral's western sections exemplify Renaissance and neo-Gothic styles). From 1500 to the early 1600s, the Italian Renaissance style prevailed.

Many of the best-known structures are Baroque and rococo, sharply tailored in the high Austrian style inspired by the Habsburgs of the 17th and 18th centuries.

Some of the most flamboyant buildings are Art Nouveau, popular from 1900 to 1918. The movement that swept across Europe developed with the Industrial Revolution.

Innovative building materials—primarily steel and glass—opened endless possibilities for artistic embellishments. Architects abandoned traditional stone structures, built in a pseudo-historic style. Art Nouveau is characterized by rich, curvaceous ornamentation that seems sadly to have vanished in the push for functionalism later in the 20th century.

Several intriguing cubist designs from that era have also been hailed for their ingenuity. As an architectural style, cubism thrived in Bohemia, and you can find many examples in the neighborhood below Vyšehrad Park.

The late 20th century played havoc with Prague's architecture. Communists were partial to functionalism with virtually no character. Their buildings shed all decorative details. You shouldn't leave Prague before taking the metro out to Prosek to see the thousands of Communist-era flats, called "rabbit huts" even by their occupants. Created partly out of socialist dogma and partly out of economic necessity, these prefabricated apartment buildings *(paneláks)* were named after the concrete slabs used to build them. Cheap and unimaginatively designed, the apartment buildings are surrounded by a featureless world. Exteriors were made of plain, unadorned cement, and halls were lined with linoleum. The same room, balcony, and window design was stamped over and over.

But *panelák* living wasn't always viewed as a scourge. Unlike the larger, older apartments, *paneláks* had modern plumbing and heating and were once considered the politically correct way to live.

Two major post-Communist projects have already triggered a new debate among the progressives and the traditionalists. The Myslbek shopping/office complex on Na Příkopě near Wenceslas Square is the business district's first attempt at blending the new with the old in a functional yet elegant way. And the so-called Dancing Building on the embankment at the Rašínovo nábřeží has conservative tongues wagging. Its design strays from the 19th-century Empire classical houses lining the river, but in a most peculiar way. Controversial U.S. architect Frank Gehry, who designed the American Center in Paris, and New Wave designer Vlado Milunič have created a building that ironically pays tribute to the most classic of film dancing pairs: Fred Astaire and Ginger Rogers. Built as the Prague office of a Dutch insurance company, the building depicts the two intertwined in a spin above the Vltava.

Recommended **Films & Books**

Films

Czech filmmaking has a long tradition. The Prague studios in the Barrandov Hills churned out glossy pre-Communist romantic comedies and period pieces rivaling the output of Paris, Berlin, and even Hollywood at the time.

While Czech literature and music have carved their places in classical culture, the country's films and their directors have collected the widest praise in the mid– to late 20th century. Cunning, melancholy views of Bohemian life (before the Soviets moved in for a few decades) were captured by some of the finest filmmakers in the era known as the "Czech New Wave" of the 1960s.

Directors Jiří Menzel and Miloš Forman were in the vanguard. An easy-to-find example of this period's work (with English subtitles) is Menzel's Oscar-winning *Closely Watched Trains*, a snapshot of the odd routine at a rural Czech train station.

Forman made his splash with a quirky look at a night in the life of a town trying to have fun despite itself. *The Fireman's Ball* shows Forman's true mastery as he captures the essence of being stone-bored in a gray world, yet he still makes it strangely intriguing. Of course, this was made before Forman emigrated to the big budgets of Hollywood and first shocked Americans with *Hair*. He then directed the Oscar-winning *One Flew Over the Cuckoo's Nest*. For *Amadeus*, Forman sought authenticity, so he received special permission from the Communists to return to Prague; while filming, he brought back to life the original Estates' Theater (Stavovské divadlo), where Mozart first performed. Forman also consulted a friend, then-President Václav Havel, before choosing Courtney Love as the pornographer's wife in the Oscar-nominated *The People vs. Larry Flynt*. Havel loved the choice but refused to attend a private 1996 screening in Prague along with Flynt himself.

Czech-based directors after the New Wave mostly disappeared from view, but one stunningly brave film was made in 1970, as the repressive post-invasion period known as "normalization" began its long, cold freeze of talent. In *The Ear (Ucho)*, director Karel Kachyňa presents the anguished story of a man trapped in an apartment wired for sound, subject to the Communist leaders' obsession and paranoia with Moscow. That *The Ear* was made in the political environment of the time was astounding. That it was quickly banned wasn't. Fortunately, local TV

has dusted off copies from the archives, and it has begun playing to art-house audiences again.

But maybe a new Czech wave has begun. The father-and-son team of Zdeněk and Jan Svěrák won the Best Foreign Film Oscar in 1997 for *Kolja*, the bittersweet tale of an abandoned Russian boy grudgingly adopted by an aging Czech bachelor on the cusp of the 1989 revolution. After a previous Oscar nomination for the 1992 *Elementary School (Obecná škola)*, the 30-something director Jan and his actor father are making an industry out of golden reflections about Czech life.

Prague has become a popular location for major motion pictures, in spite of itself. Producer/actor Tom Cruise and director Brian De Palma chose it for the stunning night shots around Charles Bridge in the early scenes of *Mission: Impossible*. During shooting, a verbal brawl broke out with Czech officials, who jacked up the rent for use of the riverside palace that acts as the American Embassy in the film (the palace is actually claimed by the von Liechtenstein family). *Immortal Beloved*, a story of Beethoven, made use of Prague's timeless streets (shooting around the graffiti).

Finally, *The Beautician and the Beast*, starring "Bond" hunk Timothy Dalton and nasal-siren Fran Drescher, uses Prague as a mythical East European capital invaded by a Brooklyn hairdresser (who makes pretty good use of her Frommer's guidebook while traveling through faux-Prague).

Still, the film about Prague probably most familiar to American audiences is *The Unbearable Lightness of Being*, based on the book by émigré author Milan Kundera. Set in the days surrounding the Soviet invasion, the story draws on the psychology of three Czechs who can't escape their personal obsessions while the political world outside collapses around them. Many Czechs find the film disturbing, some because it hits home, others because they say it portrays a Western stereotype.

Books

Any discussion of Czech literature with visiting foreigners usually begins with Milan Kundera. Reviled among many Czechs who didn't emigrate, Kundera creates a visceral, personal sense of the world he chose to leave in the 1970s for the freedom of Paris. In *The Unbearable Lightness of Being,* the anguish over escaping the Soviet-occupied Prague he loves tears the libidinous protagonist Dr. Tomáš in the same way the love for his wife and the lust for his lover do. More Czech postnormalization angst can be found in *The Book of Laughter and Forgetting* and *Laughable Loves.* Kundera's biting satire of Stalinist purges in the 1950s *The Joke,* however, is regarded by Czech critics as his best work.

Arnošt Lustig, a survivor of the Nazi-era Terezín concentration camp and author of many works, including *Street of Lost Brothers,* shared the 1991 *Publishers Weekly* Award for best literary work with John Updike and Norman Mailer. In 1995, he became the editor of the Czech edition of *Playboy.*

The best work of renowned Ivan Klíma, also a survivor of Terezín, is translated as *Judge on Trial,* a study of justice and the death penalty.

Jaroslav Hašek wrote the Czech harbinger to *Forrest Gump* in *The Good Soldier švejk,* a post–World War I satire about a simpleton soldier who wreaks havoc in the Austro-Hungarian army during the war.

Bohumil Hrabal, noted for writing about the Czech Everyman and maybe the country's all-time favorite author, died in early 1997 when he fell (so they said officially) out of a fifth-story window while trying to feed pigeons. His death was eerily similar to the fate of a character in one of his stories. He had two internationally acclaimed hits: *Closely Watched Trains* (also translated as *Closely Observed Trains,* on which the Menzel film was based) and *I Served the King of England.* When then-President Bill Clinton visited Prague in 1994, he asked to have a beer with Hrabal in the author's favorite Old Town haunt, the pub U Zlatého tygra (At the Golden Tiger). Clinton may have gotten more than he bargained for, as the gruff but lovable Hrabal, who turned 80 that year, lectured the president on his views of the world.

No reading list would be complete without reference to Franz Kafka, Prague's most famous novelist, who wrote his originals in his native German. *The Collected Novels of Franz Kafka,* which includes *The Castle* and *The Trial,* binds his most claustrophobic works into a single volume.

If it's contemporary philosophy you want, there is, of course, the philosopher ex-president. Václav Havel's heralded dissident essay, "The Power of the Powerless," explained how the lethargic masses were allowing their complacency with Communism to sap their souls. His "Letters to Olga," written to his wife while in prison in the 1980s, takes you into his cell and his view of a moral world. Available are two solid English-translated compilations of his dissident writings: *Living in Truth* and *Open Letters. Disturbing the Peace* is an autobiographical meditation on childhood, the events of 1968, and Havel's involvement with Charter 77. His first recollections about entering politics are in "Summer Meditations," a long essay written during a vacation.

While he hasn't had much time to write since his presidency, Havel says that his speeches given around the world continue a dialogue about morality in politics. If you read the anthology of his presidential speeches, *Toward a Civil Society,* you'll find it clear that Havel hasn't stopped being the dissident. However, now his target is incompetence and corruption in politics and society, including in democracies.

Madeleine Albright's father, diplomat Dr. Josef Koerbel, wrote a definitive contemporary history of his homeland in his final book, *Twentieth Century Czechoslovakia,* before his death in 1977. More than an academic study, it reads as a personal memoir of Prague's chaotic events, many of which he witnessed.

Finally, for an epic intellectual tour of the long, colorful, and often tragic history of the city, try the 1997 release of *Prague in Black and Gold* by native son and Yale literature professor Peter Demetz.

Fast **Facts**

APARTMENT RENTALS **Apartments In Prague** (Petřinská 4; ☎ 251-512-502; www.apartments-in-prague.org) has a good selection of nicely furnished short-term rentals in excellent areas like Malá Strana and near the Charles Bridge. **Residence Belgicka** (Belgická 12, Prague 2; ☎ 221-401-800; www.mamaison.com) offers high-end apartment rentals for short- or long-term stays in the upscale suburb of Vinohrady.

ATMS/CASHPOINTS The easiest and best way to get cash abroad is through an ATM—the Cirrus and PLUS networks span the globe. Bank fees average about 1%–2% of the transaction.

BABYSITTING **Prague Family** (☎ 737-749-019) offers special hotel babysitting as well as activity programs for young children.

BANKING HOURS Most banks are open Monday to Friday from 8:30am to 5pm.

BIKE RENTALS Try **City Bike Prague** (Královdvorská 5, Prague 1; ☎ 776-180-284; www.citybike-prague.com).

BUSINESS HOURS Stores are typically open Monday to Friday from 9am to 6pm and on Saturday from 9am to 1pm; those in the center often keep longer hours and may be open on Sundays and holidays as well. Museums are often closed on Mondays.

CLIMATE Prague has a continental climate with four distinct seasons, including often cold and snowy winters and occasionally hot summers, though temperatures rarely exceed about 32°C (90 °F).

CONSULATES & EMBASSIES **United States Embassy,** Tržiště 15 (☎ 257-530-663); **Canadian Embassy,** Muchová 6 (☎ 272-101-800); **United Kingdom Embassy,** Thunovská 14 (☎ 257-402-111); Irish Embassy, Tržíště 13 (☎ 257-530-061); **Australian Embassy,** Klimentská 10 (☎ 251-018-359).

CREDIT CARDS Credit cards are a safe way to carry money. They also provide a convenient record of all your expenses, and they generally offer good exchange rates. You can also withdraw cash advances from your credit cards at banks or ATMs, provided you know your PIN. (Call the number on the back of your card if you don't know yours.) Keep in mind that when you use your credit card abroad, most banks assess a 2% fee above the 1% fee charged by Visa, MasterCard, or American Express.

CUSTOMS Baggage checks at airports are rare. You're permitted to bring in reasonable amounts of tobacco products and alcohol for personal use.

DENTISTS & DOCTORS See "Emergencies," below.

DRUGSTORES After regular hours, ask at your hotel where the nearest 24-hour pharmacy is. You'll also find the address posted on the doors or windows of other drugstores in the neighborhood. One all-night drugstore is **Lékárna U Svaté Ludmily,** in Vinohrady, Belgická 37 (☎ 224-237-207).

ELECTRICITY The Czech Republic operates on the standard European 220V with a two-pronged plug with round pins. U.S. appliances will need a transformer and a plug adapter. Laptops usually require only a plug adapter.

EMBASSIES See "Consulates & Embassies," above.

EMERGENCIES Dial the following telephone numbers in an emergency: 112 (general emergency, equivalent to U.S. 911); 155 (ambulance); 158 (police); 150 (fire); 1230, 1240 (emergency road service). For emergency medical treatment, go to the **Nemocnice Na Homolce** (Hospital Na Homolce), Roentgenova 2 (☎ 257-271-111). If you need nonurgent medical attention, practitioners in most fields can be found at the **Canadian Medical Center,** Veleslavínská 1, 9e (☎ 235-360-133). For dental service, call **American Dental Associates,** V Celnici 4 (☎ 221-181-121), Monday through Friday from 8am to 6pm, and Saturday from 8am to noon.

EVENT LISTINGS The best source of weekly information in English is *The Prague Post* (www.praguepost.com), available at newsstands for Kč 50 a copy. The Prague edition of the *In Your Pocket* guides—updated quarterly—is available at bookstores and is a good source of restaurant, hotel, and club listings, as well as an entertaining, opinionated overview of what's out there.

FAMILY TRAVEL (www.familytravel.com) is an independent, U.S.-based website offering reviews, sightseeing suggestions, and more.

GAY & LESBIAN TRAVELERS The Czech Republic is a tolerant society, and gay and lesbian travelers should have no particular problems. The website **prague.gayguide.net** is a useful resource for events, clubs, and gay-friendly hotels and restaurants.

HOLIDAYS Public holidays include New Year's Day (Jan 1); Easter Monday (Mar or Apr); Labor Day (May 1); Liberation Day (May 8); Sts. Cyril & Methodius Day (July 5); Death of Jan Hus (July 6); St. Wenceslas Day (Sept 28); Founding of the Czechoslovak Republic (Oct 28); Student Demonstration of 1989 (Nov 17); Christmas (Dec 24, 25); and St. Stephen's Day (Dec 26).

INSURANCE North Americans with homeowner's or renter's insurance are probably covered for lost luggage. If not, inquire with **Travel Assistance International** (☎ 800/821-2828) or **Travelex** (☎ 800/228-9792). These insurers can also provide trip-cancellation, medical, and emergency-evacuation coverage abroad. The website www.money supermarket.com compares prices across a wide range of providers for single- and multitrip policies. For U.K. citizens, insurance is always advisable.

INTERNET CAFES Central Prague is filled with Internet cafes. Rates run about 1 Kč a minute. To surf the Net or check e-mail, try **Bohemia Bagel** at Masná 2 (Old Town)

(☎ 257-310-694; www.bohemia bagel.cz).

LIQUOR LAWS You can buy alcohol (beer, wine, and spirits) at supermarkets, convenience stores, cafes, and bars. The legal age for buying and consuming alcohol is 18, though ID checks are practically unheard of. The blood-alcohol limit for driving a car is zero, and motorists face a stiff fine.

LOST PROPERTY If your luggage is lost, immediately file a lost-luggage claim at the airport, detailing the luggage contents. For most airlines, you must report delayed, damaged, or lost baggage within 4 hours of arrival.

MAIL & POSTAGE Most post offices in Prague are open Monday through Friday from 8am to 7pm. The main post office (Hlavní pošta), at Jindřišská 14, Prague 1 (☎ 221-131-111), is open 24 hours a day. Stamps can sometimes be purchased from your hotel reception desk.

MONEY The Czech currency is the crown (koruna in Czech, noted as Kč in shops and CZK in banks). One crown, in theory, is divided into 100 haler. Coins come in denominations of 1, 2, 5, 10, 20, and 50 crowns. Bills come in denominations of 50, 100, 200, 500, 1,000, and 5,000 crowns. The euro is not in circulation in the Czech Republic, though euros are sometimes accepted at large hotels and at some shops. Dollars are usually not accepted as payment. At press time, one U.S. dollar was worth about Kč 20; one euro was worth about Kč 27; and one pound was worth about Kč 38.

ORIENTATION TOURS See "Tours," below.

PARKING Parking in Prague is a nightmare. To park in the center requires a special permit available only to residents. Parking garages and paid parking lots can be very expensive. In public parking areas, there are no parking meters; instead buy temporary parking permits at machines and display the piece of paper on your dashboard. Parking rates in the center run about Kč 40 an hour. Parking on streets outside the immediate center is free, but good luck finding a spot.

PASSES The **Prague Card** offers free entry to 55 attractions, including Prague Castle (but not the Jewish Museum), for 740 Kč for adults and 490 Kč for students. You can buy the pass at select hotels and travel agencies, and at Prague Information Service offices (see "Tourist Offices" below).

PASSPORTS If your passport is lost or stolen, contact your country's embassy or consulate immediately. (See "Consulates & Embassies," above.) Before you travel, you should copy the critical pages and keep them in a separate place.

PHARMACIES Pharmacies (*apteka* in Czech) are recognizable by the big green cross on the door. Pharmacies sell both prescription and over-the-counter medicines. Most are well stocked, though pharmacists may not always be willing to fill an out-of-country prescription (so be sure to carry extra medication if need be). Most pharmacies are open from 8am to 6pm, though a few maintain 24-hour service. Your hotel should be able to locate an all-night pharmacy in a pinch.

SAFETY Violent crime against tourists is rare, but pickpockets and scams are common. Watch your purses and wallets while on crowded trams and metro cars. Tram no. 22 is especially notorious for pickpockets. Report any theft to police for insurance purposes, and immediately cancel all credit cards. For more information, consult the U.S. State Department's website at www.travel.state.gov; in the U.K., consult the Foreign Office's website, www.fco.gov.uk; and in Australia, consult the government travel advisory service at www.smarttraveller. gov.au.

SENIOR TRAVELERS Mention that you're a senior when you make your travel reservations. As in most cities, people over the age of 60 qualify for reduced admission to theaters, museums, and other attractions, as well as discounted fares on public transport.

SMOKING Restaurants are now required to offer nonsmoking seating, but this is often forgotten about in practice. Ask the manager to seat you in a nonsmoking area if you are bothered by cigarette smoke. Pubs, particularly the older, more traditional pubs, can be very smoky, and little provision is made for the nonsmoker.

SPECTATOR SPORTS The Czech Republic is an ice hockey superpower, and the two local Prague teams, **Slavia** and **Sparta,** traditionally sport NHL-quality sides. Buy tickets at the arena on game day. Slavia plays at **Sazka Arena,** metro line B: Českomoravská (☎ 266-121-122). Sparta plays at **T-Mobile Arena,** Za Elektrárnou 419, Holešovice (☎ 266-727-443). Soccer is also very popular, with the season running from August to May (and a break during the coldest months of Dec and Jan). The city's main team is **Sparta Praha.** It plays its home games at **Axa Arena** (formerly called Toyota Arena), Milady Horákové 98, Letná (☎ 296-111-400). This is also where the Czech national team plays its home games. Buy tickets at the box office on game day.

STAYING HEALTHY Prague poses no particular health hazards. Tap water is safe to drink, but if in doubt, drink bottled water, which is cheap and abundant.

TAXES value-added tax, or VAT (DPH in Czech), is 19%, but non-E.U. visitors can get a partial refund if you spend 2,000 Kč or more within 1 day at shops that participate in the VAT refund program. The shops will give you a form, which you must get stamped at Customs. (Allow extra time.) Mark the paperwork to request a credit card refund; otherwise, you'll be stuck with a check in euros. An option is to ask for a **Global Refund form** (☎ 800/566-9828; www.globalrefund.com) when you make your purchase, and take it to a Global Refund counter at the airport. Your money is refunded on the spot, minus a commission.

TAXIS Watch for dishonest drivers. Avoid hailing cabs on the street or in popular tourist areas like Wenceslas Square. The best bet is to have someone phone for a taxi or to call one yourself. Two reliable taxi companies include AAA (☎ 222-333-222; www.aaa-taxi.cz) or City Taxi (☎ 257-257-257; www.citytaxi.cz).

TELEPHONES Working public phones are few and far between thanks to the rapid growth of mobile phones. To use a pay phone, you must buy a prepaid card from tobacco and magazine kiosks (cards are available for Kč 200). Simply insert the card, listen for the dial tone, and dial. You can use pay phones with prepaid cards to dial abroad.

The country code for the Czech Republic is 420. To dial the Czech Republic from abroad, dial the international access code (011 in the United States) plus the unique nine-digit local number (there are no area or city codes in the Czech Republic). Once you are here, to dial any number anywhere in the Czech Republic, simply dial the nine-digit number.

To make a direct international call from the Czech Republic, dial 00 plus the country code of the country you are calling and then the area code and number. The country code for the U.S. and Canada is 1; Great Britain, 44; Ireland, 353; Australia, 61; and New Zealand, 64.

TICKETS   See "Buying Tickets," p 132.

TIPPING   The Czech Republic is not a tipping culture, but waiters still expect small gratuities at restaurants. As a rule of thumb, on small bills round up to the next 10 Kč interval (if the bill comes to Kč 74, for example, give the waiter Kč 80). On larger bills or in very nice places tip up to 10% (but not higher) for good service. Tip taxi drivers a few crowns, but no more (if the bill is Kč 152, give Kč 160).

TOILETS   Every large metro station has a passably clean public toilet that you can use for Kč 5. Otherwise, search out restaurants or cafes and use the facilities in return for the price of a coffee or soft drink.

TOURIST OFFICES   The official Prague Information Service has several locations around town: Staroměstské nám. 1 (inside the Old Town Hall), Hlavní Nádraží (the main train station), and the Malá Strana bridge tower (☎ 236-002-562; www.prague-info.cz). In addition to dispensing maps and advice, the staff can help book tours, excursions, concert tickets, and hotel rooms.

TOURIST TRAPS   Prague has its share of scams. Don't be tempted to change money on the street; you'll inevitably get ripped off. Be very wary of anyone who might approach you claiming to be a police officer and asking for identification. Also, be sure to watch wallets and valuables on crowded tram and metro cars. Pickpockets abound.

TOURS   Several companies offer bus and walking tours (often combined) of Prague. Martin Tour at Štěpánská 61 (☎ 224-212-473; www.martintour.cz) and Premiant at Palackého 1 (☎ 296-246-070; www.premiant.cz) have a similar range of tours at similar prices. Precious Legacy Tours at Široka 9 (☎ 222-321-951; www.legacytours.net) specializes in Judaica and cultural tours. Most tours leave from bus stops near Náměstí Republiky.

TRAVELERS WITH DISABILITIES   Wheelchair-bound travelers or those with restricted mobility will have endless problems with Prague's stairs, cobblestones, and curbs. Though some newer buildings, and many four- and five-star hotels, are wheelchair-accessible, the city is years behind in making its streets and public buildings available to all.

VAT   See "Taxes," above.

WEATHER   See "Climate," above.

Useful Phrases & Menu Terms

Although Czech is a very difficult language to master, you should at least make an attempt to learn a few phrases. Czechs will appreciate the effort and will be more willing to help you out.

Czech Alphabet

There are 32 vowels and consonants in the Czech alphabet, and most of the consonants are pronounced about as they are in English. Accent marks over vowels lengthen the sound of the vowel, as does the *kroužek,* or little circle "˚," which appears only over "o" and "u."

A, a	father	N, n	no
B, b	boy	Ň, ň	Tanya
C, c	gets	O, o	awful
Č, č	choice	P, p	pen
D, d	day	R, r	slightly trilled r
Ď, ď	Dior	Ř, ř	slightly trilled r + zh as in Persian
E, e	never	S, s	seat
F, f	food	Š, š	crush
G, g	goal	T, t	too
H, h	unhand	Ť, ť	not yet
Ch, ch	Loch Lomond	U, u	room
I, i	need	V, v	very
J, j	yes	W, w	vague
K, k	key	Y, y	funny
L, l	lord	Z, z	zebra
M, m	mama	Ž, ž	azure, pleasure

Everyday Expressions

ENGLISH	CZECH	PRONUNCIATION
Hello	Dobrý den	doh-bree den
Good morning	Dobré jitro	doh-breh yee-troh
Good evening	Dobrý večer	doh-bree veh-chair
How are you?	Jak se máte?	yahk seh mah-teh
Very well	Velmi dobře	vel-mee doh-brsheh
Thank you	Děkuji vám	dyek-ooee vahm
You're welcome	Prosím	proh-seem
Please	Prosím	proh-seem
Yes	Ano	ah-no
No	Ne	neh
Excuse me	Promiňte	proh-min-teh
How much does it cost?	Kolik to stojí?	koh-leek taw stoh-ee
I don't understand.	Nerozumím.	neh-roh-zoo-meem
Just a moment.	Moment, prosím.	moh-ment, proh-seem
Good-bye	Na shledanou	nah skleh-dah-noh-oo

Traveling

Where is the . . . ?	Kde je . . . ?	gde yeh . . .
bus station	autobusové nádraží	au-toh-boos-oh-veh nah-drah-zhee
train station	nádraží	nah-drah-zhee
airport	letiště	leh-tyish-tyeh
baggage check	úschovna zavazadel	oo-skohv-nah zah-vahz-ah-del
Where can I find a taxi?	Kde najdu taxi?	gde nai-doo tahks-eh
Where can I find a gas station?	Kde najdu benzínovou pumpu?	gde nai-doo ben-zeen-oh-voh poomp-oo
How much is gas?	Kolik stojí benzín?	koh-leek stoh-yee ben-zeen

ENGLISH	CZECH	PRONUNCIATION
Please fill the tank.	**Naplňte mi nádrž, prosím.**	*nah*-puln-teh mee *nah*-durzh, *proh*-seem
How much is the fare?	**Kolik je jízdné?**	*koh*-leek yeh yeesd-neh
I am going to . . .	**Pojedu do . . .**	*poh*-yeh-doo doh . . .
One-way ticket	**Jízdenka**	*yeez*-den-kah
Round-trip ticket	**Zpáteční jízdenka**	*zpah*-tech-nee *jeez*-den-kah
Car-rental office	**Půjčovna aut**	*poo*-eech-awv-nah ah-oot

Accommodations

I'm looking for . . .	**Hledám . . .**	*hleh*-dahm . . .
a hotel	**hotel**	*hoh*-tel
a youth hostel	**studentskou ubytovnu**	*stoo*-dent-skoh oo-beet-ohv-noo
I am staying . . .	**Zůstanu . . .**	*zoo*-stah-noo . . .
a few days	**několik dnů**	*nyeh*-koh-leek dnoo
2 weeks	**dva týdny**	dvah tid-*neh*
a month	**jeden měsíc**	*yeh*-den *myeh*-seets
I have a reservation.	**Mám zamluvený nocleh.**	mahm *zah*-mloo-veh-ni *nohts*-leh
My name is . . .	**Jmenuji se . . .**	*meh*-noo-yee seh . . .
Do you have a room . . . ?	**Máte pokoj . . . ?**	*mah*-teh *poh*-koy . . .
for tonight	**na dnešek**	*nah* dneh-sheck
for 3 nights	**na tři dny**	*nah* trshee dnee
for a week	**na týden**	*nah* tee-den
I would like . . .	**Chci . . .**	khtsee . . .
a single	**jednolůžkový pokoj**	*jed*-noh-loosh-koh-vee *poh*-koy
a double	**dvojlůžkový pokoj**	*dvoy*-loosh-koh-vee *poh*-koy
I want a room . . .	**Chci pokoj . . .**	khtsee *poh*-koy . . .
with a bathroom	**s koupelnou**	*skoh*-pehl-noh
without a bathroom	**bez koupelny**	*behz* koh-pehl-nee
with a shower	**se sprchou**	*seh* spur-choh
without a shower	**bez sprchy**	*bez* sprech-eh
with a view	**s pohledem**	*spoh*-hlehd-ehm
How much is the room?	**Kolik stojí pokoj?**	*koh*-leek *stoh*-yee paw-koy
with breakfast?	**se snídaní?**	*seh* snee-dan-nyee
May I see the room?	**Mohu vidět ten pokoj?**	*moh*-hoo *vee*-dyet ten *paw*-koy
The key	**Klíč**	kleech
The bill, please.	**Dejte mi účet, prosím.**	*day*-teh mee *oo*-cheht, *praw*-seem

Getting Around

ENGLISH	CZECH	PRONUNCIATION
I'm looking for . . .	**Hledám** . . .	*hleh*-dahm . . .
a bank	**banku**	*bahnk*-oo
the church	**kostel**	*kohs*-tell
the city center	**centrum**	*tsent*-room
the museum	**muzeum**	*moo*-zeh-oom
a pharmacy	**lékárnu**	*lek*-ahr-noo
the park	**park**	*pahrk*
the theater	**divadlo**	*dee*-vahd-loh
the tourist office	**cestovní kancelář**	*tses*-tohv-nee *kahn*-tseh-larsh
the embassy	**velvyslanectví**	*vehl*-vee-slahn-ets-tvee
Where is the nearest telephone?	**Kde je nejbližší telefon?**	gde yeh *nay*-bleesh-ee *tel*-oh-fohn
I would like to buy . . .	**Chci koupit** . . .	khtsee *koh*-peet . . .
a stamp	**známku**	*znahm*-koo
a postcard	**pohlednici**	*poh*-hlehd-nit-seh
a map	**mapu**	*mahp*-oo

Signs

No Trespassing	**Cizim vstup zakázán**	No Smoking	**Kouření zakázáno**
No Parking	**Neparkovat**	Arrivals	**Přijezd/Přílet**
Entrance	**Vchod**	Departures	**Odjezd/Odlet**
Exit	**Východ**	Toilets	**Toalety**
Information	**Informace**	Danger	**Pozor, nebezpečí**

Numbers

1	jeden (*yeh*-den)	16	šestnáct (*shest*-nahtst)
2	dva (dvah)	17	sedmnáct (*seh*-doom-nahtst)
3	tři (trzhee)	18	osmnáct (*aw*-soom-nahtst)
4	čtyři (*chtee*-rshee)	19	devatenáct (*deh*-vah-teh-nahtst)
5	pět (pyet)	20	dvacet (*dvah*-tset)
6	šest (shest)	30	třicet (*trshee*-tset)
7	sedm (*seh*-duhm)	40	čtyřicet (*chti*-rshee-tset)
8	osm (*aw*-suhm)	50	padesát (*pah*-deh-saht)
9	devět (*deh*-vyet)	60	šedesát (*she*-deh-saht)
10	deset (*deh*-set)	70	sedmdesát (*seh*-duhm-deh-saht)
11	jedenáct (*yeh*-deh-nahtst)	80	osmdesát (*aw*-suhm-deh-saht)
12	dvanáct (*dvah*-nahtst)	90	devadesát (*deh*-vah-deh-saht)
13	třináct (*trshee*-nahtst)	100	sto (staw)
14	čtrnáct (*chtur*-nahtst)	500	pět set (*pyet* set)
15	patnáct (*paht*-nahtst)	1,000	tisíc (tyee-seets)

Dining

ENGLISH	CZECH	PRONUNCIATION
Restaurant	**Restaurace**	*rehs*-tow-rah-tseh
Breakfast	**Snídaně**	*snee*-dah-nyeh
Lunch	**Oběd**	*oh*-byed
Dinner	**Večeře**	*veh*-chair-sheh

ENGLISH	CZECH	PRONUNCIATION
A table for two, please. (Lit.: There are two of us.)	**Jsme dva.**	*ees*-meh dvah
Waiter	**Číšník**	*cheess*-neek
Waitress	**Servírka**	ser-*veer*-ka
I would like . . .	**Chci . . .**	khtsee . . .
a menu	**jídelní lístek**	*yee*-del-nee *lees*-teck
a fork	**vidličku**	*veed*-leech-koo
a knife	**nůž**	noosh
a spoon	**lžičku**	lu-*shich*-koo
a napkin	**ubrousek**	*oo*-broh-seck
a glass (of water)	**skleničku (vody)**	*sklehn*-ich-koo (vod-*dee*)
the check, please	**účet, prosím**	*oo*-cheht, *proh*-seem
Is the tip included?	**Je v tom zahrnuto spropitné?**	yeh *ftohm*-zah *hur*-noo-toh *sproh*-peet-neh

Menu Terms

GENERAL

Soup	**Polévka**	*poh*-lehv-kah
Eggs	**Vejce**	*vayts*-eh
Meat	**Maso**	*mahs*-oh
Fish	**Ryba**	*ree*-bah
Vegetables	**Zelenina**	*zehl*-eh-nee-nah
Fruit	**Ovoce**	*oh*-voh-tseh
Desserts	**Moučníky**	*mohch*-nee-kee
Beverages	**Nápoje**	*nah*-poy-yeh
Salt	**Sůl**	sool
Pepper	**Pepř**	*peh*-psh
Mayonnaise	**Majonéza**	*mai*-o-neza
Mustard	**Hořčice**	*hohrsh*-chee-tseh
Vinegar	**Ocet**	*oh*-tseht
Oil	**Olej**	*oh*-lay
Sugar	**Cukr**	*tsoo*-ker
Tea	**Čaj**	chye
Coffee	**Káva**	*kah*-vah
Bread	**Chléb**	khlehb
Butter	**Máslo**	*mahs*-loh
Wine	**Víno**	*vee*-noh
Fried	**Smažený**	*smah*-sheh-nee
Roasted	**Pečený**	*pech*-eh-nee
Boiled	**Vařený**	*vah*-rsheh-nee
Grilled	**Grilovaný**	*gree*-loh-vah-nee

Soup

Potato	**Bramborová**	Tomato	**Rajská**
Lentil	**Čočková**	Chicken	**Slepičí**
Goulash	**Gulášová**	Vegetable	**Zeleninová**

Meat

Steak	**Biftek**	Sausage	**Klobása**
Goulash	**Guláš**	Rabbit	**Králík**
Beef	**Hovězi**	Mutton	**Skopové**
Liver	**Játra**	Veal	**Telecí**
Lamb	**Jehněčí**	Veal Cutlet	**Teleci kotleta**
Duck	**Kachna**	Pork	**Vepřové**

Fish

Carp	**Kapr**	Pike	**Štika**
Caviar	**Kaviár**	Cod	**Treska**
Fish Filet	**Rybí filé**	Eel	**Úhoř**
Herring	**Sled'**	Oysters	**Ústřice**

Eggs

Scrambled Eggs	**Míchaná vejce**	Soft-boiled Eggs	**Vejce na měkko**
Fried Eggs	**Smažená vejce**	Bacon and Eggs	**Vejce se slaninou**
Boiled Eggs	**Vařená vejce**	Ham and Eggs	**Vejce se šunkou**

Salad

Bean Salad	**Fazolový salát**	Cucumber Salad	**Okurkový salát**
Mixed Green Salad	**Hlávkový salát**	Beet Salad	**Salát z červené řepy**

Vegetables

Potatoes	**Brambory**	Cauliflower	**Květák**
Celery	**Celer**	Carrots	**Mrkev**
Asparagus	**Chřest**	Peppers	**Paprika**
Onions	**Cibule**	Tomatoes	**Rajská jablíčka**
Mushrooms	**Houby**	Cabbage	**Zelí**

Dessert

Cake	**Koláč**	Apple Strudel	**Jablkový závin**
Cookies	**Cukroví**	Pancakes	**Palačinky**
Chocolate Ice Cream	**Čokoládová zmrzlina**	Vanilla Ice Cream	**Vanilková zmrzlina**

Fruit

Lemon	**Citrón**	Apple	**Jablko**
Pear	**Hruška**	Plum	**Švestka**

Beverages

Tea	**Čaj**	Red	**Červené**
Coffee	**Káva**	White	**Bílé**
Milk	**Mléko**	Water	**Voda**
Wine	**Víno**		

Toll-Free Numbers & Websites

AER LINGUS
☎ 800/474-7424 in the U.S.
☎ 01/886-8844 in Ireland
www.aerlingus.com

AIR CANADA
☎ 888/247-2262
www.aircanada.ca

AIR FRANCE
☎ 800/237-2747 in the U.S.
☎ 0820-820-820 in France
www.airfrance.com

AIR NEW ZEALAND
☎ 800/262-1234 or -2468 in the U.S.
☎ 800/663-5494 in Canada
☎ 0800/737-000 in New Zealand
www.airnewzealand.com

ALITALIA
☎ 800/223-5730 in the U.S.
☎ 8488-65641 in Italy
www.alitalia.it

AMERICAN AIRLINES
☎ 800/433-7300
www.aa.com

AUSTRIAN AIRLINES
☎ 800/843-0002 in the U.S.
☎ 43/(0)5-1789 in Austria
www.aua.com

BMI
No U.S. number
☎ 0870/6070-222 in Britain
www.flybmi.com

BRITISH AIRWAYS
☎ 800/247-9297
☎ 0870/850-9-850 in Britain
www.british-airways.com

CONTINENTAL AIRLINES
☎ 800/525-0280
www.continental.com

DELTA AIR LINES
☎ 800/221-1212
www.delta.com

EASYJET
No U.S. number
www.easyjet.com

IBERIA
☎ 800/772-4642 in the U.S.
☎ 902/400-500 in Spain
www.iberia.com

ICELANDAIR
☎ 800/223-5500 in the U.S.
☎ 354/50-50-100 in Iceland
www.icelandair.is

KLM
☎ 800/374-7747 in the U.S.
☎ 020/4-747-747 in the Netherlands
www.klm.nl

LUFTHANSA
☎ 800/645-3880 in the U.S.
☎ 49/(0)-180-5-838426 in Germany
www.lufthansa.com

NORTHWEST AIRLINES
☎ 800/225-2525
www.nwa.com

QANTAS
☎ 800/227-4500 in the U.S.
☎ 612/131313 in Australia
www.qantas.com

SCANDINAVIAN AIRLINES
☎ 800/221-2350 in the U.S.
☎ 0070/727-727 in Sweden
☎ 70/10-20-00 in Denmark
☎ 358/(0)20-386-000 in Finland
☎ 815/200-400 in Norway
www.scandinavian.net

SWISS INTERNATIONAL AIRLINES
☎ 877/359-7947 in the U.S.
☎ 0848/85-2000 in Switzerland
www.swiss.com

UNITED AIRLINES
☎ 800/241-6522
www.united.com

US AIRWAYS
☎ 800/428-4322
www.usairways.com

VIRGIN ATLANTIC AIRWAYS
☎ 800/862-8621 in the continental U.S.
☎ 0870/380-2007 in Britain
www.virgin-atlantic.com

Index

See also Accommodations and Restaurant indexes, below.

Photo **Credits**

To find out more about Avi, visit
his website at www.avi-writer.com

ERETH'S BIRTHDAY

AVI

illustrated by Brian Floca

HarperTrophy®
An *Imprint of HarperCollinsPublishers*

Harper Trophy® is a registered trademark of HarperCollins Publishers Inc.

Ereth's Birthday
Text copyright © 2000 by Avi
Illustrations copyright © 2000 by Brian Floca
Interior illustrations by Brian Floca
The illustrations are drawn with Eberhard Faber Design Ebony
pencils on Stonehenge paper.

Library of Congress Cataloging-in-Publication Data
Avi, 1937–
    Ereth's birthday / Avi ; illustrated by Brian Floca.
        p.   cm.
    Summary: Feeling neglected on his birthday, Ereth, the cantankerous old porcupine, sets
out looking for his favorite treat and instead finds himself acting as "mother" to three young
fox kits.
    ISBN 0-380-97734-6 (alk. paper)—ISBN 0-380-80490-5 (pbk.)
    [1. Porcupines—Fiction. 2. Foxes—Fiction. 3. Animals—Fiction. 4. Parent and
child—Fiction.] I. Floca, Brian, ill. II. Title.
PZ7.A953 Er   2000   99-46481
[Fic]—dc21   CIP
                                                                          AC

First Harper Trophy edition, 2001

Visit us on the World Wide Web!
www.harperchildrens.com

FOR ELISE, BETH AND RUTH

Contents

ERETH'S
BIRTHDAY

I
A Special Day

In Dimwood Forest, in the dark, smelly log where the old porcupine Erethizon Dorsatum lived, Ereth—as he preferred to call himself—woke slowly.

Not the sweetest smelling of creatures, Ereth had a flat face with a blunt, black nose and fierce, grizzled whiskers. As he stirred, he rattled his sharp if untidy quills, flexed his claws, yawned, frowned, and grumbled, "Musty moose marmalade," only to suddenly remember what day it was and smile. Today was his birthday.

Ereth had given very little thought to what *he* would do about the day. As far as he was concerned, his birthday meant others would be doing something for *him*. And the one he was quite certain would be doing all the providing was his best friend, Poppy.

Poppy, a deer mouse, lived barely an acorn toss from Ereth's log in a gray, lifeless tree—a snag with a hole on one side. She resided there with her husband, Rye, and their eleven children.

Ereth, in a *very* private sort of way, loved Poppy. He had never told anyone about this love, not even her. Enough for him to live near her. But since the porcupine was certain that Poppy thought of him as her best friend, he assumed she would be making a great fuss over his birthday. A party, certainly. Lavish gifts, of course. Best of all, he would be the center of attention.

So it was that when Ereth waddled out of his log that morning he was surprised not to find Poppy waiting for him. All he saw were her eleven children playing about the base of the snag, squeaking and squealing uproariously.

"Why can't young folks ever be still?" A deeply disappointed Ereth complained to himself. "Potted pockets of grizzly grunions, it would save so much trouble if children were born . . . old."

Agitated, he approached the young mice. "Where's your mother?" he barked. "Where's your wilted wet flower of a father?"

"They . . . went . . . looking for . . . something," one of them said.

Though Ereth's heart sank, he made a show of indifference by lifting his nose scornfully and moving away from the young mice.

Snowberry, one of the youngsters, glanced anxiously around at the others, then cried out, "Good morning, Uncle Ereth!"

This greeting was followed by the ten other young mice singing out in a ragged, squeaky chorus, "Good morning, Uncle Ereth!"

Ereth turned and glowered at the youngsters. "What the tiddlywink toes do you want?" he snapped.

"Aren't you going to stay and play with us, Uncle Ereth?" Snowberry called.

"No!"

"Why?"

"I'm . . . busy."

"You don't look busy."

"I'm trying to find some peace and quiet," Ereth snapped. "With all the noise you make, buzzard breath, what else do you think I'd be doing?"

One of the mice—her name was Columbine—slapped a paw over her mouth in order to keep from laughing out loud.

Ereth glared at her. "What are you laughing at?"

"You," Columbine sputtered. "You always say such funny things!"

"Listen here, you smidgen of slipper slobber," Ereth fumed. "Don't tell *me* I talk funny. Why don't you stuff your tiny tail into your puny gullet and gag yourself before I flip you into some skunk-cabbage sauce and turn you into a pother of butterfly plunk?"

Instead of frightening the young mice, Ereth's outburst caused them to howl with glee. Sassafras laughed so hard he fell down and had to hold his stomach. "Uncle Ereth," he cried, "you are so hilarious! Please say something else!"

"Belching beavers!" Ereth screamed. "I am not hilarious! You're just a snarl of runty seed suckers with no respect for anyone older than you. How about a little consideration? As far as I'm concerned you mice have as much smarts as you could find in a baby bee's belly button."

"But you *are* funny, Uncle Ereth," cried another of the young mice, whose name was Walnut. "Nobody else talks like you do. We love it when you swear and get angry at us."

"I am not angry!" Ereth raged. "If I were angry, I'd turn you all into pink pickled pasta so fast it would make lightning look

like a slow slug crawling up a slick hill. So listen up, you tub of tinsel twist."

This was too much for the young mice. They laughed and squeaked till their sides ached.

"Uncle Ereth," said Sassafras between giggles, "please—*please*—say something funny again. You are the funniest animal in the whole forest!"

Staring wrathfully at the young mice, Ereth considered uttering something unbelievably disgusting—dangling doggerels—thought better of it, and wheeled about, heading north as fast as he could.

"Uncle Ereth!" the mice shouted after him. "Please stay and say something else funny. *Please* don't go!"

But Ereth refused to stop.

Sassafras watched the porcupine plunge into the forest, then turned to the others. "But what are we going to tell Mom and Dad?" he cried. "They told us to make sure he didn't go anywhere."

"Oh, don't worry," Columbine assured her brother. "Uncle Ereth always comes back."

2

Ereth Makes a Decision

"Kids," Ereth muttered as he hurried away. "They think they're so wonderful. Truth is, they do nothing but make their elders work hard, eat their food, ask for things, break them, then proclaim all adults stupid! And what do kids give in return? Nothing!

"All that baby-sitting I do . . . all that listening to their endlessly boring stories, dumb jokes, what they learned today . . . hearing Poppy and Rye talk about this one's problems, that one's doings . . . attending their parties . . . finding presents for them . . .

"Well, here it is, *my* birthday. At least I only have one a year. But do those kids notice? No! Not so much as a gill of grasshopper gas. Do they care what I feel, think, am? Not one pinch of pith pills! Right! The whole world would be better off without kids. So all I say is, keep kids to the rear, blow wind, and turn on the fan!"

With such thoughts and words churning in his mind, Ereth

rushed on. Once, twice, he passed a rabbit, a squirrel, a vole, but when they saw the mood the porcupine was in they retreated quickly, not willing even to call a greeting. After all, the creatures of Dimwood Forest knew Erethizon Dorsatum quite well. Very few had any desire to interfere with him when he was in one of his bad moods—which was clearly the case that morning.

The old porcupine pressed on, his mind taken up by a careful composition of the things he hated, the insults he had endured, the slights he had suffered. The list was very long. The more he recalled, the grumpier he became, and the faster he hurried on.

It was an hour before Ereth allowed himself to pause. All his emotion and running had quite worn him out and made him ravenous. Spying a young pine tree, he scrambled over to it and began to peel away the outer bark, then chew on the green layer underneath.

"Good, good," he babbled as he gobbled. "This is more like it."

Suddenly he lifted his nose, sniffed, and frowned. "Squirrel-splat soup! The air has changed."

It was true—the air *was* different. It had become crisp and had a deep, tangy smell. And now that Ereth thought about it, the days had been growing shorter, the nights longer. It was only a question of when the first snow would arrive.

"Seasons," Ereth thought to himself. "Boiled bat butter! Just when you get used to one way, everything changes. Why can't things ever stay the way they are? Phooey and fried sala-mander spit with a side order of rat ribbon. I hate change!"

More than ever, Ereth was convinced that he needed *something* to mark the day. But what? It had to be something special. Something just for him. Then, in a flash, he knew exactly what would please him most. *Salt.*

Just to think about salt turned Ereth's longing into deep desire and dreamy drools. For Ereth, salt was the most delicious food in the whole world. He could shut his eyes and almost taste it. Oh, if only he had a chunk! A piece! Even a *lick* of salt would salvage the day. No, there was nothing he would not do for the smallest bit of it.

The old porcupine sighed. Since no one else was going to pay attention to him, he owed it to himself to find *some*

birthday treat, and salt was the perfect thing. But where was he going to find any?

Though Ereth, with his great knowledge of Dimwood Forest, knew exactly where *he* was, finding salt was quite another matter. He considered New Farm, a place where some humans kept a whole block of salt in the middle of a lawn. Once, when the block had shattered and fallen to the ground, Ereth had gorged himself for days. Though truly fabulous, that salt was long gone. Moreover, when the humans replaced the block they put it at a height convenient for deer—not porcupines.

"Deer dainties!" Ereth snarled with contempt. "Why couldn't they have put the salt out for *me?*"

So the question remained, Where could Ereth find salt?

Then Ereth remembered: on the far northern side of Dimwood Forest was a lake. Long Lake, the animals called it. On its shore humans had built a log cabin. Rather crudely constructed, it did not even sit on the earth, but on a platform a few feet off the ground. The cabin was used rarely, only when humans wanted to hunt or trap animals. Every year brought frightening stories of deer, fox, and rabbits, among others, being killed, hurt, or maimed by these humans. Hardly a wonder that the cabin—though more often than not deserted—was a place the animals of Dimwood Forest avoided. Just thinking about it made Ereth shudder. And yet . . .

As Ereth also knew, these humans often left traces of salt on the things they used. Sometimes it was nothing more than a smear of sweat on the handle of a tool, a canoe paddle, or an odd bit of clothing like a hatband. These objects were often

stored in that space beneath the cabin.

Scanty though these tastings were, they were tempting enough for Ereth to venture to the log cabin now and again to satisfy his salt cravings. Once he had been rewarded by finding an almost full bag of salty potato chips. That was a day to remember.

Hardly a wonder then, that just the possibility of finding even a lick of salt stirred Ereth.

He looked around. Overhead loomed the great trees that kept the ground dim and give the forest its name. Such sky as he could see was gray, while the sun itself seemed to have turned dull. White mist curled up from the earth's murky nooks and crannies.

"It's almost winter," Ereth told himself. "This may be my last chance to get salt for a while. Besides," he reminded himself yet again, "it's my birthday. I deserve something special."

Even so, the porcupine hesitated, all too aware of the risks involved. Fooling around with humans, especially if they were hunters or trappers, was risky.

"Bug bubble gum," he swore. "What do I care if there are humans at the cabin? Nothing scares *me*."

With that thought Ereth continued making his way in a northerly direction toward Long Lake, the cabin, and the salt.

3
Marty the Fisher

As Ereth rushed on he passed beneath a particularly large oak tree. So quickly did he move by it, he had no notion that two dark eyes were looking down at him. The eyes belonged to Marty the Fisher.

About three feet in length, and more than a foot tall, Marty the Fisher had short, brown fur and small, round eyes almost blank of emotion. His legs were stubby but powerful. With his sharp claws he could climb trees and leap about branches as nimbly as a squirrel. On the ground he was just as agile.

The only thing Marty feared was humans. With reason. Human hunters, attracted by the fisher's glossy brown fur, had all but exterminated his family. Marty was the only one left, a fact that filled him with enormous rage. Even so, he kept to a stern, self-imposed rule: never, ever tangle with humans. They were far too dangerous.

Though he killed birds—even ate their eggs—what Marty

liked to hunt were other four-legged creatures, like mice, rats, rabbits, and squirrels.

Marty chose his victims with care, stalking them silently and patiently, wanting to be certain he could overwhelm them with the savagery of a single attack.

Once he chose his prey, Marty pursued it for however long it took to bring the creature down. It could be hours. It could be days. Or weeks. The most patient of hunters, Marty loved nothing more than to devise clever strategies to fool his victims, luring them into places where he could surprise them and they would be defenseless. Those whom he assaulted barely had time to know what hit them.

To further insure his success Marty traveled alone, keeping to trees, rocks, and leaves, where his dark fur blended in. Such

tactics made him almost invisible. Indeed, Marty was rarely seen—until it was too late.

Though he never bragged about it, never gloated, rarely even smiled—in fact, had almost nothing to do with any other creature—Marty's solitary tactics almost always worked.

Hardly a wonder that Marty gained the reputation for being the most patient hunter in all of Dimwood Forest. Indeed, he rather liked to consider himself Death on four paws.

And of all the forest and woodland animals Marty hunted, it was porcupines he enjoyed hunting the most. It was not that porcupines had injured Marty in any way. They did not insult him. They did not compete for food or space. No, it was their vanity that infuriated Marty the Fisher. Porcupines believed that no one could interfere with their lives, that they could

do whatever they wished. How dare any creature think itself immune from Marty's anger?

What's more, Marty had found a way to successfully attack porcupines. By careful observation, he had discovered that porcupines had no quills on their bellies. The belly was the porcupine's most vulnerable spot. If Marty picked his moment with care, moved with complete surprise, a porcupine could be successfully attacked from *below*.

Thus it was that whenever Marty came upon a porcupine, he liked nothing better than to hunt it down and kill it.

Hardly a wonder that when Marty the Fisher looked down from his perch in the old oak tree and saw old Ereth lumbering along beneath him, he became very excited.

"Ahhh," he whispered to himself. "It's Ereth! If ever there was a self-centered porcupine, he's the worst. Look at the way he's waddling along! Not a worry in the world. Acting as if he could live forever. Well, I'll teach him a thing or two!"

From that moment, Marty the Fisher began to stalk Ereth.

4
In Pursuit of Salt

The day grew colder. Not that Ereth cared. He rushed on, completely absorbed in the anticipated pleasures of salt. At times, his desire was so great he began to salivate, producing great drools of spit, which he sucked up noisily.

So focused were his thoughts on salt that he failed to notice when it began to snow. Coming with a breathless, hurried hush, the snow's silence was intense, swallowing every sound like a sponge absorbing water. Within moments, the entire forest became utterly still.

The snow was an inch deep before Ereth even realized it was there. Suddenly he could not see his own paws. Surprised, he gazed up. For just a moment Ereth imagined that it wasn't snow falling, but salt, and his heart leaped with joy. Then a particularly large flake of snow landed on his nose and made him sneeze. That brought him to his senses.

"Stupid snow," he complained. "You would think it would

have the decency to wait until I got to where I was going before it started."

Though Ereth knew the snow would make traveling harder, not for a moment did he consider returning home. "What do I care?" he told himself. "It's my birthday. Who needs noisy mice? The salt will taste even better when I get there."

With an angry shake of his head—as if *that* could get rid of the snow—Ereth pushed on.

Leaping silently from tree branch to tree branch, Marty the Fisher followed.

The snow tumbled from the sky like confetti from a barrel. It sleeved tree branches in white. It hid rocks and stumps. It covered the land until its surface became round and soft, melding into one continuous undulating form. It was as if an enormous eraser were rubbing out the world, leaving nothing but one vast sheet of blank, white paper. Only Ereth, like a solitary, dark dot, moved across it.

Becoming weary, Ereth paused and looked back over his shoulder at the trail he was making. To his surprise it did not extend very far. Like a ghost, he left no tracks. The thought startled him. Then he realized it was only that the snow had covered his paw prints.

Shifting his gaze forward, the porcupine tried to calculate how far he would have to go before he reached the cabin. A good way. Sighing with frustration, he told himself yet again that the salt would make his efforts worthwhile.

He went on.

•

The snow became so deep, it was increasingly difficult to keep his chin above the surface. "Elephant elbows," Ereth swore, beginning to falter for the first time. He glanced back. For just a second he thought something was following him. "Nonsense," he muttered. Reminding himself yet again of the tasty treat that lay ahead, he pushed on, one step at a time.

The sky grew darker, the air colder, the snow deeper. The trip was taking hours.

"Stop snowing!" Ereth shouted at the unrelenting sky. "Can't you see I'm trying to get some salt?"

There was no reply.

Pausing to catch his breath, Ereth began to wonder if he would ever reach the cabin. As he recalled, the trail led over a small hill. Beyond that, right on the shores of Long Lake, was the cabin.

Perhaps he should go home. He turned to look back. Once again he had the brief sensation that something was stalking him. "You're acting like an old creature," Ereth chided himself. "Imagining things." And he moved on.

Marty the Fisher, high in a tree, seeing Ereth look back, ducked away in haste. He need not have bothered. Ereth merely glanced back before continuing on.

"Good," Marty muttered. "All I need to be is patient. *Very* patient."

"No," Ereth said under his breath as he trudged along. "I've come too far to go back." Besides, he reminded himself for the

millionth time, it was his birthday. Back home there was nothing but raucous children. Better to be alone than in the midst of a crowd and ignored.

The porcupine did consider climbing a tree to wait out the storm. He shook his head. "I'm too close to salt."

On he went.

Ereth blinked open his eyes. Had he fallen asleep? Had he stopped? Had he walked in his sleep? If so, how far had he gone?

Ereth peered to the right and the left. The landscape revealed nothing. The forest was just as white as the last time he had looked. For all he knew he might have gone a mile. Or ten. Or perhaps he'd fallen asleep and hadn't moved at all. He looked back. Was something there? No. He was getting silly.

With a shake of his quills—sloughing off what felt like a ton of snow—Ereth forced himself forward again. But it had become very hard to walk. Perhaps, he told himself by way of encouragement, he was just climbing the hill, the last obstacle before reaching the cabin. He did know he was feeling light-headed. Hadn't he thought something was following him? Even so, he took one slow step after another slow step, like a wind-up toy running down.

Suddenly, his way seemed easier. Lifting his head Ereth looked forward. With the swirling snow in his eyes, it took a moment for him to realize he was looking down a hill, beyond which was an open space. At the bottom, Ereth saw a large mound of snow. In one or two places, light seemed to glow

from within the mound. Sticking up from the top of the mound was a silver pipe, from which dark smoke drifted. The smoke carried the smell of roasting meat. Ereth, a vegetarian, curled his lips in disgust.

But the evidence was plain: the open space was Long Lake. Buried in the snow was the log cabin. The cabin would have salt. But inside the cabin were . . . *humans*.

5
The Cabin

There was almost no animal or bird in the world Ereth feared. Owls, foxes, beavers—they were all one to him. True, only rarely would any of them bother him. His sharp quills assured him of that. And if the need came, he was more than capable of defending himself.

Humans were quite another matter. Sometimes they merely watched the animals in the forest. Other moments they wanted to touch them. Or run away. On still other occasions, however, the humans stayed and killed. People were that unpredictable.

The last thing the tired Ereth wanted to do was confront one. Besides, if humans were in the cabin, most likely it was because they were hunting. No, it did not bode well at all. And yet, there was the salt . . .

Staring at the cabin, Ereth tried to make up his mind what to do.

•

Marty the Fisher, perched high on a branch forty yards behind Ereth, looked on with troubled interest. He, too, realized that humans were in residence. As he had followed Ereth through the forest, Marty had wondered where the porcupine was so doggedly heading. Now that he saw the destination, he could guess what the porcupine was after. "Salt," Marty said to himself. "That stupid beast has come out in a storm in search of human salt."

Just to know he was close to humans made Marty anxious. He had little doubt these humans were hunters, the worst kind of humans from his point of view. For all he knew, they might even be looking for him, just as they had tracked down his whole family. It made him recall his ironclad rule: *keep far away from humans and all things human.*

"If Ereth has any brains," Marty thought, "he'll back off from that cabin and those people. I hope he does. He's acting tired. He's probably cold and hungry. Good! When he turns back from the cabin, he won't have the energy to resist when I strike.

"Of course, if he's idiot enough to go forward, I'll wait him out. There are always ways to lure someone like Ereth to where I'd like him to be."

Marty flexed his sharp claws, watched, and waited.

Ereth gave a shake of his head. There was, all in all, no choice to be made. He was cold, tired, and hungry. As far as he could determine, the best shelter would be directly under the cabin. Relatively speaking, it would be warm and dry there.

It was probably the best place to find some food too. And of course, there was the whole purpose of the trip to consider: *salt*. How could he come so far without so much as a lick to show for it? Besides, though he did not like to mess with humans, he thought it most unlikely they would go under the house.

Moving downhill slowly, his breath a cloud of frosty vapor, Ereth watched and listened with every step he took. He was halfway there when, with a flash of golden light, the cabin door burst open. A man so bundled in furs he looked more bear than human stepped onto the porch, gathered up the last load of logs that lay by the door, then returned to the cabin. The door banged behind him, shutting in the light.

After a brief pause, Ereth continued downhill. Moving as fast as the deep snow and his short legs allowed, he waddled across the open space between hill and cabin. Heart racing, panting for breath, he ducked under the structure.

He was there. The heat radiating down from the house above was instantly soothing.

Ereth took a deep breath and looked around. Only a little snow had collected, and that on the northern side. He noticed a broken chair, a blue plastic tarpaulin bunched up in a corner, a canoe, a snowmobile, a pile of long logs, and, on the pile, an *axe*.

Unable to restrain himself, Ereth rushed forward, climbed the log pile, sniffed at the axe handle, and all but swooned. The axe handle bore the remains of human sweat: salt.

Heart aflutter, Ereth stuck out his tongue and began to lick

the handle as a human would attack an ice cream cone. Oh, rapture! Oh, bliss! Oh, *salt!* It was all he had imagined. The struggle through the snow had been worth it!

In a dreamy mood, he had just begun to chew on the axe handle when he was interrupted by the sound of a human voice from above.

"I'm telling you, Wayne," the voice said, "I'm so hungry I could eat a live porcupine!"

"Pulsating puppy pimples," Ereth snarled. "He can start by chewing my tail!"

Despite brave thoughts, Ereth, wondering if it might be better to bolt from the cabin while escape was still easy, looked around nervously. Though everything in him told him to run, the idea of doing *something* to teach that human a lesson was hard to resist.

Turning back to the axe handle, an angry Ereth gnawed furiously. As he chewed, he cast his eyes around in search of something else to mangle.

That's when he spied the snowmobile. Ereth was perfectly aware what it was. He had experienced just how much noise they made, the ghastly fumes they left in their wake, the way they chewed up the forest floor. Having seen them from a distance he also knew how humans used them: by sitting on the long black seat that ran down the middle, then twisting the handlebars, which caused the machine to shoot forward at enormously loud and smelly speeds.

Though Ereth did not like snowmobiles, humans, he knew, loved them. As far as he was concerned, that made the snowmobile the perfect target.

Having chewed the axe handle almost in two, the porcupine waddled over to the snowmobile. Using his front paws, he hoisted himself onto the black seat. It was soft and pliable. Twisting around, he lifted his tail and whacked it a few times. When he was done, a goodly number of quills remained sticking straight up from the seat. "Burping bird burgers," he muttered. "That'll fix them."

That accomplished, Ereth used his high perch to observe the rest of the area. In doing so he noticed a cardboard box and wondered if there was anything in it worth eating.

Climbing down from the snowmobile, he waddled over to the box and peered inside, only to recoil in fear. The box held four black, metal spring traps, the kind human trappers use to catch animals by their legs. There was also a box trap, designed to catch larger animals alive and transport them elsewhere.

"Killers," Ereth whispered in fury. "They're nothing but killers!"

"Hey, Parker," one of the human voices suddenly said from above. "We need to get some more firewood. Where'd you leave that axe?"

"Under the cabin. On the log pile."

"If we're going to keep from freezing tonight I better chop us some more wood. It's getting colder."

"Suits me."

"Fine," the voice said. "I'm going to get some wood from under the cabin. Be right back." The conversation was followed by the sound of one of the humans moving toward the cabin door.

Ereth, close to panic, looked for a place to conceal himself. He caught sight of the blue plastic tarpaulin off in a corner.

From above came more footsteps as well as the sound of a door opening and closing. Hurriedly Ereth clawed his way under the plastic.

6
Ereth's Revenge

From beneath the tarpaulin Ereth could see nothing. But he could hear someone stomp out onto the porch, then crunch through the snow around the cabin.

There were some grunts and groans, which Ereth presumed were the sounds of the human lifting one of the logs. For a moment all Ereth could hear was breathing. Then he heard a *snap*, followed by a cry: "Gol darn! Who did this?"

A smiling Ereth knew the man had tried to use the axe.

"Must have been a porcupine!" the man snarled. "Stupid jerk!"

Ereth grinned.

The human swearing was followed by the sound of steps that suggested the man was going back around the cabin to the porch.

Ereth poked his head out from under the plastic and listened intently. Within moments there came the sound of a human voice.

"Hey, Wayne! Some blazing idiot of a porcupine chewed through the axe handle. Busted on my first stroke. Can't use it."

"Oh, oh."

"And hey, man, with night coming on and the temperature dropping, we're going to run out of heat. Maybe we better head out while the going is good. Not much point in hanging around here anyway."

"What about the rest of the traps?"

"How many we set? Sixteen out of twenty? Not bad, considering the weather. We can take care of the rest later."

"Just have to move quickly," the second man agreed. "Better not travel in the dark."

"Fine with me. We'll just leave everything and go."

Ereth, feeling quite satisfied with himself, retreated as far back under the tarpaulin as he could go.

For a while he heard footfalls crisscrossing directly overhead. These sounds were followed by movement on the porch and the sound of the humans crunching through the snow.

"Hey, Wayne," a voice called. "Give me a hand with the snowmobile."

Ereth heard sounds of pushing, and shoving and hauling.

"Come on, get on. We gotta move."

Ereth held his breath.

"Yoooooow!"

"What's the matter?"

"Holy . . . look at that! Porcupine quills! I sat on them! Ow!"

The other man laughed. "Hey, you said you could eat a porcupine alive, didn't you? Guess he heard what you said and got to you first."

"Yeah, right."

Ereth grinned and nodded.

There was a loud roar as the snowmobile's motor kicked in.

"You going to sit or stand?"

"Hurts too much to sit."

"Sure, but it'll hurt a lot more if you stand and fall off. I'll go as fast as I can."

The noise rose and fell as the snowmobile roared off. The stench of gas fumes made Ereth gag. Soon the machine—and the humans—were gone. The deep winter silence returned.

From his place on the hill Marty the Fisher watched the snowmobile race away.

Though surprised, he was very pleased. "Good," he said to himself. "The humans are gone. Now if I can get Ereth away from the cabin, he'll be an easy target." He put his mind to finding a way to lure the porcupine back into the woods.

Beneath the cabin, Ereth waddled about sniffing, in hopes of finding something to eat. It was while lifting his nose up toward one corner of the cabin that he suddenly caught a powerful scent. *Salt.* Such a strong smell could mean only one thing: there was a *lot* of salt inside the cabin. He began to tremble with excitement.

The next moment Ereth rushed out from beneath the cabin, bounded through the snow drifts, scrambled up the front steps, made his way to the door, then thrust his black nose into the crack where the door met the frame. He inhaled deeply.

"Penguin peanuts," he whispered in awe. "There must be a

ton of the stuff in there." His teeth chattered with anticipation.

Struggling to contain himself, Ereth examined the door intently. When he realized it was padlocked, he began to shove it with his forehead as well as his front paws. It wouldn't budge.

Furious, he backed off and studied the walls of the cabin. About four feet off the ground—to the right of the door—was a small glass window. Perhaps he could get in that way.

Since Ereth climbed trees with ease, working his way up the side of the log cabin to the window ledge proved no problem. Once there he pressed his face to the glass pane and peered inside. A small table stood in one corner of the room. It was littered with plates, knives, and forks—even food. In the middle of the table stood a glass jar filled with salt.

"*Salt*," Ereth murmured even as he began to drool. "A whole jar of salt." In a frenzy now, he began to butt his head against the window.

Ereth worked harder, certain that just a little more effort would shove it in entirely. "Pitted potwallopers!" he cried, as he thumped away. "Open up!"

Even as the window began to give, Ereth heard a voice from the woods behind him. "Help!" came the cry. "Someone help me! *Please!*"

"Mosquito mung," Ereth grunted angrily as he tried to ignore the cry from the woods. Intent upon his task, he worked feverishly, poking his claws in and around the edges of the cabin window, trying to push it in. "Open up!" he shouted.

"Won't someone help me?" came yet another call.

"No, I won't!" Ereth replied out loud. "I've got better things to do."

Butting against the window as well as shoving with his paws, he gave a great grunt of exertion. The window fell in, striking the wood floor with the sound of shattering glass.

The smell of salt saturated the air. "Oh, my, oh, my," the porcupine crooned with excitement. "A room of salt! It's heaven. It's bliss."

"Help! I'm hurt," came the wail from the woods, more desperate than ever.

Prepared to leap down into the room, Ereth felt compelled to look back over his shoulder.

"I'm dying," came yet another cry. "Please. Help me."

"Donkey doughnuts," Ereth griped, glaring in the direction of the woods. "Why does everybody have to call on *me* for help? Used to be, taking care of yourself was what the world was about. It's not as if anybody cares about *my* life!" he added with exasperation.

"Please help!" came the cry again.

Ereth shook his head in frustration. "Buckled badger burgers!" he complained. "I'm never going to enjoy eating this salt with that racket in my ears." Angry and frustrated, Ereth crawled down from the window, tail first.

For a moment he stood at the edge of the porch and gazed furiously at the still falling snow. Every tree and bush was coated with thick white frosting. Branches were bent, small shrubs partially flattened. In the deepening dusk the whiteness seemed to be turning purple with cold.

"Maybe it's a trick," Ereth suddenly thought. "Maybe somebody wants to get me away so he can have the salt for himself. Or maybe . . ." it suddenly occurred to him, "somebody is

trying to lure me into the woods."

Ereth considered that notion only briefly. "Anybody mess-ing with me gets a quill up his snoot faster than a diving owl with lead claws."

With another look back at the cabin and a deep sniff of the salt, Ereth waddled down the steps and plunged into the snow.

The snow had become deeper. To make any progress Ereth had to leap forward by fits and starts. Every few leaps he paused to catch his breath. But now that he had committed himself to finding the creature, the cries for help had ceased.

"I'll bet anything the dunce who was calling is better," Ereth muttered. He pushed on almost out of spite. "Catastrophic coyote culls! If it wasn't for this idiot I could be eating that salt

right now. But no. Kind, old Ereth always puts others before himself. Blessed saint is what I am. Busted bird bloomers!" he cried, lashing his tail about in anger. "I never think of myself. *Never!* Well, when I find whoever called I'll give him a piece of my mind—and tail—so he won't ever send out false alarms again." With such thoughts, Ereth plunged in among a cluster of trees.

Suddenly he stopped. Directly ahead, but hidden by a cornice of snow, he heard the sound of thrashing and clanking, followed by a soft whimpering. This was followed by a piteous *"Please."*

Whoever had been calling was not only still in trouble, it sounded as if he was growing weaker.

Ereth lifted his nose and sniffed. An animal was right in front of him. The question was, what kind? He couldn't tell because another smell filled the air. Though this second smell was familiar, Ereth could not quite grasp its nature. "Wilted wolf waffles," he muttered, "what is it?"

His frustration abetted by curiosity, Ereth took two more leaps forward in the snow, then stopped and gasped in horror.

7

Ereth Makes a Promise

On the ground lay a slim fox with tawny red fur and a long, bushy tail. The lower part of her delicate, pointed face and much of her muzzle were white. Her few remaining whiskers were as black as her nose. Black too was the outline of her almond-shaped, orange-colored eyes. Her pointed ears were limp. All around her, the beaten-down snow was red with blood, for the fox's left front paw was gripped in the jaws of a steel spring trap.

In an instant Ereth understood: she had been caught in one of the traps that the hunters from the cabin had set.

The trap consisted of a pair of metal jaws, which—once sprung—had crushed the fox's paw, biting savagely through fur, flesh, muscles, and tendons. All were exposed. The amount of blood that lay about suggested the fox had been trapped for a long time. It was the blood that had confused Ereth's sense of smell.

Just to look upon the scene turned Ereth's bone marrow colder than the snow.

The fox, not yet realizing anyone else was there, whimpered softly to herself as she tried to move her paw. Though extremely weak, she managed to lift the trap an inch or two. It was connected to a stake by a metal link chain. When the trap moved the chain jangled. Her effort—small as it was—was an enormous struggle, so much so that after a painful moment, she dropped paw, trap, and chain and lay panting with exhaustion.

As Ereth, horrified, continued to watch, the fox leaned forward and tried to gnaw at the chain, then at the trap itself.

"Murdering mud malls," Ereth growled under his breath.

His words were just loud enough for the fox to hear. Slowly, she turned her head.

Her nose was dry, caked with blood. Her whiskers were bent and broken. Her eyes were so glazed over with pain and tears, Ereth was not certain she grasped that he was there. "Can . . . can I . . . do anything?" he managed to say.

The fox cocked her head slightly, taking in the words as if they came from a distant place. This time Ereth was sure she saw him. "I'm . . . caught . . ." she said in a weak voice. "Please help . . . me."

Ereth, fighting waves of nausea, drew closer. The smell of blood, the sight of the fox's mangled paw, were making him feeble. "I'm . . . awful sorry," he whispered.

"Yes . . ." was all the fox could reply.

Gingerly stretching his head forward, Ereth attempted to bite the chain, the trap itself, and the spike which held the trap to the ground. Bitterly cold, iron hard, the metal would not give.

"How long have you been here?" he asked.

"All day."

"Mangled moose marbles," Ereth whispered with fright.

"It's been . . . so long," the fox said.

"I . . . see."

"The moment it happened I knew I would never get free," the fox went on. The snow, fluttering softly through the trees, clung to her fur like a delicate shroud. "I'm going to die," she said after a few moments. The words took a great deal of her energy to speak.

For once in his life Ereth did not know what to say. Though he wished there was something he could do, he had no idea what it might be.

"But—" the fox went on, gazing at Ereth with dark-rimmed

eyes, "I want to ask you . . . to . . . promise me something."

"Oh, sure," Ereth blurted with relief. "Whatever it is, I'll do it."

"You're . . . very kind," the fox whispered.

Ereth was about to ask her how she knew he was kind but decided against it.

"Not far from here . . . " the fox went on, speaking with increasing difficulty, "is my . . . den."

"Yes . . ."

"In the den are my . . . three kits. They're only a few months old."

"Three kits?" Ereth echoed, not grasping what the fox was leading to.

"Two sons, one daughter," the fox explained. "They don't know . . . what's happened to me. I went out in search of some fresh food for them when . . . I stepped on this . . . trap and . . . got caught."

"Salivating skunk spots," Ereth whispered. In spite of himself he looked anxiously about in search of other traps. How many had those humans said they set? Was it sixteen? Twenty?

"The snow hid it," the fox went on. "And . . . took away its smell."

Ereth licked his lips nervously.

"Would . . . you," the fox continued, "could you . . . be kind enough . . . to go to my kits. They . . . need to be told what's become of me."

"I . . . suppose," Ereth stammered, taken by surprise.

"They are very young. Helpless," the fox went on. "If you could just . . . take care of them . . ."

"Take care of them!" Ereth cried.

The fox blinked tears. "It would be so generous. Just knowing that you . . . would . . . I might . . . die with some measure . . . of peace."

"But . . . buttered flea foofaraws!" Ereth cried. "Where's . . . where's their father? Isn't he around?"

The fox turned away. "I don't know where he is," she said. "He's . . . gone off."

"Puckered peacocks," Ereth said indignantly. "That's not right. Or fair. I mean . . . it's absolutely un—"

The fox turned and gazed at Ereth with such sorrowful eyes he shut his mouth and wished he had not spoken so loudly.

"Would you . . . please, *please*, promise you'll take care . . . of my kits? Show them some . . . kindness? I love them so much. They're not old enough to take care of themselves . . . yet."

"But . . . oh, chipped cheese on monkey mold," Ereth growled, feeling sick to his stomach. "I suppose . . . I . . . could . . . for a bit. But only a bit," he added hastily.

"Thank you," the fox said. "They will be . . . so . . . appreciative. And so . . . will I. You are a saint to do so." The fox's eyes were closed now. Her breathing had become more difficult.

"Zippered horse zits," Ereth swore as he realized the fox was doing worse and worse.

"My den . . . is about . . . " the fox said, paying no mind to Ereth, " . . . a mile from here. Due east . . . in a low bluff. Behind . . . a pile of boulders. Just behind . . . a big blue rock."

"*Blue?*"

"A little . . . bit." The fox was fading rapidly.

"Low bluff . . . due east . . . blue rock," Ereth repeated.

"Thank you," the fox murmured, "thank you . . . so very much."

"I'll do it," Ereth sputtered. "But only for a short time, you understand. Only until their father gets back. I mean, I've no intention, none whatsoever, of taking the place of real parents who have the responsibility to—"

Ereth stopped speaking. It was obvious—even to him—that the fox had died.

For a long while Ereth stared at the dead fox. Twice he swallowed hard and sniffed deeply.

The smell of death filled the air. It frightened him deeply.

"Jellied walrus warts," he mumbled as he hastened away from the scene.

For a while he went on silently, only to suddenly halt, lift his head, and bellow, "Dying! It's such a stupid way to live! It makes no sense at all!"

Taken aback by his own outburst, Ereth gave himself a hard, rattling shake. "It has nothing to do with me. *Nothing!*" he added savagely. "I'm going to live forever!"

He gazed up at the sky. It had stopped snowing. In the darkness a dull moon revealed rapidly moving shreds of clouds. It made the sky look like a torn flag. Stars began to appear, cold and distant. "Waste of time, stars," Ereth complained.

He went on, only to stumble into a ditch and sink up to his neck in snow. "Suffocating snow!" he screamed with fury. "Why does it have to be cold and wet?" With a furious snort he hauled himself up and shuddered violently.

Grudgingly, painfully, he recalled his promise to the fox, that he would help her three kits. His heart sank. He groaned.

"Oh, why did I ever say I would do it?" he reproached himself. "I didn't mean it. I only said it to make her feel better. Fact is, I should have ignored her cries. I'm old enough to know better. Help someone and all you do is get into trouble. Always. I don't even like to be my own friend. But then I befriended Poppy. And accepted her husband. Then I was nice to their children. I should have kept to myself. Better to be alone. To stay alone.

"Helping others," he snarled viciously. "Being good! It's all broccoli bunk and tick toffee. Oh, pull the chain and barf three buckets. What am I going to do?"

8
Following and Moving On

Marty the Fisher had been as surprised as Ereth when the fox's call came out of the woods. He looked from Ereth to the woods, from the woods to Ereth, wondering what he should do.

Of course, Ereth had made the decision for him. When the porcupine broke away from the cabin and went lumbering through the snow toward the sound of the call, a puzzled Marty followed from a safe distance.

Then he saw Ereth disappear behind a mound of snow and heard low voices.

Alarmed, he swiftly, silently crawled up a tree and out along a branch, then looked down. When he saw the trapped fox, he was so startled he almost fell out of the tree.

As the fox and Ereth talked, Marty watched. He could not hear what they were saying. Then the fox slumped down, and the porcupine backed away. The next moment Ereth hurried off.

Staring at the scene below, Marty was filled with anger. The fox was dead. He knew who she was, too. Leaper. He knew of her kits, and her husband. "Humans . . ." the fisher hissed with fury. Then he saw where Ereth had gone, and his anger redoubled. "Look at him! He thinks he's beyond all that! Just runs off, the self-centered good-for-nothing . . . " More than ever, Marty resolved to catch the porcupine.

"Most likely I'm only going to get one chance," he reminded himself. "It has to be right. As long as he stays beneath the trees I'll be fine.

"Be patient Marty, be very patient," he told himself as he resumed his stalking.

Ereth plunged on through the thick, soft snow. "She said they were kits," he mumbled to himself with disgust. "Three months old. Babies. Nothing but poop and puke, puke and poop. Helpless. Brainless. Useless. The only thing I hate more than children is babies. *Babies*," he sneered with contempt. "Never could figure out why there are so many babies. They can't *do* anything . . .

"Right," he said, halting in his tracks. "And that means I should forget the whole thing, head back to the salt, and for once, do something nice for myself!"

Then Ereth had a terrible thought. *The traps.* Hadn't the humans said they had staked out many of them? With so much snow the traps would be as invisible and odorless to him as they had been to the fox. They could be anywhere. He could be caught.

Engulfed by rising panic, he began to move forward again,

but now each step he took was a cautious one.

Now and again he paused nervously to check over the trail he had made. It looked as if someone had dragged a bulky bag through the snow. "I could follow my own trail back," he told himself. "Safe once, safe twice." He turned around.

"Except . . ." he muttered, "I suppose *somebody* needs to tell those kits what happened to their mother. If they come looking for her . . . they might get caught, too." The thought was too ghastly for Ereth to contemplate.

Besides—he told himself—if he did not tell the kits what happened, they might never know. Being stupid youngsters, they were liable to just sit there and wait for her to come back. Doing nothing for themselves, they would starve to death. "That's the way the young folks are," Ereth thought, "always waiting for someone to give them a handout—even if the waiting kills them."

He turned back around and continued in the direction of the fox den.

"Of course," his thoughts continued, "if they did know what happened—I mean, if they had any brains, which isn't very likely—they could go out and find their father. That's what they should do. Let *him* take care of them.

"Wonder where the father is. Gone for a holiday, probably. Foxes are such idiots. But then, all meat eaters are jerks!"

Ereth groaned. "All that incredible salt sitting there and . . . I could use some sleep."

Once again he looked back in the direction of the log cabin. For a second he thought he saw what appeared to be a shadow moving high among the branches. It startled him.

"You're getting jumpy," he told himself. "No, not jumpy. Gilded carrot quoits," he swore. "The truth is, I don't want to do what I promised to do."

He rubbed his nose and sniffed. "Then again, I suppose it won't hurt me to drop by and tell those kits what happened. The salt isn't going to walk away. And maybe I could sleep in their den—long as it doesn't stink of meat—then get back to the salt in the morning.

"Now where did she say those kits were?" the porcupine wondered out loud as he peered around. "About a mile east from where I found her. In a low bluff. Behind some rocks. A blue rock. Oh, boiled badger boogers!" he growled in exasperation. "I hate this!"

He studied the scene before him. With everything buried in snow, it was hard to distinguish anything—rocks, boulders, bushes—much less determine where he was.

Coming out from the woods Ereth found an open field stretching before him. Blanketed in snow, it lay in perfect stillness. The new snow—untouched, untrod upon—appeared to have been there since time began. Moonlight gave it a radiant glow.

At the far end of the field was a bluff. It rose up sharply, as if half a hill had simply dropped away. Peering at it, Ereth could see the lumpy outline of rocks and boulders beneath the snow.

"Chipmunk tail squeezers," Ereth said. "I bet that's where her den is." It fit the fox's description and seemed logical. Anyone approaching the den from across the field would be seen from a safe distance. And it wasn't likely anyone would

drop down to the den from the top of the bluff. It was too steep.

"But how am I, in the middle of the night, supposed to find a blue boulder that's buried in the snow?"

With a snarl that was half anger, half weariness, Ereth moved out across the field. Suddenly he stopped. "Goat gaskins and maggot mange!" he cried. "What am I supposed to say to those kits?" The thought of it made him groan out loud.

"Tell it to them straight," he told himself. "Right off. They'll have to face the mucus some time or other. It's a rough world. No sentimental slip-slop for me.

"I'll say: 'Hello! Guess what? Here's the news. Your mother's dead. Go find your father. Goodbye.'

"Yes. That's the way it's going to be. If they don't like it, they can eat my quills."

Grimly determined, Ereth continued to push forward. As he went he kept practicing his speech. "Hello! Guess what? Here's the news. Your mother—"

It took him a while to reach the base of the bluff. Once there he halted and searched for some clue that might tell him where the fox's den was. But now that he was close he could see that there were *many* boulders embedded in the bluff. Every one was jagged and irregular. In the best of weather the den's entryway would be masked. Now it was further hidden by snow. "Lazy lizard lips," Ereth complained bitterly. "If those kits are deep inside some den, I'll never find them!"

More weary than ever, the porcupine waddled along the base of the bluff in search of some meaningful sign.

Suddenly he heard a single yelp. It seemed to come from

within the bluff itself. Ereth had no doubt it was one of the kits. He was close. He held his breath in the hope that the sound would be repeated.

Though it took some time—Ereth was shivering by now—it came. This time the yelp was behind him. With a grunt of exasperation the old porcupine wheeled about, trying to determine the exact location of the sound. Once again there was only silence. "Bat bilge," the porcupine muttered angrily. "Since I'm spending so much time looking for them, the least they could be is helpful!"

He took another step and paused. From almost right over his head he heard an explosion of yelps.

He peered up the bluff to see a particularly jagged group of rocks. He began to move up. Upon reaching the first of the boulders he scratched the snow away to expose the surface. The rock was dark, but in the moonlight it had a blue cast.

Ereth had no doubt he was close to the den. But where was the entry?

He crawled higher. Twice he slipped back and had to struggle to keep himself from tumbling all the way to the bottom. The more he looked, the more exasperated he became. There didn't seem to be an entry. If there was one—and there had to be—it was so cleverly hidden he would never be able to find it.

Sighing deeply, Ereth wondered what he should do. He was exhausted. Angry. "Wet worm water," he whispered between chattering teeth. "Why did I ever agree to do this! Why did I ever leave home? Oh, Poppy, why did you abandon me?"

He took some deep breaths and shut his eyes. He had hardly done so when he felt a sharp smack on his nose.

9
Ereth Speaks

"Hello, Porky! You looking for someone?" yelped a high-pitched voice.

Ereth opened his eyes. A young female fox, head cocked to one side, was looking at him quizzically with bright, orange eyes. Her fur was fuzzy red, her muzzle white, her ears too large for her young head. Her front paws seemed oversized too, while the dark fur that covered them made it appear as if she were wearing baggy knee socks.

Ereth blinked. "Sparrow spittle," he sputtered. "What did you call me?"

"Porky," the fox said cheerfully. "Isn't that what you are, a porcupine?"

"My name is Erethizon Dorsatum," Ereth returned with hot dignity.

"Are you a male or female?"

"Male, needle nose!"

"My name isn't needle nose, it's Nimble," returned the fox.

"And I'm a female."

"Do you live here?"

"Oh, sure," Nimble returned. "There's me and my brothers, Tumble and Flip. Then there's our mother. Her name is Leaper."

"Do you have a father?"

"Silly. Of course we do. His name is Bounder."

"I suppose that's him," Ereth muttered even as it was perfectly clear that he had found the fox's den and her three kits.

"When we heard you coming," Nimble said, "we thought you were Mom."

"Why?"

"She's been away an awfully long time."

"Oh, right," Ereth said nervously.

"Bet you'll never guess what happened today?" Nimble said.

"What?"

"Some humans came by. They were walking around the field and the base of the bluff. Doing stuff. We don't know what."

"The trappers," Ereth thought with dread. "What did you do?" he asked.

"Nothing. Hid like Mom told us to do. Don't worry. They never saw us."

Ereth took a deep breath and said, "Guess what?"

"What?"

"Here's the news . . . " But Ereth could not go on. Tongue-tied, he could only mutter, "I'm not your mother."

"Oh, I know that," Nimble said, laughing. "I may be young, but I'm not stupid. You don't look like her at all. I mean, she's very beautiful. And, no offense, you're ugly. No way I'd confuse you with her. But by any chance, have you seen her? See, Mom went hunting this morning. To get us some fresh food. Like she always does. Only, like I said, she hasn't been back for a very long while. We think it was this white stuff."

"You mean . . . the snow?" Ereth asked.

"Oh. Is that what it's called? We never saw snow before."

"Why not?"

"Because we were born only a couple of months ago, silly."

"Lungfish loogies," Ereth said.

"What did you say?"

"I said, *lungfish loogies!*" Ereth barked.

Nimble cocked her head to one side. "Why did you say that?"

"Because I wanted to, bean head!"

The young fox stared open-mouthed at Ereth, trying to understand him. "Oh," she said with a sudden grin, "I get it. You're trying to be funny."

"Gallivanting glowworms!" Ereth roared. "I am not trying to being funny! I'm serious."

The next instant two more fox faces popped up behind Nimble and stared at Ereth. They looked very much like their sister, with red coats, white muzzles, ears much too big for their heads, and very large paws. Ereth could hardly tell them apart. When they looked at him, their faces showed disappointment.

"Who is that?" one of them asked Nimble.

"That, Flip, is a very funny old porcupine," Nimble replied. "His name is Earwig Doormat."

"It is not Earwig Doormat! It's Erethizon Dorsatum!"

Nimble grinned. "But *Doormat* is easier to say."

"He smells nasty," the other young fox whispered to Nimble. Ereth assumed it was Tumble.

"Has . . . has he seen Mom?" Flip asked.

"I asked him."

"What . . . what did he say?"

"He didn't."

"Mr. Doormat," Flip asked shyly, "have you seen our mother?"

"Look here, brush tails," Ereth cried. "The name is Ereth,

not Doormat, and I've been out in the snow all day and night. I'm cold. I'm wet. I'm hungry. Do you think you could show some manners and invite me into your den? Or don't foxes know how to be polite?"

"Of course we do," Nimble said brightly. "Mom taught us. I just didn't think you'd want to. Come on in and make yourself at home."

With that the three foxes whirled around and disappeared. Though it happened right before Ereth's eyes, he was not sure where they had gone.

"Where the frosted frog flip-flops are you?" he screamed.

Nimble stuck her head up from behind a boulder. "Right here, Doormat."

"Stop calling me 'Doormat'!" demanded Ereth as he lumbered up to where the young fox, a saucy look on her face, was waiting. "The name is Ereth."

"Perish?"

"Ereth!"

"Oh, okay," Nimble returned. "Whatever you say is fine with me. Just watch your step."

Ereth scrambled over a mound of snow, then poked his nose down into a hole. Out of it wafted a smell of rotting meat so strong he gagged.

"Are . . . are you coming?" Flip called.

Deciding he had no choice, Ereth yelled, "Of course I'm coming!"

The porcupine lumbered down a steeply sloped tunnel some six feet in length. At the bottom it opened up into a large, roomy area. It was warm but rank with the stench of old meat.

As Ereth came into the den, the three young kits—lined up side by side—were sitting on their haunches, tongues lolling, heads cocked to one side, eyes bright and eager, staring at Ereth with curiosity.

Trying hard to recall who was who, the porcupine looked around.

In one corner, old leaves had been heaped together into a mound. Ereth assumed it was where the foxes slept. In another corner lay a small pile of gnawed bones. From the look of them Ereth guessed it was the remains of small animals, voles, mice, and the like: meals. Ereth, who hated even the thought of eating meat, felt revulsion.

Nimble said, "I'm sorry we can't offer you any food. We've eaten everything. That's why Mom went out."

"But she'll be back any minute," Tumble insisted in his sulky way.

"She doesn't usually stay away so long," Flip offered.

"Which is okay," Nimble added, "except we're pretty hungry. We think," she went on, "that with all this white stuff—it's called snow"—she explained to the others—"that covered everything, Mom probably had to go a long way. That's why she hasn't gotten back yet."

"What . . . what . . . do you think?" Flip asked Ereth in a quavering voice.

Ereth hardly knew what to say. Twice he opened his mouth and tried to deliver his prepared speech, only to have the words stick in his throat.

"Are you trying to say something?" Tumble demanded.

"I was going to say, 'Giraffe gas.'"

The young foxes looked at one another in puzzlement.

"What?" Tumble asked.

"I said, 'Giraffe gas'!" Ereth shouted.

For a moment no one said a thing. Then Tumble demanded, "Mr. Perish, how come you're here?"

"The name," the porcupine yelled, "is Ereth! As for why I'm here . . . Well, I . . . I like taking walks. That's why."

"In all that . . . snow?" Flip cried.

"Do you have a problem with that, dribble nose?"

The foxes looked at one another again. Nimble giggled. Flip grinned shyly. Even Tumble—though he seemed more reserved and serious than the other two—smiled.

"I guess not," Flip replied.

Ereth shifted uncomfortably on his feet. "Look here," he began, trying to find the courage to speak the truth. "I've got something to say to you. Something . . . really important."

"Oh, that's nice," Nimble said. "We'd really like to hear it. What is it?"

"It's . . . it's . . . Oh, sugared snail spit . . . I . . . spoke to your mother."

"You did! Where is she? Why hasn't she come home?" the kits cried out.

"She . . . she . . . won't be coming home," Ereth blurted out.

The young foxes stared at him in bewilderment.

Ereth swallowed hard. "And that's . . . because . . ."

"Because of *what?*" Tumble asked sharply.

"Great gopher underpants!" Ereth cried out. "What makes you think I know?"

"Because you just said you did," Nimble pointed out.

"Moth milk." Ereth sighed. He stared at the kits. They were gazing at him with rapt attention. Nimble had her mouth open, panting gently. There were lines of anger over Tumble's eyes. Flip's eyes were full of tears.

The emotion was too much for Ereth. "Sour snake sauce on spaghetti!" he suddenly cried. "Forget it!" Whirling around, he scrambled for the entry tunnel.

"Mr. Perish Doormat," Flip called after him, "did . . . did something happen to Mom?"

Ereth stopped in his tracks. Slowly, he turned back to face the young foxes.

"We . . . need to know," Flip said.

"No, you don't!" Ereth snapped.

"We do too!" Tumble insisted.

"No!"

"But why?"

"Because," Ereth shouted with complete exasperation, "Oh, fish feather fruitcakes . . . because your mother is dead, that's why!"

10

Ereth and the Kits

The three young foxes gazed at Ereth with eyes full of disbelief. No one spoke.

It was Flip who finally stammered, "Would . . . would you repeat that?"

"Sorry," Ereth grumbled. "I . . . ah . . . didn't mean to say it that way." Flustered, wishing he could be anywhere else in the world but where he was, he backed up a step. "And I wouldn't have either if . . . you hadn't made me. I mean, I'm . . . sorry. I am. . . ." His voice faded away.

"But," Flip asked in a quavering cry, "did you say that Mom . . . died?"

"Yes."

"How . . . how do you know?"

"It had nothing to do with me," Ereth said. "I was an innocent bystander."

"*Died?*" Nimble echoed, her voice rising tremulously.

"I said yes, didn't I?"

"But how's that possible?" Tumble wailed. "Moms . . . can't die. They're supposed to take care of us. *Always*."

Ereth swallowed hard. "There is this cabin. With salt. And it's my birthday. Except that has nothing to do with it. Only, because I was there, I heard her. She . . . stepped into a trap. And . . . she . . . couldn't get out. She bled . . . badly . . . too much."

"Did . . . did you speak to her?" Flip asked. "Before she . . . died?"

"Yes."

"What did she say?" Nimble asked.

"Look here," Ereth sputtered. "I never had to . . . do this before. Never wanted to. And I . . . oh, spread peanut butter on pink poodle!" he screamed. "I don't know what to say!"

"I don't care what *you* have to say," Tumble barked angrily. "Just tell us what *she* said!"

"Oh, right," Ereth muttered. "She . . . said a . . . lot of things. Mostly . . . sentimental slip-slop. No! I didn't mean that. I mean, well, she said you were helpless. That you couldn't take care of yourselves. Wanted me to find you and tell you . . . what happened. Asked me to take care of you. It was all . . . well, ridic—I mean, sad. And I suppose I will stay . . . but only until your father comes home. Understand that? Only till then. That's what she said."

"Nothing . . . else?" Flip asked after a moment.

"Well . . . she also said . . . she . . ."—Ereth almost choked on the word—"loved . . . you."

Nimble stared at Ereth dumbly. Tumble, tail between his legs, backed away. Flip's eyes filled with tears.

Ereth turned away and shuffled into a corner. Hearing nothing from the trio, he looked back over his shoulder. The young foxes were gazing after him as if they could not believe what had been said.

Then Flip slowly lifted his head, squeezed his eyes shut, opened his mouth, and let forth an earsplitting, dismal yowl that saturated the den with its misery. The two other foxes did the same until all three were howling together. Howl after howl they cried, filling the den with their anguish. On and on they went, with such a volume that Ereth, becoming fearful that he would lose his mind, spun about and shouted, "Stop it! Stop it at once!"

As if a switch had been flicked, the foxes ceased their cries and just sat and sniffled.

"Food!" Ereth cried in desperation. "You have to eat food."

The foxes looked at him blankly.

He said, "You said you hadn't eaten all day."

"That was because Mom . . ." Nimble stopped in midsentence.

"Right," Ereth snapped. "She went out to get you some. Now, just tell me, what do you eat?"

Tumble shrugged. "Whatever she brought us. Chipmunks, moles, and voles. Rabbits if she was lucky. Mice, too. They're great appetizers. But then I'm very particular about what I eat."

Ereth grimaced. "I *hate* meat eaters," he said.

"Well, we love meat," Tumble threw back defiantly. "It's what Mom always gave us."

"Don't you eat anything else?"

"Bugs," Tumble snapped.

"Oh, green goose cheese!" Ereth cried with disgust. "How about some decent food? Like . . . like vegetables."

Nimble wrinkled her nose. "Only if we have to. You know, berries and stuff. No offense, but we like meat a whole lot better."

"In fact," Tumble said, "we hate vegetables."

"Yeah," Flip agreed. "They're really nasty."

Ereth studied the faces of the young foxes. They were looking at him as if he knew what to do, as if he had answers. "Do you do any hunting for yourselves?" he asked.

"I . . . I caught a grasshopper once," Flip said with pride. "It was crunchy."

Ereth almost threw up.

"Did your mother hide any food?" he asked. "Foxes do that, you know."

"They do?" Nimble said. She turned to her brothers with a questioning look. They seemed equally surprised.

"'Course they do," Ereth snarled. "Everybody knows that. She probably had another den, too. Or more. A just-in-case den. Am I right?"

"Oh, that," Nimble replied. "Sure. It's down along the bluff a bit. Not too far from here."

"Would there be any food there?"

Nimble shrugged. "Mom only told us what we needed to know."

"Can you find it?"

The foxes exchanged glances again. "Yes . . . I suppose. Maybe."

"Then why the mangy muskrat mites, if you were so hungry,

didn't you go look there for food?"

There was a moment of embarrassed silence. "I guess we didn't think of it," Flip offered after a moment.

"We were waiting for Mom," Tumble said belligerently. "The way she told us to."

"And we always do what she tells us," Nimble explained more softly.

"Anyway, the . . . white stuff came," Flip added.

"Snow," Nimble reminded him.

Ereth said, "I suppose we'd better check that place. Now you, Nimble, take the lead. You seem to know where this place is. Then Tumble, Flip, you follow. I'll come behind. Come on, let's hit it."

For a moment the foxes just looked at him.

It was Flip who said, "Mr. Doormat are . . . are you going to be our mother from now on?"

"Look here, you simple smear of wallaby wax," Ereth

roared, "the name is *Ereth*, not Doormat. Secondly, I am not your mother. I can't be a mother. I don't want to be a mother. I'm only taking care of you until—" Ereth stopped.

"Until what?" Tumble prompted quickly.

"Until . . . your father gets back. Which better be fast as bees buzzing buttercups. Do you understand?"

The foxes stared at him.

Exasperated, Ereth asked, "Do you have any idea where he is?"

"He happens to be doing his business!" Tumble returned hotly. "He's got a lot of it."

"Sorry I asked," Ereth returned in the same tone. "Just hop it! To the other place."

The three foxes, energized by Ereth's yelling, tumbled out of the den. The weary porcupine followed, close enough to hear Tumble whisper to the others, "Wow, he's a nasty one, isn't he?"

II

Marty the Fisher

n the field below the bluff sat Marty the Fisher, up to his neck in snow. The skies had cleared. The moon was full. The air was still. Not a sound could be heard. The world glowed with a serene whiteness.

Not that Marty the Fisher cared or even noticed any of that. He was angry at himself for allowing Ereth to get away. His strategy, once he realized that the porcupine was heading toward the far side of the field, was to trap the prickly creature against the wall of earth. He was quite sure this would work. But to Marty's great puzzlement, Ereth had simply vanished. It was as if he had been swallowed up by the bluff itself.

"Perhaps," he thought, "he found an old badger's den. Or a cave. Maybe he's holing up till morning. Sleeping.

"Should I wait?" he asked himself. "Should I come back tomorrow? Should I forget all about this annoying Ereth? How irritating that he should get away from me!

"No," Marty decided. "I'll wait a bit. Until the moon's

shadow goes from over there to over here."

He was still studying the scene when he saw three young foxes burst out of the bluff, followed momentarily by the porcupine.

"Not good," Marty said to himself with a frown. "I can deal with the porcupine, but not if those foxes are with him. They look young, but the four of them together will be too much to handle."

Even so, Marty told himself to be patient. "Porcupines and foxes do not mix," he reminded himself. "Sooner or later Ereth will be alone again." From a safe distance Marty watched to see where the quartet was going.

The Other Den

t was Nimble who led the way to the other den. Tumble and Flip followed on her heels. Last to come was Ereth. He could see right away why the foxes had been named the way they were. Each one of them moved through the snow in short, frolicking jumps. So energetic were they, they sometimes landed on one another's backs, or collided. Ereth, who could do nothing but plod stolidly after them, kept crying, "Slow down. Wait for me!" He was terribly nervous. What if one of the kits put a foot into a trap? What if *he* did?

But whenever the weary Ereth caught up to them the kits were off again, leaving the porcupine to mumble disparaging remarks about foxes and the world in general.

Though the second den was only some twenty yards from the one he had first entered, Ereth never would have found it on his own. In fact, when he finally caught up with the kits they were hastily scraping back the snow from between two large

boulders. Only when the snow was removed was a small hole revealed—smaller than the one that led into the other den.

"Is this it?" Ereth demanded, panting from exertion.

"It's what we told you about," Flip assured him.

"Are there others?" Ereth asked, eyeing the narrow entryway.

"Don't know," Tumble said. Without another word, he scurried down the hole. Nimble followed.

"Are . . . are you coming?" Flip asked.

"I'll try," Ereth replied.

"I'd like you to," the young fox said shyly before he darted down the hole.

"Monkey muumuus," Ereth grumbled, as he braced himself to follow.

No sooner was he inside the tunnel than he felt himself squeezed from all sides. Grunting and groaning, scraping and pushing at the dirt, he found it hard to breathe.

"Are you still coming?" he heard one of the foxes call.

"Of course I am!" Ereth shouted.

"Hurry up. There's food down here!"

Ereth continued to kick and pull, gradually working his way forward. Suddenly Flip appeared in his face.

"Need some help?" he asked.

"Buzz off, you bowl of burro barf!" he cried. "I never need help! Never!"

"Sorry," Flip said quickly and retreated, leaving Ereth to struggle.

Twenty minutes later the exhausted porcupine squeezed into the den, bringing with him a shower of pebbles and dirt.

The three foxes were on their bellies, holding bones in

their paws and gnawing at them.

Nimble looked up. "What took you so long?" she asked.

Ereth only said, "Did you find something to eat?"

"A lot," Tumble enthused, with his mouth full. "A really great half-eaten rabbit."

"Would . . . would you like some?" Flip offered.

"No!" roared Ereth. Though famished, he could only think about sleep.

He looked around the new den. Slightly smaller than the first, it was the same messy, nasty-smelling kind of a place.

Without a word, the porcupine moved as far from the foxes as possible, then lay down. "I'm going to sleep," he announced. "And I just want you to know, this is the worst birthday of my life."

"What's a birthday?" Flip asked his sister in a low voice.

"It's the day you're born," Nimble explained.

"Oh, wow! Does that mean that Doormat was just born today?"

"No way," Tumble said. "He's got to be ancient."

Ereth closed his eyes, curled up, and tried to act as if he were already asleep.

"Really? How old do you think he is?" Flip asked in a whisper.

"From the way he's acting," Tumble asserted with great authority, "I'd say two hundred years, at least."

"Does that mean he'll die soon?"

"Probably."

"Shut up!" Ereth screamed.

For a moment there was silence.

"Sir," Flip said in a small voice. "Mr. Perish?"

Ereth sighed. "I'm sleeping," he said.

"Oh."

A few quiet moments passed. Just as Ereth felt himself drifting off, he felt a nudge. He opened his eyes. The three foxes were standing next to him.

"What is it?" Ereth asked numbly.

Nimble said, "Mr. Earwig, when we sleep at night, Mom lets us snuggle up close to her. She even wraps her tail about us. It keeps us very warm."

"Chewed over cow cuds," Ereth mumbled. "Will this day never end?"

"What should we do?" Tumble asked.

"Have you even looked at my tail?" Ereth snapped.

"What about it?"

"It's full of quills."

"Are you *completely* covered with quills?" Flip asked.

Ereth hesitated. "No," he admitted.

"Where aren't you?" Tumble demanded.

"My belly."

"Can we snuggle *there?*" Nimble asked.

"No!" Ereth roared.

"But we can't sleep," Tumble said after a moment. "Our mother . . ."

"I am not your mother!" Ereth shouted, turning his back to the foxes. "I'm a porcupine who wants to be left alone! Beat it!"

The foxes stared at him for a while. Then Flip turned and, with head bent low, trotted off to the farthest side of the den.

Sighing, he flung himself down with his back to Ereth and curled up in a ball.

After a moment the other two followed their brother. In moments they were rolled up together like a flower bud.

Despite his exhaustion Ereth could not sleep. He kept thinking of all that had happened that day. "So help me," he muttered, "this'll be the last birthday I ever celebrate."

He began to drift off, only to hear a sound: a long, sad sigh. He tried to ignore it, but more sighs followed. The foxes were whimpering.

"Barbecued bear beards," Ereth swore to himself. Heaving himself up, he waddled over to where the foxes lay.

"Move over, you piebald pooper snoopers!"

He flung himself down and tried to flatten his quills as

much as possible. Then he rolled over, exposing his soft, plump belly. Within moments he could feel first Flip, then Nimble, and, after a pause, Tumble push up against him, uttering sleepy sighs of comfort.

As he lay there the old porcupine's mind drifted to visions of his own snug, private log. He thought of Poppy and Rye's children. Those children were a nuisance too, constantly talking, asking him needless questions. "But," he thought wistfully, "I never had to be in charge of them. And at the end of the day they always went away."

"Baked birthday boozers," Ereth managed to say before he succumbed to deep and needed sleep. "I'm trapped. Completely, utterly, miserably trapped."

13
Marty the Fisher

The morning dawned as bright as ice. New snow lay thick, softening everything jagged, even as it absorbed almost every noise. In all the landscape the only sound to be heard was the high, piping *dee-dee-dee* of a tiny black-and-white chickadee flitting among the tree branches along the edges of Dimwood Forest.

That small sound was enough to wake Marty the Fisher from his sleep. He had gone to bed beneath a pile of old leaves he'd found heaped against a rock by the forest rim. Before burrowing in and falling asleep, he'd vowed to wake as early as possible, promising himself that on the morrow he would catch that very annoying Ereth.

In fact the fisher was more determined than ever to catch the old porcupine. He was not going to give up now.

When Marty had last seen Ereth—beneath the light of a midnight moon—the porcupine had been moving clumsily along the bluff in the wake of three tumbling young foxes.

Even as Marty watched, the whole group had suddenly disappeared—into a den, or so the fisher presumed.

Afterward, Marty spent a good amount of time trying to guess why Ereth was with the foxes in the first place. He decided it must have something to do with Leaper.

Quickly throwing off remnants of sleepiness, Marty crept silently along the forest fringe. When he saw an aspen tree with a thick branch that stretched over the open field, he climbed it, then moved along the branch as far as he could safely go. From this high vantage point he had a complete view of the field—and that included the bluff.

"Be patient . . . " Marty urged himself yet again. "Be *very* patient. Ereth is doomed."

14
The Kits

Deep within the fox den it was not noise that aroused Ereth from his fitful sleep, but immense aggravation. "Snake-smell soup," the porcupine protested as he recollected the appalling situation in which he'd placed himself.

Then he sensed his hunger. It seemed like forever since he'd eaten a decent meal. He had to get up. But when he made an attempt to move his cramped legs he only bumped into the three young foxes.

Slowly, not wanting to wake them, Ereth eased himself away from the leggy hugs of the kits. Once free, he shook himself all over—producing a soft rattling sound—then turned to look at the sleeping youngsters.

"Wanting me to be their mother!" Ereth shook his head violently. "Rabbit earwax! What I need to do is get out of here before they get up."

Then and there Ereth made up his mind to head back to

the log cabin before the trappers returned, have himself a feast of salt worthy of his efforts, then continue on. These kits could take care of themselves.

Moving as noiselessly as he was able, Ereth crept to the entryway. When he reached it he paused. Recalling how difficult it had been to get through when he came down into the den, he eyed the hole anxiously. But no sooner did he brace himself to go forward than a twinge of guilt held him back.

Murmuring "Phooey on being decent," he turned to take one final look at the kits—just to make sure they were sleeping. To his surprise, Nimble had raised her head and was staring at him with sleepy eyes.

"Mr. Earwig, sir," Nimble asked with a yawn, "are you going out?"

An indecisive Ereth stood by the entryway. The only

response he could come up with was, "The name, banana brain, is Ereth."

"Oh, right. I forgot. But, Ereth, *are* you going out?" Nimble asked again.

Ereth made a noncommittal grunt.

"I mean," the young fox inquired, "will you be coming back?"

"'Course I will," Ereth said gruffly. "Do you think I'd just abandon you?"

"I was only asking," Nimble said with a friendly wag of her tail. She yawned, revealing white teeth, red tongue, and gullet.

Ereth said, "I was just thinking about . . . food."

Nimble got up on all fours, stretched, and gave herself a shiver to loosen her stiff muscles. "Mr. Perish . . . I mean, Ereth . . . I think you're too fat for the entryway. Would you like me to make it bigger? I'm pretty good at digging. That way you could come and go much more easily. You know, when you get us food."

Ereth grimaced but said nothing.

The young fox trotted up to the tunnel and made her way up to the ground surface. Within moments Ereth could hear her scratching and digging furiously. Gradually, she worked her way back down. When she emerged her face and fur were covered with dirt.

"There!" she offered with a grin. "It's a whole lot wider now."

"Thanks," Ereth grumbled as he moved toward the entryway. Pushing and shoving, he got through the tunnel with somewhat less difficulty than the night before.

Outside, the dazzling whiteness of snow, the cloudless sky, and the golden sun made him blink. The field before the bluff lay smooth and undisturbed. And at the far side of the field was the edge of Dimwood Forest.

Though Ereth looked at the forest trees longingly—and dreamed of the tender under-bark that he knew was there for the eating—he worried about the kits. "Where the blazing baboon balloons can I find them some food?" he asked himself with exasperation.

As he fretted, Nimble came out of the hole and sat beside him.

"Ereth, do you like snow?"

"No."

The young fox thought about this, and then said, "Do you like anything?"

"Salt."

After another interval, the fox asked, "Ereth . . ."

"What?"

"I may be wrong, but I don't think you want to stay with us."

Ereth made a noncommittal grunt.

"You know, it'll be fine with us if you leave. I mean, I don't think we need you."

Ereth said, "You're wrong."

"Why?"

"Because," Ereth said, "youngsters don't do well alone. You're takers, not givers. If there's no one to take from, you'll die."

"Oh, okay," Nimble said agreeably.

"Look here, elephant ears," Ereth suddenly barked, "I'm a vegetarian. I don't eat meat. I hate it. Just the thought of eating it makes me ill. So I don't have the slightest idea how to go about getting the kind of food you want."

"Mom used to go out into this field and listen."

"Listen?"

"Oh, sure. She could hear the most amazing things. I mean, pretty much anything that moved. She was wonderful. There were crunchy voles and tasty mice—"

"Stop!" Ereth snapped.

Nimble turned. "What's the matter?"

"No mice!"

"Are they bad for you?"

"Eat a mouse and you've had it," Ereth snarled. "Worst food in the world for foxes. Or anyone else for that matter. One hundred percent poison."

"Thank you. I didn't know that."

Side by side, the two stared at the snow-covered field.

Then Nimble suddenly whispered, "Ereth! There's something moving right down there."

"Where?"

"In the snow," Nimble said. "At the bottom of the bluff. I'm pretty sure I can hear it." She dropped into a crouch, belly low to the ground.

"It would be a whole lot better if you ate bark," Ereth muttered.

Nimble was not listening. Ready to pounce, she began to move forward.

"I don't want to watch," Ereth said, feeling ill. With that he turned around and crept back down into the den.

The other two foxes had woken up.

"Where's Nimble?" Tumble demanded right away.

"Outside. Getting food."

"Why didn't you tell me?" groused Tumble, who bounded up the tunnel, leaving Ereth alone with Flip.

"Don't you want to hunt for food too?" Ereth asked him.

"I don't feel well."

"What's the matter?"

"I . . . I have a stomachache," the fox said.

"Galloping goat giggles," Ereth sneered. "*Why* do you have a stomachache?"

"I just do."

"Well, that's your problem, mustard mold. I have no idea what to do about it."

"Can I come lie near you?" Flip asked.

"Do whatever you want."

Flip came over to where Ereth was and stretched out, chin resting on his forepaws, large ears tilted forward, big eyes staring up at the porcupine.

Feeling uncomfortable under the gaze, Ereth shifted slightly.

"Mr. Ereth . . . " Flip said.

"What?"

"I'm . . . glad it was you who brought us the news about . . . Mom."

"Oh, well, sure . . . fine," Ereth replied gruffly.

Neither fox nor porcupine spoke for a while.

Flip sighed. "I figured out something," he said.

"Yeah? What?"

"You don't like us very much."

"I do like you," Ereth growled.

"Do you like us enough to stay with us?"

"I told you I'd stay, didn't I? But the minute your father gets back, I'm out of here."

"Oh." Flip wiggled a little closer to Ereth. "Mr. Ereth," he said, "I like you."

Ereth grunted. "Why?"

"You're nice, but I don't think you like it when I say that."

"Shut up!" Ereth snapped.

Tumble popped down from the entryway. "Ereth!" he cried.

"What?"

"Nimble couldn't catch that vole. So we're really hungry. It's your job to get us some food."

15
Chores

The three foxes sat side by side, tails wagging, tongues lolling, big eyes staring at Ereth.

"All right," the porcupine said. "It's perfectly obvious to anybody but a belching boomerang that there's a whole lot to get done. That means you've got work to do."

"*Work?*" Tumble asked, irritation in his voice. "What are you talking about?"

"Maybe you haven't noticed, sludge foot," Ereth snapped, "but there's a need to collect food, and to clean the mess around here. Look at those bones scattered about. And the floor! Messy! We need to get the meat stink out. I can't stand it. There's your sleeping pile too. It needs to be made neat. Just because you hung around me last night doesn't mean that it's going to happen again. From now on—as long as I'm around—you'll sleep on your side of the den, in your own bed. Am I making myself understood?"

The foxes stared at him blankly.

"All right then, who does what? What chores do you each have?"

The foxes exchanged puzzled looks.

"What's the problem?" Ereth demanded. "All I'm asking is, who does what around here?"

"We don't do any of that stuff," Tumble said disdainfully.

"Moose midges on frog fudge!" Ereth barked. "All I'm asking is, who does what chores?"

Flip said, "Mr. Ereth, all we do is play. And eat."

"And sleep late," Nimble added.

"Then who the puppy pancakes does all the work around here?" Ereth demanded.

"Mom," Nimble replied.

"Right," Tumble said angrily. "So if you're going to be our mother, you should be doing all that stuff too."

"I am not your mother!" Ereth roared. "If you think I'm going to take care of you like some servant while you do nothing, you go can go take a slide on the sludge pile.

"This is your den, not mine," he raged on. "And it's absolutely disgusting. So first of all, you're going to clean up."

"But I hate work," Tumble announced. "It gives me a headache."

"Look here, stinkweed," Ereth said. "You hankering to turn your nose into a pin cushion?"

"No."

"Then you'll work like everyone else."

Tumble glowered but said nothing more.

Ereth said, "Who's the best hunter?"

"I am," Nimble piped up. "I almost caught that vole. Next time I'm sure I'll get something."

"Fine, after we do the den you can go hunting. As for you," Ereth said to Tumble, "you'll keep the den floor clean. And you," he told Flip, "will make sure the bed is kept neat. Now hit it!" the porcupine roared.

The foxes didn't move.

"What's the matter?" Ereth demanded.

"What chores are *you* going to do?" Tumble asked.

"Look here," Ereth roared, "you wasted wedge of wood-chuck wallow, this is your den, not mine!"

"But Mr. Ereth sir," Flip asked cautiously, "don't you clean up your own den?"

"One more word out of any of you, and you'll get fifteen quills in each of your backsides." Ereth waved his tail ominously. "Now move it!"

With much sighing and grumbling as well as dirty looks at Ereth, the foxes set about their tasks.

Flip began by pushing the bed leaves into a pile, then went about the den picking up stray bits of leaves and twigs with his teeth and depositing them on the heap. Nimble, meanwhile, gathered gnawed bones and carried them one by one—and slowly at that—out of the nest, where she deposited them a short distance from the den's entryway. As for Tumble, he set about trying to smooth down the dirt floor of the den with his tail. In fact, he spent most of the time cleaning his tail of any twigs, leaves, and bone bits he happened to pick up.

A glowering Ereth watched the work progress. Now and again he called out useful suggestions, such as, "You missed that

bone over there, sack foot!" Or, "Hey, armpit brain, don't forget to smooth down that corner."

The three foxes worked slowly, resting more often than they labored. They also spent a considerable amount of time complaining about what they were doing. Then, whenever they got close to one another, they fell into bickering and snapping. More than once Ereth had to come between them.

"Mr. Ereth?" It was Flip who called.

"What is it?" Ereth growled.

"Could you help me? I can't get the leaf pile right."

"What's the matter with it?"

"It's all lopsided. I need you to tell me what to do. Please."

With a grunt Ereth heaved himself up and waddled over to the corner where Flip was working. Balefully he surveyed the pile of leaves. It was as the fox had said. The leaves had simply been shoved into a corner where they were still quite a mess.

"Typical," Ereth muttered. "Youngsters don't know how to do anything right." In a fury of frustration the porcupine pushed the leaves from first one side, then another, shaping the mass into an orderly pile. As he worked Flip looked on approvingly, but did not lend a paw.

"There!" Ereth said, when he had finished. "Did you see how I did it?"

"Oh, wow!" Flip cried. "It looks so much better than I ever could have done. And you did it faster too."

Tail wagging with pleasure, he waded clumsily into the pile, then threw himself down right in the middle. "Oh, this *is* wonderful," he barked with delight as he squirmed down so that the leaves were all about him. "You do it so well. You should do this chore all the time."

Flip lifted his head. "Hey, guys," he cried. "Look what nice Mr. Ereth did to our bed."

As soon as Nimble and Tumble saw how cozily Flip had settled himself, they dashed over and leaped, paws first, into the pile.

As Ereth looked on in dismay, the three foxes began to tumble joyfully, wrestling, snarling, and snapping at one another until the entire leaf pile that Ereth had shaped had become a complete mess. With leaves scattered everywhere, the den was worse than it had been before.

"Stop!" Ereth cried. "Stop!"

The kits, however, paid not the slightest attention to him, but continued their romp. A disgusted Ereth turned his back on them and went outside.

"Impossible," he kept saying to himself. "Completely, totally impossible. I can't do it. I just can't. I've been with them only one day, but if this keeps up, I'll be dead in a week."

16
Hunting

Ereth was staring glumly over the snowy field, trying to decide what to do next, when Nimble popped out of the hole.

"I'm ready," she announced brightly.

"Ready for what?"

"Don't you remember? You said hunting was to be my job."

"Is the den cleaned up?"

"Oh, sure," Nimble assured him. "Do you want to see?"

"No."

"Okay. But if you want to teach me how to hunt, I'm ready to do it now."

"Antelope uncles!" Ereth swore. "I told you, I don't know anything about hunting."

"I should be a good hunter," Nimble said. "My mother was. And my father's really, really great."

Ereth looked around. "You have any idea when this father of yours is coming back?"

"Nope," Nimble said earnestly. "He just comes and goes. He's a very busy fox."

"Busy at what?"

Nimble's eyes narrowed. "Are you suggesting he isn't busy?"

Ereth decided not to pursue the matter. Instead he asked, "Where do you usually hunt?"

"Right down along the bluff here. Mom always said we mustn't go too far. Should I go then?" Nimble asked.

Ereth was about to say yes, when he thought about the human hunters' traps. "I'd better go with you," he announced.

"Great!" Nimble bounded off.

"Don't go so fast!" Ereth shouted after the fox, as his short

legs struggled to carry him through the snow, over the rocks, and around the boulders.

Pausing, Nimble looked around and grinned to see how awkward Ereth was.

After much panting and scowling, Ereth caught up with the young fox. "Listen here, flea brain, your legs are a lot longer than mine. So keep it down to a decent crawl."

"I will. But—" She stopped speaking suddenly.

"What is it?" Ereth asked.

"I smell something."

"What? Where?"

"Right down there at the bottom," Nimble whispered.

Ereth looked, but could see nothing.

The young fox made her way down the face of the bluff, pointing her nose now this way, now that, sniffing.

Suddenly she froze. With her belly low to the ground, she stretched out to her full length.

"Be careful!" Ereth cautioned.

"Shhh!" Nimble replied. Tail stiff behind her, the young fox moved one step at a time, all but slithering toward whatever it was she had detected.

Ereth, trying to keep his eye on the kit but feeling more clumsy than ever, struggled hard to catch up, skidding and slipping over the rough terrain.

Below, Nimble prepared to pounce.

Suddenly, Ereth broke through the snow, only to strike a patch of rocks and boulders. His legs went out from beneath him. As he tried to right himself he caused a small landslide. Rocks and snow cascaded past the fox. One rock popped up

into the air. It came down in front of Nimble's nose.

No sooner did the stone hit the snow than two jaws of steel rose up and snapped together, clamping on the rock with a horrifying metallic *clack!*

"Don't move!" Ereth screamed.

A baffled Nimble came up out of her crouch and stared at the object. "What . . . what is it?" she asked.

Ereth, heart hammering, shouted, "It's a trap! Don't breathe! Don't think!"

Nimble leaned forward and sniffed.

"Didn't you hear me, you busted bottle of chicken clots? There may be other traps near you." Moving with great caution, Ereth inched toward the exposed trap, his small black eyes looking this way and that.

"But . . . what's a trap?" Nimble asked.

"It's . . . made . . . by humans," Ereth said, struggling to get his breath back. "To catch . . . animals like you and me. It's what caught your mother. That's what killed her."

Nimble's eyes grew very big. "Oh," she said.

Ereth leaned forward toward the sprung trap. It had a hard, oily reek that turned his stomach. When he thought of their walk last night from one den to the other—and Nimble's pursuit of a vole—it made him feel faint to realize how lucky they had been.

Nimble came forward and sniffed at the trap again. "But . . . but it smells like good food," she said, still baffled.

"That's the bait," Ereth said. "And there are fourteen more of them."

"Oh, dear," Nimble said. In a small voice she said, "Where?"

"That's just the point, pug pill! I don't know!" Ereth was so upset he was shouting.

"But . . . why are you so angry at *me*?" Nimble asked, backing away.

"I am not angry at you!" Ereth screamed. "I'm angry at the whole world!"

"But . . . does that mean we can't go . . . anywhere?"

"It means we have to be super careful. The snow makes everything worse. You can't see anything. You'll have to think!

Get it? For once in your life you're going to have to use your brindled bit of baby brain."

"I'm not a baby!"

"You're a child!" Ereth raged on. "It's the same thing. And I'm the one who has to take care of you!"

"No, you don't."

"No? If I hadn't thrown that rock right there, you would have never seen that trap."

"You didn't throw it, you fell, and it rolled down," Nimble pointed out. "It was nothing but stupid luck."

"Never mind luck! There are other traps around. Waiting to grab you. I can't be easy until we get them all."

"But . . . but how do we do that?"

"That's the point, elbow eyes!" Ereth screeched in frustration. "I don't know!" He turned away to hide the angry tears in his eyes. "All I know is that I have to do something. Fast!"

17
Traps

Ereth and the three kits were sitting outside, next to the entryway to the den.

"Look here, fur balls," Ereth said to them. "I know you're impatient to get about. But as Nimble here can tell you, you can't just bop around like a bunch of giggling glitz glumpers. Tell them what happened."

Nimble looked around sheepishly. "I was just about to pounce—I think it was a mole I was smelling—when Ereth here kicked a rock. And this thing—"

"A trap," Ereth corrected.

"A trap sprang up right out of the snow. It's . . . really nasty. Ereth says it was the same kind of trap that . . . got Mom."

Tumble and Flip, having listened in silence, turned and stared where Nimble indicated.

"Remember the day of the snowstorm? And those hunters who were around? They put down sixteen of these traps," Ereth explained. "They could be anyplace, from the bluff right back

into the forest and up to that cabin of theirs. No telling where they might be."

The kits remained silent. Then Tumble said, "I'm hungry. You should be feeding us."

"Holy horse hockey!" Ereth snapped. "I know you're hungry. But if you go ambling around you're liable to get killed."

"I don't believe you," Tumble said. "You just like to boss us around. Mom didn't boss us. Dad doesn't."

"Look here, you leaky lump of wallaby filigree, if you want

to get yourself snuffled by a trap, that's your business!"

"You old . . ." Tumble started to say, but shut his mouth when Ereth glared at him.

"Don't pay attention to him," Nimble said to the porcupine. "He's always grumpy."

"What . . . what can we do about the traps?" Flip asked.

Ereth turned to stare out over the field. It looked so free of all danger. Yet he knew that lurking beneath the snow was something truly deadly.

Turning back to the three kits he said, "We have to find those traps."

"My dad could find them, easy," Tumble said.

"Fine, anthill brain," Ereth snapped. "Go find your father. He can deal with it. That'll suit me perfectly. I'll be gone so fast you won't even remember I was here."

Tumble, backing off, muttered, "He's probably very busy . . ."

"We could throw some more rocks," Nimble suggested.

"That might work," Ereth agreed, "but only if we're lucky. If we're even just a bit off, it won't do us any good." He gazed at the huge expanse of snow again as if it could offer some answers.

"What . . . what about a snowball?" Flip asked timidly.

"That's stupid," Tumble said immediately.

But Nimble asked, "What do you mean?"

"Well . . . I was just thinking," Flip went on cautiously, looking from his brother to his sister and ignoring Ereth, "we could roll a ball in front of us, and, you know, keep it rolling. If it hit a trap it wouldn't hurt us—just the snowball. And . . . and I think it would leave a path we could walk on."

The foxes turned to Ereth.

The porcupine considered for a moment. Then he nodded vigorously. "Snap-bug salad! That's a great idea. Best I've heard in a long time."

Flip grinned with pleasure.

"I think it's dumb," Tumble said.

Ereth paid him no mind. "Come on," he urged. "Roll up a ball right now and push it down the bluff."

Flip, delighted to have his idea so quickly put into practice, used his paws to shape a ball. Nimble helped. Very soon they had a large, if lopsided, ball of snow.

"That'll never roll," Tumble announced.

"Give it a try," Ereth urged.

Standing by the entryway to the den, Flip prodded the ball with his nose, managing to nudge it enough so that it began to roll down the bluff. As it went it gathered snow and speed. In its wake it left a wide path which exposed the earth. Very quickly it reached the bottom of the bluff.

"See?" Tumble said smugly. "No traps."

"That's the whole point, hippo head!" Ereth snapped. "At

least we can walk down that way." This they did in single file, using the path the snowball had made, with the porcupine leading the way. When they came to the bottom, where the ball rested, they stopped. Having gathered snow during its roll, the ball was very much bigger.

"Now," Ereth commanded, "push the ball back toward the other den. Where I first met you."

Flip stood up on his hind legs and placed his front paws near the top of the ball. Nimble did the same.

As usual, Tumble held back. "There's no room for me," he announced.

"Just push," Ereth said to Flip and Nimble, as he added his own weight to the effort.

The three proceeded to roll the ball forward. The heavier ball was much harder to push. Even so it inched along. Suddenly, there was a loud *snap!* The ball exploded. The stunned foxes—

as well as Ereth—jumped back.

Ereth, his face white with snow, peered cautiously forward. There, amid the remains of the snowball, was another trap, its teeth clenched ferociously together.

"Thirteen to go," the porcupine announced. There was relief in his voice, but also worry.

Tumble edged forward, sniffed the trap, then touched it gingerly with a paw. He said nothing.

"What do we do now?" Flip asked.

Ereth sighed. "Make another snowball," he said.

At that Tumble barged forward and rolled up a new ball. Then he began to push it forward with his nose. "Come on," he called hotly to his brother and sister. "I need some help. Don't be so lazy."

The others joined in. Slowly they moved the ball along the base of the bluff. As it went forward it gathered more snow. It was after they had gone some thirty more feet that another trap sprung.

"Twelve," Ereth said. He looked around anxiously. "Is the area along the base of this bluff where you and your mother walked a lot?" he wanted to know.

"I guess so," Nimble said.

"Well that explains one thing," Ereth said.

"What's that?"

"It wasn't an accident they caught your mother. Those trappers—those humans—were *trying* to snare you foxes."

"But . . . why would they do that?" Flip asked, his voice full of astonishment.

"Your fur," Ereth said glumly.

The foxes inspected their coats in puzzlement.

"Okay," Ereth said. "Let's put together another ball, and this time we'll roll it up the bluff to the entry of your regular den."

"Up there?" Tumble cried. "Up the bluff? That's too hard!"

"Go lick a lemon tree," Ereth snapped. "We don't have any choice."

It took all four of them to push the snowball up the face of the bluff. It was extremely hard work. More than once they ran into boulders and had to manipulate the increasingly heavy ball around them. Once it got away from them and rolled back to the bottom of the bluff, forcing them to start over.

At last, however, they reached the main den, without uncovering any more traps.

"Well," Ereth said. "At least you can go from one den to the other without any danger."

"But . . . Ereth . . ." Nimble asked plaintively, "what about food?"

Ereth sighed and looked back over the field again. He too was very hungry. He would have given anything to get back into the forest where the bark was plentiful. Instead he said, "We'll have to mark out more paths first. A lot of them. Otherwise it won't be safe."

Neither Flip nor Nimble objected.

But Tumble said, "You're all too slow. I know what to do." Before anyone could object, he scrambled down to the base of the bluff along the path that had just been cleared. Ereth and the other two foxes watched him go.

"Why is he always crabby?" Ereth demanded.

Nimble exchanged looks with Flip.

"He misses Dad a lot," Flip blurted out. "I mean we do too. But that's all Tumble ever talks about. You know, how he wishes Dad would come home."

A glum Ereth made no response. He merely watched Tumble.

At the base of the bluff the young fox was hastily putting together another ball of snow. Then, using his nose as well as his front paws, he began to shove it erratically across the field in the direction of Dimwood Forest. Clearly frustrated, he did not always stay behind the ball.

Ereth watched in dismay. "That worm wit is going to get himself killed," he said. With that he turned to the other two foxes. "Stay here," he commanded. Slipping and sliding, he scurried down the bluff after Tumble.

"Hey, wait!" he called.

Tumble did not even look around, but continued to roll his snowball forward.

Ereth, breathless from the exertion, caught up with the young fox. "Hey, you putrefying packet of parsnip pips, didn't you hear me?"

Tumble paid no attention. Instead, with his back to the porcupine, he struggled even harder with the ever-growing ball of snow, stubbornly inching it forward.

"Don't you understand?" Ereth cried after him. "This is dangerous work. Listen to me. You're going to get yourself killed."

Suddenly Tumble let go of the snowball, turned, and snapped, "Why don't you leave me alone! You're such a know-

it-all. I'm sick and tired of being ordered around by you. Who are you? Nobody. We never asked you to come around here in the first place. We were perfectly fine until you stuck your nose in. Why don't you just go away? That'll make everybody happy."

"Do you think I *want* to be here?" Ereth roared back. "Let me tell you something, cheese blister. I've got three billion better things to do. I'm only here because your mother asked me."

"She did not!"

"Suffocating snake slime! Why else would I have come here? She said you were helpless. That you needed me to look after you. That you couldn't get by on your own."

"That's not true!" Tumble shrilled, eyes hot with tears. Furious, he spun about and resumed pushing the snowball across the field, away from Ereth.

Ereth followed right after him.

When Tumble, with a darting glance over his shoulder, saw

Ereth was at his heels, he cried, "We're old enough to be on our own. The only reason you came to us was to get out of the snow, get warm, and eat our food. You're just too lazy to go back to your own home. You're nothing but an old, ugly, fat porcupine. And you stink, too!"

Ereth, taken aback by the new onslaught of words, stopped in his tracks. For a moment he was speechless.

"See?" Tumble went on. "You insult whoever you want, but you can't take it, can you?

"Didn't you hear me? We don't need you," Tumble insisted, going forward again. "My sister and brother feel the same way, only they're too nice to say it. Well, I'm *not* nice or polite. I say what I think. Anyway, my father will get here soon and when he does, you can—"

At that precise moment the snowball exploded, hurling snow into Tumble's face.

The young fox, taken by surprise, stood in place, trembling. Poking up through the snow were the sharp steel jaws of another trap.

"There," Ereth said angrily. "Didn't I tell you to be careful?"

Tumble whirled around. "Oh, can't you ever be quiet!" he said into Ereth's face. Then he burst into tears.

Ereth blinked. "But what . . . what's the matter?"

The fox couldn't speak. He was sobbing too hard.

"Talk!" Ereth barked.

"I . . . want my mom . . ." Tumble whispered. "So badly. I miss her so much . . . "

Ereth paled. "But . . . she's . . ."

"I know she's dead!" Tumble cried, switching back to anger,

though the tears continued to flow. "Stop telling me things I know. Oh, why don't you just go away! You're awful to have around. You're bossy. You're sarcastic. And do you know what you are most of all? You're so old your brain has turned gray. Yeah, that's what you are. Old!" With that Tumble lifted his nose, opened his mouth wide and began to howl. "I want my daddy!" he cried again and again.

An appalled Ereth looked back over his shoulder to see if Flip and Nimble were watching and listening. To his great relief they were nowhere in sight. He could only hope they had gone down into the safety of the den and had not witnessed any of this.

Ereth turned back to Tumble. The young fox was just sitting there, his head low, looking miserable.

"Tumble . . ." Ereth began, not knowing what else to say.

"Go away!" the fox screamed, not looking up. "I hate you. I wish you were dead!"

"I'm just . . ." Ereth looked around again to see if anyone else was listening. When he saw no one he said, "I'm just trying to help."

"We don't need your help!" Tumble bayed.

Ereth sighed. "Someone had to tell you about your mother."

"Right. But you just barged in and blurted it out like the stupid animal you are. I mean, it was our mother, not yours!"

Cringing, Ereth struggled to find a reply. "But," he finally got out, "you needed to know about the traps, didn't you?"

"I . . . suppose," Tumble conceded through renewed sobs. "But now that Flip—not you—figured out a way to find them, you're not necessary."

"What . . . what about food?" Ereth asked.

"We don't like vegetables!" Tumble cried. "We like meat! But you don't hunt. So you're as useless as . . . as parboiled pumpkin puke!"

Shocked, Ereth's mouth opened wide but no words came out. The next moment he sputtered, "That's it. I give up. Do what you want. Drop dead for all I care!" With that, he pushed past Tumble and began to stumble through the snow toward Dimwood Forest.

Tumble did not look around, but continued to stare down at his feet and the exposed trap just a few inches away. Only when he was certain that Ereth had gone by did he lift his head and gaze after the retreating porcupine.

"Goodbye," Tumble whispered. The tears began to flow again.

"Salamander-sap salad!" Ereth cried as he breasted through the snow in the direction of the forest. Deeply upset, he was breathing heavily, snorting wrath with every trembling step he took. "Try and help idiots and it gets idiotic," he reminded himself. "Kill yourself for kids, and they'll kill you first. Ungrateful, spoiled brats! Phooey on all children with a squashed boll weevil on top. Let 'em do what they want. They aren't *my* responsibility."

He paused and looked around to see where he was going. "I'll go back into the forest the way I came, get myself some decent food, then head right for that log cabin. Gobble up some salt. I mean, why should I care about a bunch of bungling, unappreciative babies . . ." Ereth, swearing all the while, pushed steadily across the field.

From his lookout on the aspen tree branch, Marty the Fisher spied Ereth moving toward the forest. "At last!" he cried, barely able to suppress his excitement. "I knew I was right to wait. And he's coming in my direction. Well, Ereth, you're in for one big Marty the Fisher surprise."

With that, the fisher checked to make sure he was certain of the exact spot where Ereth would enter the forest. Then he scrambled down from his tree and raced for a hiding place. "Now I've got him!" he exulted.

18
Ereth Has Some Other Thoughts

Ereth was halfway across the field on his way to the forest when he suddenly came to a stop. "Bouncing balls of beeswax!" he muttered with horror. "The traps! I'm so furious I've forgotten all about them. I'm acting blind and brainless. Any moment now I could be stepping right into one of those things. If I do I'll maim myself. Kill myself!"

Anxiously, he swung about and took a step back along the trail he'd made through the snow. He had been, he now realized, lucky to come as far as he had without harm. It would be best to return. By walking in the same steps he had just made, he could get safely back.

But no sooner did he take one step back than he spied Tumble. The young fox, head low, was walking slowly toward the den. Just to see him filled Ereth with rage.

"Monkey marbles!" he shouted out loud. "No way I'm going back there." With that he spun about and faced the trees, only to have his nerves fail him again. "But if I'm caught in a trap . . .

"I know: I'll make a snowball, just the way those idiot kits did. If I have to, I'll push it all the way home."

Ereth set about to shape a ball, only to quickly realize his legs were too short for the job.

"Great galloping guppy gunk!" he cried with a rage that brought tears to his eyes. "I don't know which way to go!" Trembling, Ereth stood in the middle of the field facing the forest. More than anything else, he wanted to lose himself in the trees, then find a way back to his own lovely log. How he yearned to return to his gloomy, stinky home, to wallow in his own muck, to have a soothing talk with Poppy. Oh, to be anywhere but where he was!

And yet, he could not make himself go forward. He was too afraid. Better to go back to the safety of the den. No! He didn't want to do that either. The kits hated him. Didn't want him. He turned about. Even as he stood there, a breeze swept across the field, carrying snow. To his horror, the tracks he had just made began to disappear. If he didn't go back immediately he'd have to break a new trail, with the danger of stepping into a trap.

One moment Ereth was in a rage. The next moment he felt soft and weepy. What was happening to him? His helplessness was frightening. "Oh, sloth-swill soup with bird-drop stuffing!" he shouted to the air. "I can't go anywhere!"

Then all of a sudden an even more terrible thought came to him. What . . . what if . . . even *some* of the things Tumble had said were true? Could he really be so dreadful? Was he really a

bad creature? Had he, in fact, become old without noticing?

The answer came in the form of a cold shiver that went through his whole body. Yes, it *was* so. Everything the young fox had said was true. He *was* an awful creature. He *was* old. He *was* bossy. No one bothered about his birthday because he wasn't worth bothering about. What's more, there was nothing he could do about it. He was too set in his ways to change. He was worthless. He might as well be dead. Ereth shut his eyes against his thoughts.

"Ereth . . . ?"

At first Ereth was not sure he heard his name. But the call came again, slightly more insistent.

"Ereth?"

Someone was calling to him.

Ereth opened his eyes. No one in front of him. Nor to either side. He looked back. It was Flip.

In spite of himself, Ereth scowled.

Flip stood some way off, afraid to come any closer.

"Ereth . . . ?" he called again cautiously. It sounded like a question, as if he were unsure he should even say the name.

Ereth felt his anger returning. "What is it?" he growled.

"Can . . . can I talk to you . . . ?"

"About what, tinkle brain?" the porcupine said, though he immediately regretted having spoken so.

"Ereth . . . Tumble came back to the den."

"What about it?"

"He . . . he told us what he said to you. He's very upset."

Ereth thought of saying, "What about *me?*" but held his tongue.

"He said that he yelled at you," Flip went on. "That he said a lot of . . . awful things. That he made you go away."

Ereth grunted.

"I . . . I just wanted to tell you that what he said isn't . . . the way Nimble and I . . . feel."

Ereth, unprepared for the searing pain he felt, stared at the young fox. Turning, he shifted away from Flip and gazed longingly at the forest.

Flip drew a little closer. "Ereth," he called. "I'm . . . I'm glad you came to us. I like you."

Ereth sniffed.

"I . . . wish you'd come back . . . " Flip coaxed. "We found two more traps."

"You did?" Ereth said.

"How many did you say there were?" Flip asked.

After a moment Ereth said, "Tumble just found another one. With the one you found before it adds up to five altogether. Then there was the one your Mom . . . found. Those trappers said they had put down sixteen. If we can believe them, that means there's just nine left."

"We could find them," Flip said. "I'm sure we could. But, Ereth, don't you think it would be better if you stayed with us?"

Ereth continued to face the forest. Perhaps he should live alone, the way he had spent most of his life before he met Poppy. When he was alone no one hurt him. No one ignored him. Being alone was safe.

"I mean, maybe you could just stay until our dad gets back," Flip said.

"Caterwauling catfish," Ereth cried. "For all you know

he may never come back."

"Oh, sure he will," Flip said. "He cares for us a lot. He does. It's just that he's very busy. I mean, he has to take care of his business."

"What about *my* business?"

"Ereth," Flip pleaded. "Tumble is very upset. I don't think he meant what he said."

Ereth sighed.

"Did you hear me?" Flip asked.

"Maybe . . . it was true," Ereth whispered.

"Well, even if what he said was . . . a *little* bit true . . . Please, I still think we need you."

Ereth turned around and faced him. "You really want me to stay?"

"Yes."

Ereth sighed. "All right. But only until we find the rest of the traps. Or till your father gets back. Whichever comes first."

"Oh, wow. That's so great of you," Flip said excitedly. "I'll go tell the others." With that he turned and bounded back along the trail toward the den. He had not gone ten steps when he stopped and returned to Ereth.

"Now what?" Ereth demanded.

"There's something else I want you to know."

"What?" Ereth said, preparing for the worst.

"I really like you," Flip said. "I mean, you're really . . . sweet." With that the young fox hurried on back to the den.

Ereth stared after the young fox. Reaching up, he touched his nose on the spot where Poppy had once kissed it. "Sweet," he muttered with a grimace. "*Sweet* is a word for nitwits and gumdrops. . . . Not . . . me.

"It'll only be for a short time," he told himself. "A very short time." With that he began to waddle back along the trail Flip had just made, telling himself that it was, after all, the safest way to get anywhere.

Marty the Fisher watched with bitter disappointment as Ereth headed back toward the bluff.

"He's gone back to them," he growled. "That means I'm going to have to find some other way to get him alone."

He thought for a while. Then he smiled.

"Maybe it's time I found father fox. Yes, I think I'll let Bounder know exactly what's going on. He'll flush that stupid porcupine out."

With that thought, Marty whirled about and raced into the forest.

19

In Search of Food

When Ereth reached the den, the three foxes were sitting side by side near the entryway. Suddenly uncomfortable, Ereth gazed at them. Nimble and Flip returned his look. Tumble avoided eye contact altogether.

For a moment no one said anything.

It was Nimble who called, "Hi, Ereth, where you been?"

"Out," Ereth said. "Walking."

"Oh."

"See anything interesting?"

"No."

Silence.

"Listen here," Ereth snapped, "you tasteless tubs of toad twaddle, if you think . . ." Hearing himself, Ereth paused, cleared his throat, and began again. "What I mean is that if you willow wallows think I'm going to do all the work, while you loaf and soak up the sun like a bunch of cross-eyed octopuses—

No! I didn't mean that. I . . ."

"What would you like us to do?" Flip said. "Chores? Hunt? Clean up? Whatever you say, Ereth. We'll be glad to do it."

"How about making some more snowballs?" Ereth continued testily. "Start rolling them along the base of the bluff, then go across the field in any direction you want. Just stay *behind* the balls. Do you understand? *Behind!*

"If there are any trails you and your mother used a lot, make sure you roll the balls those ways. Any questions? Problems? None? Good. Then get going!"

Yapping and braying, the foxes hurried down along the trails they had already made, packed up some new snowballs, and began to roll them in different directions.

When the three foxes returned to the den and Ereth, they were exhausted but elated.

"We found three more traps," Nimble cried with glee as she bounded up the bluff.

"Fine," Ereth said. "Good. We're making progress. It won't be long before you've found them all. We just need to search some more."

"Ereth . . ." It was Tumble who spoke.

"What?"

"We're really starving."

"Mom always brought home lots," Nimble added plaintively.

"More than we could eat," Flip agreed.

"More?" Ereth's ears perked up.

"There were times," Tumble said, "she brought us rabbits so big we couldn't even finish everything."

"What happened to the extra?" Ereth asked. "Did she take them off and eat the rest herself?" He knew that's what he would have done.

Flip shook his head. "Mom said dinnertime was family time, that it was rude to go off and eat alone. So we always ate together."

"Then, where did she put the leftovers?"

The foxes looked at one another in puzzlement.

"I guess we don't know," Nimble said with a shrug. "She just did what she did."

"Do you think she could have stored them somewhere?" Ereth asked. "She ever mention having still another den? You know, an emergency storehouse?"

"She never said," Flip replied.

A frustrated Ereth turned to look over the field. If there was a storage den stuffed with food it would make all the difference in the world. The problem was, such a place was likely to be well hidden. It could be *anywhere*.

He turned back to the waiting kits. "There must be one. I think we'd better go look for it," he said. "The point is, I can't teach you anything about hunting. But you need food. So think hard. Did your mother even hint about another place?"

"Nope," Nimble said.

"Okay," Ereth said. "Then here's what we're going to do. We've got those trails you've made. Instead of looking for traps, go back along them. Keep your noses to the ground. Sniff. Smell. See if you can find a storehouse. But, whatever you do, *don't go off the safe trails!* If you think you smell something, come back and we'll investigate together."

The kits needed no further encouragement. They bounded off, each one going in a different direction.

As he waited, Ereth scrutinized the field, trying to guess where, if *he* were to build a secret storehouse, he might put it.

Then he craned around to look behind him, at the crest of the bluff in particular, which rose up some five feet over his head. He doubted if the kits would even think of looking there. A shrewd mother like Leaper, knowing that, might well put a storehouse in just such an out-of-the-way spot.

Ereth eyed the area carefully, trying to figure out a way he could haul himself to the top. It was steep. But as he looked around he noted that not very far from where he sat was a natural cleft worn into the face of the bluff. If he could work his way up that cleft, he should be able to get beyond the bluff.

Still he hesitated. What about traps? There were still six to be uncovered. So far, however, they had all been found along the base of the bluff, in the forest, or out in the field. That suggested they wouldn't be beyond the bluff. Maybe.

Ereth looked over the field. The kits remained hard at work. Should he tell them what he was doing? No. It would take too long. Besides, it would be a lot more enjoyable to greet them with news of his discovery—if he made one.

Ereth headed for the cleft, working his way across the bluff. It was not easy to reach. First there was snow with which to contend. Then too, the face of the bluff was studded with rocks and boulders, all of which slowed him down. More than once Ereth needed to stop and rest.

Once he reached the lower end of the cleft, he started up, clawing and scratching at the loose gravel and snow. Twice he

had to stop, panting heavily. But when he pulled himself over
the final bit, he faced a stand of pine trees. His heart skipped a
beat. Food! Trailing drools of spit and ignoring all caution, he
ran right toward the trees.

Upon reaching the pines he attacked them with nothing
less than savagery, ripping away the outer layers of bark to get
at and gnaw at the sweet under-bark.

After twenty minutes of nonstop eating, Ereth felt so
stuffed, so crammed full of food, he had to rest and allow himself to digest his meal. Then, with a start, he recalled his
original mission: food for the kits.

He sat up and looked about. The first thing he realized was

that there were enough trees in the area to keep him satisfied for a long time. That is to say, *his* food problem had been solved.

But where, he asked himself again, if he were a fox, would he place a secret den?

Ereth searched among the trees. The ground was hard, frozen in spots, though without many rocks. The snow was sparse here, and he was able to make his way with relative ease. Still, there didn't seem to be any logical place for a secret den.

Then he noticed, within a tightly woven grove of trees, a large pile of rocks. He lumbered over to it and eyed it with care, searching for a hole or anything to suggest an entry to an inner cache of food. But though he walked completely around the

pile, he saw nothing that even hinted at it.

He was about to move on when he decided he should climb atop the pile. Perhaps—though he doubted it—he might see something more from up there.

He clambered up the rocks. It was not easy, and he kept swearing to himself. Then, as he climbed higher, he began to detect the smell of something distinctly unpleasant.

Ereth reached the top of the pile, and suddenly the smell of meat was much more pungent. Poking about the top, he found a hole. It was not a very large hole, but when he put his nose to it he had to jump back, so repellent was the stench. It was the stink of meat. A *lot* of meat.

Excited now, Ereth scratched about the hole, trying to enlarge it. The edges gave way quickly, as if they had been but loosely packed in the first place.

Very soon Ereth was able to poke his head down into a bigger hole. What Ereth saw in the dim light made him blink. The pile of rocks enclosed an entire storeroom of food: partially eaten rabbits, voles, chipmunks, and even, to his horror, mice. All were frozen.

It was as he had guessed and hoped: Leaper *had* carefully provided emergency rations for her family to last for a good part of the winter. No one would starve.

Caught between total revulsion and complete glee, Ereth wheeled about and dashed back toward the bluff and the foxes. "Bouncing bear burps!" he cried, "I've found it. We're saved." He was so excited he hardly noticed he was using the word "we."

20
Bounder

oward the other end of Dimwood Forest was a
small, shallow glen. All but circular in shape, the
hollow was surrounded by tall ponderosa pines,
their heavy limbs bent with snow. Near the center of the place—like the hub of a wheel—was a rock. Atop the
rock, bathing in the warm sun beneath the blue sky, was a large,
handsome fox. It was Bounder, the father of the three kits.

Head high, majestic tail curled about his body, Bounder
was in perfect repose. His coat of ruby red fur was as thick as
summer grass. His paws were powerful. His noble face, long and
pointed, bore deepset eyes and sharp whiskers.

Indeed, he was quite prepared to believe that the rock upon
which he rested and even the sun in the sky were there for him,
so as to show him at best advantage. All that was missing was
a pool of water in which he might admire his own image.

A few days ago Bounder had heard a rumor that the humans
at New Farm—at the eastern end of Dimwood Forest—had

built a brand-new chicken coop. The coop was full of plump chickens—or so the fox had been informed. With visions of many tasty meals in his future, the fox was determined to visit the coop. Just thinking about it made him lick his lips in anticipation. For Bounder did what he wanted, how he wanted, when he wanted. It was only the snowstorm that had interrupted his journey.

Though the storm was now over and he was still planning to go, the soothing sun upon his back detained him. The warmth provided such sweet contentment, he had shut his eyes and given himself over to random thoughts.

Even as the fox's eyes were shut, his ears were working, listening to the sounds of the forest, on guard for the slightest hint of any disturbance to which he should attend.

As time went by he caught the sound of a mouse burrowing under the snow. Bounder decided the mouse was not big enough for him to bother with.

Not long after that, he was certain a baby rabbit was hopping by the rock. Though the fox knew the rabbit was easy prey, once again he decided that the animal's small size did not justify making any effort to catch it.

It was his awareness of the young rabbit, however, that caused him to think—momentarily—about his wife, Leaper, and his three kits, Nimble, Tumble, and Flip.

Regarding Leaper, Bounder had no great depth of feeling. When he thought of her, it was to acknowledge that she was a good mother to these kits of his. That, as far as he was concerned, was the only thing important about her. For Leaper's good mothering meant that he, Bounder, did not have to con-

cern himself very much about his youngsters. That in turn allowed him to go about his business freely without the least hindrance. And so he did.

As for the kits, he did care for them, but on his own terms. He enjoyed visiting them from time to time. He liked to bring them special treats, like a freshly killed chicken—something their mother would not risk providing. He also enjoyed engaging the kits in a bit of rough play—just enough to let them experience *his* strength.

But what Bounder liked most, in regard to his kits, was to allow his children to gaze upon him with adoring eyes. Once that was accomplished, he would go off again on his private business.

All that, in Bounder's opinion, was the proper life for a father fox.

So it was that as the fox continued to lie beneath the warm sun, he deliberately dismissed thoughts of home and family. Life was too good for him to be disturbed by such things.

But then Bounder heard the sound of something much larger than a baby rabbit. Opening his orange eyes a little, he sought out who it might be. There, on a branch on one of the trees overlooking the glen, was Marty the Fisher.

As soon as the fox realized it was Marty, he shut his eyes again. Bounder did not like Marty. As far as the fox was concerned, the fisher was an unpleasant creature: sly, secretive, not always to be trusted.

"Hello, Bounder," Marty called out. "Do you know what is happening?"

The fox said nothing.

"Well, then," the fisher said, "my guess is that you don't want to know what's happened to your wife, Leaper, and those three kits of yours who go by the names Tumble, Nimble, and Flip."

Bounder felt uneasy. By stating the fox's family's names, Marty had aroused his curiosity. Still, the last thing the fox wanted to do was *ask* for the story. That would put someone else in control, a thing Bounder did not like to happen. He preferred to be in charge.

When the fox neither moved or replied, Marty called, "It's a pretty tragic tale, Bounder. I don't blame you for not wanting to know."

Bounder continued to act with indifference.

"But then," Marty continued loudly, "since everyone else knows what happened, I suppose you do too. Yes, I'd guess you were the first one to hear. Well, Bounder, you *do* have my sympathy."

Bounder, no longer able to resist, turned to the fisher. "I beg your pardon. Were you talking to me?" He was very vexed, but worked hard to avoid showing it.

"Of course I was talking to you," Marty cried. "And you heard everything I said, didn't you? You foxes have a great reputation for listening. I suppose you're as good as most. Better, maybe."

Bounder sniffed loudly a few times. "Listening?" he said. "Actually, my hearing hasn't been very good lately. A kind of cold or . . . something. The snowstorm, I suspect. Even so, if you have something to say to me, I'd be happy to make an effort to hear it."

Marty studied Bounder intently with his dark, emotionless eyes, trying to make up his mind if the fox was telling the truth

or not. He decided he was not. And that annoyed him. "It's your wife, Leaper," he called bluntly. "She's been killed."

"*Killed!*" Bounder cried, taken aback, but under such self-control that he remained in place. "You're lying!"

"No. It's true. By a hunter's steel trap. Near the cabin at Long Lake. It happened just yesterday, during the snowstorm."

"What about my kits? Were they hurt?"

"Oh, no. They weren't with her."

"Do they know about her?"

"I'm not sure."

Now Bounder was concerned. "Tell me everything you know."

"All I know is that an old porcupine who goes by the name Ereth is staying with your kits!"

"*Ereth!*"

"That's him. He seems to have moved into your den."

"In *my* den!" Bounder cried. "With *my* kits?"

"I think so."

Bounder knew all about Ereth. If anything, he knew him too well. Little more than a year ago he had been chasing a mouse through the forest when she ran into a hollow log to escape. The log proved to be Ereth's home. Though all Bounder had wanted to do was to eat the mouse—porcupines, he knew, were not meat eaters—Ereth had slapped him with his tail, giving him a nose full of painful quills. So, yes, Bounder knew all about Ereth. He disliked him intensely.

"Those are *my* kits," the fox growled. "That porcupine has no business with them, none. What's he doing there?"

"I think . . . " Marty the Fisher said, "he's pretending to be their . . . father."

"Their father!" Bounder exclaimed. "Are you making any of this up?"

"Not in the least. And quite a happy family they've become. That's all I know." So saying, Marty the Fisher retreated among the branches of the tree. He was deep enough for Bounder to lose sight of him, but not so far away that he could not watch the fox.

Bounder was thinking hard about what he had heard. "Could it really be true?" he asked himself. If true, it was a dreadful thing that had happened to Leaper. He truly regretted it. He did. But at least his kits were safe and being cared for. As far as Bounder was concerned, that was the most important thing. Regarding Ereth the porcupine—Bounder grinned. It served the old porcupine right for being such a busybody. What a perfect revenge on Ereth—the old porcupine taking care of *his* kits. Acting like their father. Until of course, he dismissed him.

The more Bounder thought about it, the more it pleased him that his old foe should be stuck with the job of taking care of his children. Served the porcupine right. Moreover, it meant that he, Bounder, could get on with his business of catching the chickens from the coop at New Farm.

With that thought Bounder trotted off through the snow, his mind entirely on those plump chickens.

"Good," Marty the Fisher said to himself as he watched Bounder go off. "If I know Bounder he'll get Ereth away from those kits. And when the porcupine is alone again I'll be there, waiting for him."

21
Discoveries

I t was now a whole week since Ereth had first come to the foxes' den. With a plenitude of food available, life had settled into a steady routine.

Sleeping arrangements were something of a compromise. While the kits slept on their own heap of leaves, it worked out that Ereth slept there too. Sixteen paws, four tails, and countless quills found a way to be close without anyone's being hurt. What's more, everyone's sleep was sound.

Ereth was the first to get up each morning. Even as the sun threw golden shafts of light over the white field in front of the bluff, he could be found scrambling toward the grove of trees. There he breakfasted on tender bark, eating as much as he wanted. Only when he was fully satisfied did he return to the den to wake the kits.

It was not an easy task. "Time to wake up, you slimy slug bugs!" he'd cry out, or something equally cheerful and inviting.

Nimble was usually the first to stagger up. A very sleepy

Flip followed. As for Tumble, he almost had to be dragged to his feet. Even then he protested in his grumpy fashion all the way.

Once the three kits were up, there was considerable yawning, stretching, and bumping, not to mention bickering. Ereth, meanwhile, snapped, ordered, cajoled, and otherwise insisted that faces be washed, fur groomed, tails smoothed. Nimble had the most trouble with this, insisting she did not care what anyone thought about how she looked, that she was going to appear as she chose no matter what. Flip went the other way. He took great pains with his grooming, insisting that there was no way he would be caught dead (his unfortunate words) looking anything less than exactly as he wished. As for Tumble, he did not care one way or the other, but simply went through the motions to avoid Ereth's barbs.

Though it seemed to take forever, everyone was eventually up and ready. Then one of the foxes was sent out to the storage den to fetch breakfast. Being chosen and sent by Ereth was considered something of a privilege. Ereth tried to be careful as to his choice, rewarding now one, now another for good behavior, so no one was favored unfairly.

Whoever went brought back just enough breakfast for the other two. Ereth's orders were always the same: "Take *only* as much as we really need," he insisted. "It has to last the rest of the winter."

While the morning's breakfast was devoured—with much smacking of lips, wagging of tails, and snapping of bones Ereth made sure he went outside. Try as he might, he s could not abide a meal with the foxes—neither the food

ate nor their manners—but had decided that they were not going to change. Protest was to no avail.

Once he sensed breakfast was done Ereth returned to the den. It was time for daily chores. Everybody knew exactly what to do—not that it ever went smoothly or without complaint. If Flip was supposed to tidy the bed, it almost never failed that Tumble or Nimble messed his work up. If Nimble was smoothing down the den floor, there was Tumble or Flip to track it up. Tumble, whose job was the removal of odd bits of bone and uneaten food, almost inevitably discarded something that the other two were saving.

"You're nothing but a bunch of lazy-legged leeches," Ereth would inform them hotly. "Why do you always have to be bothering and bickering with each other?"

The kits, who had grown used to the way Ereth talked and groused, paid little attention to him, except to laugh. But once when Tumble, in imitation, actually called Ereth "a pillow of potted porcupine," Ereth was beside himself with indignation.

"You youngsters," he yelled, "are nothing more than a tribe of disrespectful renegades. All of you should be turned out in the dead of winter to fend for yourselves, and then, maybe, *maybe*, your brains would grow as fast as your appetites and that would make the world a better place."

The kits just laughed.

Once chores were done—and in the end they always did get done—they all went outside and began the daily search for the remaining unsprung traps.

The search began with a discussion as to what areas of the field they should investigate that day and how they should do

it. There was even Dimwood Forest to consider.

Ereth, for one, was wary of the forest, fearful of what might be found there. While he was fairly certain the hunters had not returned to the field, Ereth could not be certain about the forest. The problem was, if the hunters *had* returned, there was no way of knowing if new traps had been set. Though he kept it to himself, Ereth had a distinct memory of the traps he'd seen under the cabin, the four additional spring traps and the one designed to catch a large animal alive.

From time to time Ereth contemplated going back to the log cabin on his own. Once there, it would be easy to determine if the humans had returned. The idea was appealing. Besides, he had not forgotten the salt.

Yet it was the presence of the salt that held Ereth back. He preferred to keep that a secret. Not that he believed that the foxes had any interest in it. In fact he was certain they would never understand his feelings for salt at all.

Over the next six days they did find traps, four in all. By Ereth's reckoning, that meant—if the humans had spoken true—there were only two more to find.

In the afternoons, Ereth insisted that the kits take naps. This they did while he took a brief stroll back out to the grove of trees, where once again he satisfied his own appetite.

After nap time, there was dinner to fetch.

The hours after dinner were the best. Snug and warm beneath the ground, feeling safe, their bellies full, the kits settled down. Every night Ereth told the kits stories. Mostly they were about things he had done or heard about. What they loved most were the exploits of Ereth's famous friend, Poppy. The kits loved the tales about the many battles she and Ereth had

fought. With eyes wide and large ears erect, they paid close attention to them all. Indeed, they liked these stories so much, no one
objected when Ereth repeated them, even though each time the
porcupine told them they grew in length, facts, complexity.

In turn, the foxes told stories about their mother and how
she had hunted this or that creature. Though Ereth was not
really interested, he listened patiently.

Not so pleasing for Ereth to hear were tales about Bounder,
the foxes' father. These stories seemed all alike to him, tales
in which Bounder accomplished the most amazing feats with
incredible strength and astonishing brilliance.

"He's the smartest fox in the whole world," Nimble assured
Ereth, when the porcupine dared to question whether Bounder
had once truly managed to open a steel lock on a certain
farmer's barn using only his teeth.

"How do you know it really happened?" Ereth asked.

"Because Dad told us, and what he says is true," Tumble
said, defiance in his voice.

"Do you think he'd lie to us?" Flip demanded.

"Snail sauce on snake saliva," Ereth returned. "I was just asking."

At night, when the young foxes were finally abed and Ereth was at peace, he sometimes thought about how different his life had become. How crowded. How busy.

From time to time, he also thought of his home and, in particular, of Poppy. It was a long while now since he had left his log. Ereth wondered if she ever puzzled as to what had happened to him. Did she miss him? Was she worried about him? Did she regret ignoring his birthday?

Just to think about such things made Ereth unhappy. "Better to be here," he told himself. "At least the kits are beginning to appreciate me."

Early one morning, when Ereth popped out of the den, he was

startled to see two hunters walking about the field. Horrified, he watched as they moved along the trails the foxes had made. One by one they picked up the sprung traps and stowed them in a bag.

Ereth stayed to see if they would reveal the unsprung traps—or if they would put down new ones. They did neither, but retreated back into the woods.

The porcupine was not sure whether to be pleased by what he had observed. He could only hope they had not touched the salt at the cabin.

When he told the kits about the hunters they listened wide-eyed. "The danger isn't over," he warned. "Not yet."

More cold winter days passed. There were good days and bad. Sometimes winter weather raged. Sometimes it was almost balmy. Even so, one more trap was discovered, leaving, by Ereth's calculations, just one more trap to be found. He was hopeful they would find that one soon enough.

One evening, four weeks from the time Ereth had first come to the kits, right in the middle of what must have been his fourteenth telling of the famous battle between Mr. Ocax the great horned owl and Poppy the mouse, a voice boomed down the entry tunnel.

"Anybody home?" the voice bayed. "Anybody care for some fresh chicken?"

There was a moment of silence.

Then Tumble leaped to his feet. "It's Dad!" he cried, and tore up the entryway. The next moment his sister and brother followed.

"Buzzard boozers on burnt toast," Ereth mumbled. "Bounder has returned." The old porcupine felt very nervous.

22
The Return of Bounder

Below ground Ereth could hear joyful yapping and barking from the kits up above. Part of him wanted to go up and see what was happening. After hearing so many stories about Bounder from the kits, he was curious about him and wondered what he was truly like. But he worried even more how the fox would treat him.

While Ereth hesitated, a very excited Flip rushed down into the den. "Ereth," he cried, "why are you staying down here? Come on up. It's Dad. He's back. Don't you want to meet him? And guess what? He brought a whole fresh chicken. Just for us. Isn't that fantastic? It's the best thing I've ever eaten! A lot better than anything Mom or you ever got us. Come on! Look!" With that, the excited fox raced back up to the surface.

Even as Ereth knew it was good that Bounder had returned, he wished the fox had not. Ereth was not unfamiliar with jealousy. He recognized the almost forgotten feeling

in himself now. It infuriated him. "You pocket of pig poke," he accused himself. "You're an idiot! A fool! A dope!"

The force of his own barrage propelled him up the entry tunnel. Once at the top he poked his head out and looked around.

Bounder was stretched out on the ground, forepaws extended, tail straight behind him, head held high. There was an air of muscular pride about him as he gazed down at the kits.

The three youngsters were frolicking before him, yapping and growling joyfully, tails wagging wildly. They were in the midst of devouring the chicken, which they must have pulled apart as soon as it was offered. But even as they ate, they kept breaking away from the food to leap at their father, pummel him with their paws, nip at his fur, roll on his back, then rush back to their food lest they miss a delicious morsel. All the while they also were—as best they could with mouths full— jabbering away, telling Bounder everything they had been doing. They talked simultaneously, paying no heed to one another. Ereth had never seen them so happy.

There was endless chatter about tracking down the traps. "There were sixteen of them, Dad! Sixteen! They were so ugly. And really scary."

On they went: How Flip had the idea of making snowballs to find them safely. How they had managed to make the balls. How the balls had worked.

There was talk too about the big snowstorm and, in passing, the sad death of Leaper—but that talk was brief. There was much more talk about how they had managed to keep

everything going. "Mom left us a whole storage den of food, Dad," Nimble explained. "So we've had plenty to eat."

"But this is so much better than anything she left!" Tumble quickly put in, his mouth full of chicken.

The only thing the kits never mentioned was Ereth.

Bounder himself gave little response to the youngsters other than a few nods and yaps, just enough to make it apparent he was aware the kits were talking to him.

Then, quite casually—as if by accident—Bounder turned and gazed at Ereth. Their eyes met. In an instant Ereth recognized him as the fox he had met in Dimwood Forest a long time ago, when Poppy had first run into his log.

He could not help but grin at the memory, telling himself he had every reason to detest this fox, and that nothing—ever—would alter that. Nothing.

"Well, hello, Ereth," Bounder said in a low, even voice. "What a surprise to see you here."

"Nice to see you again," Ereth returned, trying to keep the snarl out of his voice, but not quite managing.

Nimble, hearing the exchange, looked up and around. "Oh, right, Dad. This is Ereth. He's been staying with us."

"Has he?" Bounder said.

"Yeah," Tumble put in as he looked up from his food. "But don't worry. Now that you're back he'll go away. That's what he keeps telling us."

Ereth flinched.

It was Bounder who grinned now. "Been keeping warm in my den, Ereth?" he asked the porcupine.

"I've been taking care of your kits," Ereth replied sharply.

"Where have you been?"

"Oh, you know how it is, Ereth," the fox said in his most casual way. "Business. Constant business. It keeps me on the go. I wish I had the time to hang around and take it easy—like you," he added with a smile. "But then, some of us have to work hard to make a living."

"Dad," Tumble said. "Do you want to see how we make the snowballs and find the traps? Do you? Please. It was our own idea."

"Be delighted to, son," he said. "Delighted." He stood up to his full height. He was much bigger than the kits, and Ereth too, for that matter.

The young foxes fell back and stared at him with wide-eyed admiration.

"Dad," Nimble said, her voice tinged with awe, "how big are you?"

"Oh, pretty big," the fox returned casually. "And someday you might be as big, too."

"As big as you?" Flip asked in astonishment.

"Could be. If you eat all the meat you can." He looked at Ereth. "We foxes are mostly meat eaters. You know, mice and such."

"Come on, Dad," Tumble cried. "I really want to show you how we get those traps."

"Be right there, son. You guys go ahead. I need to tell Ereth some things."

"Dad," Flip said.

"What?"

"I think you better stick to the paths we made. There's

still one trap we haven't found. Isn't that right, Ereth?" He looked over to Ereth.

"Right," Ereth said glumly.

Flip, sensing something was wrong, cast a worried look at Ereth, then at his father before joining his brother and sister, who were already heading down the bluff.

Left alone, Ereth and Bounder eyed each other with suspicion and hostility. Ereth, to his own horror, found himself wishing he could be so big and handsome and young, instead of being so old, small, lumpish, and covered with quills.

"So you've been looking after my kits," the fox said.

"Leaper asked me to."

Bounder lifted one eyebrow skeptically. "I thought she had passed away."

"I came upon her just before she died, broom tail," Ereth returned. "She was caught in a trap."

"Yes. Terribly sad."

"She asked me to come here, tell the kits what happened, take care of them."

"Oh?" Bounder said, again conveying doubt.

Ereth felt rage boiling up inside him. "You bet she did, you lump of lizard lung," he shot back. "Only until you got back."

Bounder grinned. "Well, here I am."

"Are you going to stay with them?"

"Well, Ereth, I don't know if that's any of your business. They're my kits. I think I can manage perfectly well without your intruding."

Ereth opened his mouth to say something. He found him-

self too furious, too upset to speak.

"Hey, Dad!" Tumble was calling from the base of the bluff. "Aren't you coming?"

"Be right there," Bounder called back. To Ereth, he said, "Look here, porky, I think it would be best if you left. Why don't you just take off right now. I'm going to be down there for a while. When we get back, I want you gone."

"But . . ."

"Hey, Ereth," Bounder said, "face it. It's me—their father—they should be with, not you. They don't care about you. Don't you see? You're no longer wanted. Or needed. In other words, pin cushion, you're fired." So saying, Bounder turned his back on Ereth, and with a whisk of the tail that managed to swipe across Ereth's nose, he trotted down the bluff.

Ereth, watching him go, felt as though he was suffocating with rage and humiliation. His eyes filled with tears. His chest was bursting with pain. "You dusty dump of dog diddle," he muttered furiously. "You stretched-out piece of wet worm gut! You bottomless barrel of leftover camel spit! You . . ." He was so enraged he could speak no more.

Even so, for a while Ereth remained in place, staring down the hill, watching the kits frolic with their father. Then, still boiling with a furious hurt, he retreated to the entryway, only to realize that was the last place he should be.

"I can't go without saying goodbye to the kits," he told himself. "I can't. And there's nothing that idiot of a fox can do to prevent me from doing that."

With that Ereth made his way along the bluff until he

reached the cleft in its side.
From there he scurried over
the bluff, after which he made his
way to Leaper's winter food stock-
pile.

Once among the trees, the old
porcupine chewed on some bark
strips, but quickly realized he had
lost his appetite. Instead of eating
he climbed into a tree in search of
sleep. In the morning he would talk
to the kits—if they came—alone.

23
Ereth Says Goodbye

I t was the first time in a long time that Ereth had slept outside and he made a poor night of it. Tossing and turning, more than once he almost fell off his perch. He kept waking and craning about to look for the first signs of dawn. Again and again there were none.

Sometimes he felt full of rage. At other moments he was so full of grief he almost could not see. Ereth's thoughts kept turning to his old life of solitude, before the kits, before Poppy, before these ridiculous feelings, all of which were a direct result of too much contact with other creatures.

"There are other places to live besides Dimwood Forest," Ereth told himself. "I'll find one and make sure no one ever sees me again. And I'll never leave that home. Never, never, never."

Dawn came at last. When it was little more than a pale pink glimmering along the eastern horizon, Ereth scrambled down from the tree. He went directly to the pile of rocks, trusting

that one of the kits would show up sooner or later to get some food.

Exactly what he intended to say if anyone appeared, he had no idea. All he knew was that he had to say *something*. He did caution himself not to say anything bad about Bounder. It would get him nowhere. Worse, it would only, in all probability, anger the kits. Nothing would be gained.

As time passed Ereth tried to wait patiently, but found himself pacing. Around and around the pile he went, pausing now and again to check the progression of the sun in the sky. It was growing late. Humph! If he were at the den those kits would have been up and about a long time ago.

Then he asked himself what he would do if they did *not* come. "No, they have to come," he kept telling himself. "But what if they don't?" he wondered. Should he stay the whole day and wait until the next? No! If they did not come soon he would go do what he needed to do, which was to find a new home for himself.

When the kits finally came—about an hour and a half later—Ereth was daydreaming about burrowing deep inside a dark, smelly log.

Startled by a sound, he swung about. Nimble, Tumble, and Flip were right before him, sitting in a row. They were looking at him. Their tails were wagging, their mouths slightly open, their large ears pricked forward.

"Ereth!" Flip said. "We didn't expect to see you here."

"Where did you think I'd be, murk mind?"

"Well, Dad said you wanted to get home right away," Nimble explained. "And that's why you didn't say goodbye."

"Is that what he said?"

"Yeah," Tumble said.

Ereth took a deep breath. There was a great deal he felt like saying. All he said, however, was, "That isn't true. He told me to go. How come you're all here?" he asked.

Tumble said, "Dad said we should have a huge breakfast together. Told us to come up and grab as much as we wanted. A feast. As much as we could carry. That's why."

Ereth said nothing.

"Ereth," Flip asked cautiously, "*are* you going home?"

"Eventually," Ereth returned. "But I needed to hang around."

"Why?" Nimble asked.

"I . . . I wanted to say goodbye."

"Oh," Flip said.

"Did you think I'd go without that?" Ereth demanded angrily.

The foxes exchanged looks, but said nothing. They had ceased wagging their tails.

As Ereth considered them, he thought they seemed a little sad. Or were they only confused? Or did he only want them to have those feelings? Maybe they were just embarrassed. Maybe they were wishing he had not been there. Flip kept looking over his shoulder, back toward the bluff, as if half expecting his father to appear.

"Look here," Ereth began, though he found it hard to speak. "I just wanted to say . . . I liked being . . . with you."

"It . . . was fun," Flip said after a moment.

"Fun . . ." Ereth echoed sadly before continuing. "I . . .

really came to . . . well . . . like you. You taught me a . . . lot."

"Taught *you*?" Tumble asked. "What could we teach you?"

"Oh . . . forget it," Ereth muttered helplessly. "I only wanted to say," Ereth repeated, "that I'm glad I stayed. You're very . . . nice."

"I'm glad you think so," Nimble said, giving a slight wag of her tail.

"And . . . and," Ereth struggled, "if you ever, well, need me for anything, you can come get me."

"You never told us where you lived," Flip said.

"Cross the field, through the forest, till you get to the log cabin at Long Lake. Follow the trail south until you reach a gray snag. It's full of mice. I live right next to it. In a log."

"Oh great," Nimble said. "Maybe we'll visit you."

"Yeah, right," Ereth returned, not sounding very encouraging or hopeful. Then he remembered that he was going to find a new home where he could live alone, so no one would find him. He didn't let them know about that.

No one spoke. The foxes gazed at Ereth, then away, then down at their paws. Ereth, not trusting himself to look at them, stared at his paws too.

"I have to go," he suddenly announced. "Be careful until you find that last trap."

"Don't worry," Tumble said. "We will."

Still Ereth hesitated. "Hope things go well."

"We'll be okay," Nimble said.

"Okay," Ereth said. Abruptly he whirled about, took three steps and banged into a tree. "Puckered pine pits!" he screamed. Then he backed off and stumbled away.

After ten yards he stopped and turned around. The foxes were still sitting there. Still looking after him.

"One more thing," the porcupine croaked. "If I ever hear that any of you gangling idiots eats a mouse, I'm coming back. And if I do, I'll make your nose look like a cactus in need of a haircut! Remember that!"

With that, Ereth, not daring to look back, ran away as fast as he could.

24
Ereth and the Salt

Ereth waddled blindly through the woods. He barged into bushes, bumped into trees, slipped, stumbled, fell into pockets of snow. Each time he stalled, he snarled, swore under his breath, picked himself up, pawed his eyes clear, and pushed on.

Only when he grew so weary that he had to rest did he stop and lean against the trunk of a tree. He did so reluctantly, gasping for breath. Briefly, he peered back along the trail he had just traveled to see if he had been followed.

For a second, he thought someone *was* there, and his heart jumped. Then he decided he was just imagining things and his heart sank again.

With an angry shake of his head, he murmured, "Alone at last," and allowed himself a sigh that he fancied was one of contentment. At the same time he felt a great swell of emotion in his chest, which he did not have the energy to suppress. The effort left him weak and shaky.

"Blue heron hogwash," he muttered. "I'm done with all this family fungus! Better to do what I want, when I want, how I want. I'm free again! Life is *good!*"

With that Ereth gave himself a shake, as if he could rid himself of whatever might be sticking to his quills. "It's about time I did something for myself," he announced out loud. Then he grinned. "Time to get some . . . salt."

Damp-eyed, he looked around. By scrutinizing the sun as well as the shadows on the ground, he determined where he was.

After careful consideration, Ereth was quite sure his head-long rush had taken him north. To the best of his judgment,

Long Lake, along with the cabin and the salt, was to be found in a southwesterly direction.

Feeling much more composed, Ereth took time to eat before resuming his journey. Yet once, twice, he gazed about, unable to rid himself of the feeling that someone was lurking in the woods, watching him.

"Fool," he muttered. "No one's there! No one will ever be there!" Still, he allowed himself the thought that it was always best to be on guard. But when he caught himself taking another peek behind, he made a stern vow to look no more.

As he went on, his spirits grew lighter. It was good, he kept telling himself, to be on the move. Good to have no

responsibilities other than himself. He tried to put his thoughts on the salt and how it would taste. He thought too about home—wherever that might be. Indeed, the old porcupine thought of many things, but never once did he allow himself to think of the kits any longer than the moment it took to regret such thoughts. All that, he insisted to himself, was over and done with. Finished. Only once did he slip from his mental discipline, when he suddenly shouted, "They didn't even say thank you!" That said, he vowed to say no more. It was done. Gone. Finished. The end.

The porcupine pushed through the woods at a steady clip. The snow had receded, leaving great patches of brown, cold earth. The pine-scented air was bright and crisp, filled with buoyant energy.

When Ereth decided he had gone far enough to avoid the field and the bluff, he swung southwest, trusting that at some point he would reach the shores of Long Lake.

It was not till late afternoon that he rested again. Early winter shadows, like grasping paws, extended a stealthy hold over what remained of the crusty white snow.

The porcupine fueled himself with a quick chew of some bark, then set off again. "That lake should be near," he told himself, trying to ignore his exhaustion.

As he hurried, there were a few times—despite his earlier resolve—that he caught himself thinking about the kits again. What had they done all day? Had they eaten well? Did they do their chores? Had they thought about him? Then, with a snarl and a muttered, "Salivating shrew slop," he angrily dismissed such thoughts and willed himself to concentrate on the

salt that soon would be his.

He reached the lake at twilight. In the dim light its surface lay white and frozen. Ereth stared at it. It looked so cold and deserted.

Suddenly, tears began to flow. "Oh, why did I ever leave home?" he asked himself. "Because of my birthday," he recalled. "No one paid any attention to me. I was forced to go and get a present for myself. And look what's happened! Well, that'll be my last birthday.

"That'll teach 'em!" he said out loud with a savage bite in his voice.

"Salt," he whispered with desperation, "I must get some salt."

With new urgency, Ereth wheeled about and hurried on. Keeping the lake to his right, he skirted the shore. Sometimes, as he scooted across low, beach-like areas, the going was easy. At other times the shore was irregular or boggy, clotted with old brambles. In those places he had to push his way through or take long detours. "Why is it always so hard to get where you want to go?" he complained.

Night wore on. The white moon rose with brilliant promise, only to be obscured by clouds. A wind rattled the bare branches like old bones. Around midnight, snow began to fall. Fearful that if he stopped he might never move again, Ereth pressed on. The snow piled up quickly, making the going slower. When dawn came, gray and hard, mantled by still-falling snow, he dared not rest.

Then, at last Ereth saw the cabin. By early morning's thin light it seemed little more than a dark lump on the snow-filled

landscape. No lights were on, though Ereth reminded himself that was no proof the hunters weren't there. It was still early. The humans might be sleeping.

He sniffed the air, trying to detect any hint of burning wood. None.

Emboldened, Ereth edged closer to the cabin. He continually looked about, seeking some sign, any sign, that would suggest the presence of people.

There were no footprints, but new snow would have covered them. Briefly, he tried to calculate the time since he'd seen the hunters on the field. Was it two weeks ago? A month?

In the growing daylight he scrambled under the cabin and peered around. No snowmobile. That, he decided, was a good sign.

Then he caught sight of the box in which he had seen the traps and was filled with revulsion. Even so, he crept forward, hoisted himself up, and peered inside. The box was empty.

Had the humans come back and set the remaining traps? Or had they returned and taken the traps away with them?

Cautiously, Ereth crept out from under the cabin and worked his way to the front porch.

He went up the steps and put his nose to the door jamb. A tremor of excitement coursed through him. The smell of salt was unmistakable. *It was still there!* His heart hammered. Oh, if only he could have some! So much would be mended!

He crawled up to the window, the one he had previously knocked in. Not only was glass back in place, bars had been placed over it. One glance and a disappointed Ereth knew there was no way he could get through it.

He dropped down and butted his head against the door. It would not give. Frantic, he raced down the steps and around the cabin, searching for any way to get inside. He found none. He even plunged under the cabin in hopes he might discover an entry there. Once again he was thwarted.

"Hit the puke switch and duck!" he shouted. "It's not fair. I deserve better. I've been treated badly. I should get *something!*"

Furious, feeling nothing but the cruel injustice of the world, he raced back to the front porch. Maybe he had given up on the window too quickly. In great haste, he crawled up and balanced himself on the windowsill. Perched precariously, he clutched the bars and tried to rattle them as if he were in a cage and trying to get out. The bars held. Increasingly desperate, he reached through the bars and pressed against the window itself. It would not budge.

Thoroughly defeated, he turned around. Only then did he see that right below him on the porch was another animal. He was about three feet in length and more than a foot tall, with short brown fur and small, round, dark eyes, which, to look at them, were almost blank of emotion.

"Got you," said Marty the Fisher. "Got you at last."

25
What Happened at the Cabin

Open-mouthed, Ereth stared at the fisher.

"You thought you were being clever, hiding with those kits for so long," Marty sneered. "But you're too stupid to know that I'm the most patient creature in the world. I've waited and watched every move you made. I saw you pretending to take care of those foxes when all you were doing was hiding from me. I saw you rush through the woods and take an indirect route back here. I saw and I followed. I'm like death. You can't escape me!

"You coward!" he went on. "I know you for what you are. You're an old, witless, selfish porcupine. But now you're going to get what you deserve. Get down from there!"

"But . . . but . . . *why?*" a very frightened Ereth stammered. "Why are you so angry at me? What did I do to you?"

"You porcupines think you can go and do anything you

want," Marty replied angrily. "You're nothing but self-centered beasts without any feeling for anyone but yourselves. You don't care what you say or do. You think nothing of others. You think your quills will keep you safe. Well, I'm here to show you, porcupine, no one can be safe from Marty the Fisher. Not even you. Now get down!"

"But . . . but . . . I'm not like other porcupines," Ereth stammered. "Or if I was, I've changed. I've become different. I have feelings. I *do* care what others think."

"Liar!" Marty snarled. "Come on down here and get what you deserve!"

Ereth, knowing perfectly well what the fisher could do to him, remained where he was. While he could put up resistance, he was hardly in a place to do so. Beyond that, he was exhausted from his long, difficult trek back to the cabin.

He looked around. The barred window was behind him. No escaping that way. Nor was there any escape right or left. He glanced beyond the porch, toward the woods. There, perhaps, lay safety. If he could climb into a tree he might be able to defend himself. But first he had to get to the tree, and the new snow would be slippery, perhaps even deep in places.

"Get down!" Marty shouted, eyes cold and hard. "Get down or I'll yank you down!" So saying, he reared back on his hind legs as though ready to attack.

"Moldering mouse marbles!" Ereth cried. "I don't deserve this. I don't!" But when he saw the fisher's muscles tense, he knew he had no choice. He had to reach the trees.

Terrified, Ereth did what he had never done in his entire life. He made a flying leap off the windowsill. Kicking back

hard, he sailed over the fisher's head, landing with a hard thump on the porch.

Marty, caught by surprise, swung around.

Paws smarting from a painful landing, a dazed Ereth struggled to his feet. He spun about, trembling with panic, and waved his quilled tail wildly, ready to smack Marty across the face if he got too close.

Marty stepped back spryly.

Seeing that he had won a brief advantage, Ereth turned again. He tried to get off the porch by running but completely forgot about the steps. Missing the first one, he tumbled head

over tail, doing three complete somersaults before landing on his back in the snow, belly exposed.

Shrieking with rage, Marty extended his claws and took a great leap off the porch, aiming right at the porcupine. Ereth saw him coming and rolled over, but not fast enough. The fisher managed to snare him with his front claws, leaving two long scratches across Ereth's belly. Blood began to flow.

"Potato pip paste!" Ereth screamed. "I'm being murdered! Help!" He continued his roll, then turned again, once more putting his tail between himself and the snarling fisher.

Marty, alert to the danger, backed off.

A frantic Ereth began to race toward the trees, taking what were for him great bounding leaps. As he went he trailed streaks of blood, which were like stitch marks on the white snow.

The fisher saw where Ereth was heading. With a burst of speed he shot past the porcupine, made a sharp U-turn, and confronted him head-on.

Ereth came to a skidding stop. He started to turn, but saw that if he did, the fisher would be herding him right back toward the cabin, the last place Ereth wanted to be.

"Give up, you stupid beast," Marty taunted. "You don't have a chance!"

"You occupational ignoramus!" Ereth screeched, huffing and puffing as he tried to recover his breath. His heart was hammering so hard it was making him dizzy.

Trying to defend himself, he tucked his head down between his front legs, shaping himself into a ball of bristling quills. Then, with mincing steps, he awkwardly waddled forward. This moved him toward Marty, but with his head so low he

could no longer see where he was going.

Marty, seeing that Ereth was attacking blindly, backed up and quickly circled the porcupine, looking for a place to attack. Noticing that the quills along Ereth's side were flattened, he leaped forward, both front paws out, trying to knock Ereth off balance.

Hit hard where he least expected it, Ereth rolled away. Once again his belly was exposed. Once again, the fisher struck, drawing more blood.

The pain was enough to force Ereth to uncoil himself. He had to see where he was, had to see where the fisher was, had to know how to escape. But when he looked about he was so confused and woozy he couldn't find his enemy. Belatedly, he saw that the fisher had jumped in front of him again. Even as Ereth realized his whereabouts, Marty attacked, this time aiming right at Ereth's face.

The porcupine ducked. He avoided the worst but received a bad scrape on one ear even as he managed to butt the fisher hard, hoping he'd poked him with a couple of quills.

Marty dropped back, coolly trying to decide where to attack next.

In that moment, Ereth stole a quick glance to see how far he was from the trees. He had covered half the distance, but it felt as if they were still miles away.

As Ereth struggled to decide what to do, Marty took another hard lunge at him, trying to knock him over. This time he missed completely and went sprawling in deep snow.

Sensing his opportunity, Ereth hurled himself toward the trees. He was beginning to think he was going to make it, when

he received a hard smash on the left side.

The stroke came so suddenly, so intensely, Ereth landed hard against an old stump, the wind knocked completely out of him.

Feeling increasing pain and growing even more muddled, Ereth knew that he must get up and defend himself.

He could not.

The best he could manage was to open his eyes. He beheld a dreadful sight. Marty the Fisher was crouching a few feet away. His face bore a cruel grin. "Now I have you," Marty hissed.

"Help!" Ereth gasped. "Help!"

"You're done, porcupine," Marty snarled. "Completely *done*. No one, absolutely no one, escapes Marty the Fisher."

Ereth strained to get up again. The pain was too great. He was too weak. He was bleeding too much. "Please," he bleated.

"I need some help . . . please. Someone help me."

As Marty the Fisher prepared his final, fatal spring, Ereth closed his eyes. "Goodbye, Poppy," he whispered. "Farewell, kits!"

He opened his eyes to see the fisher, claws fully extended, leaping at him.

The next instant there was an explosion of red. It seemed to come from nowhere, and yet it was everywhere all at once. Thinking it was his own blood he was seeing, Ereth squeezed his eyes shut. Then he heard the yelping, barking, and snarling.

Ereth opened his eyes and blinked with astonishment.

Tumble, Nimble, and Flip had burst from the woods and leaped upon the fisher, taking him completely by surprise. What's more, they were pummeling him with all the ferocity they could muster.

Tumble, with jaws tightly clamped, was holding on to the scruff of the fisher's neck and shaking hard, all the while grunting and snarling. Nimble had taken a fast hold of one of the fisher's legs and was refusing to let go, no matter how much the beast thrashed. As for Flip, he had a firm grip on the fisher's tail and was growling and yanking and pulling with all his might.

In seconds it was Marty the Fisher who was on his back, kicking and clawing frantically, trying to get away.

A weak, dazed Ereth could only mutter, "Welcome the wombats and bless all bees!"

Suddenly Marty the Fisher gave a mighty yank and freed his leg from Nimble's grasp. Though Tumble was still clinging to him and Flip refused to let go, the fisher staggered to his feet. With a violent shake, he flung Tumble away. Then he turned and snapped savagely at Flip, who was forced to let go of the fisher's tail.

Free at last, Marty, instead of staying to fight, whirled about, leaped through the bushes, and fled among the trees.

The kits, tongues lolling, chests heaving, watched him go. So did Ereth. For a moment there was nothing to hear but the sound of the fisher smashing through the underbrush. Next there came the distinct, dreadful sound of a metallic *snap*.

26

Marty the Fisher

N o one moved. Not Ereth. Not Tumble, Nimble, or Flip. Instead, they all stared in the direction that Marty the Fisher had gone.

"What . . . happened?" Nimble said at last, though she as well as everybody else was pretty sure.

Tumble, trembling visibly, began to edge forward, his nose extended, sniffing.

"Careful!" Ereth cried out from where he lay. "There may be more traps about. When I checked there were none left under the cabin."

"Do you think he got . . . caught?" Flip asked.

No one replied. Instead, the three kits crept forward into the brush. Hauling himself up, Ereth limped painfully along.

"Look!" Tumble cried. He had managed to get ahead of the others.

The two other kits went forward. Ereth came last.

What they saw was the large box trap from under the cabin.

Inside—very much alive—was Marty the Fisher. In his haste to get away he had rushed blindly into it. The moment he did, the doors at either end snapped shut.

The three kits and Ereth crept closer, their eyes glued to the sight.

Marty, his face bearing a look of terrible rage, glared out at them. "Don't just stand there gawking," he snarled. "Get me out of here!"

Neither Ereth nor the kits replied.

"You don't understand," the caged animal said, speaking with barely suppressed fury. "I'm from the great fisher family. No finer animals in all the world. We've been hunted down everywhere by humans because of our fur. Even dolts like you must be capable of seeing how beautiful I am. We're so beautiful there are very few fishers left. Every time one of us is killed or captured, the chances of our survival are reduced. If you let them take me away, we fishers shall be almost extinct. Now, get the cage open."

"But . . . you were trying to kill Ereth!" Nimble protested.

"Of course I was," returned the fisher.

"But . . . why should you want to do that?" Flip asked.

"Because," returned Marty proudly, "only fishers are smart enough to deal with porcupines. Now stop yapping and open the trap!"

The kits looked to Ereth.

"I . . . don't know how to open it," Ereth said.

"You blundering idiot!" Marty the Fisher cried out. "Can't you do anything right? Open your eyes. There's a rod lever on top. Push it down. It'll open the trap doors. The four of you can do it easily."

Once again the three kits looked to Ereth, waiting for him to decide.

"Fumigated goat fidgets," Ereth muttered, not knowing what to do.

"Will . . . you promise not to hurt Ereth?" Tumble asked.

"And just go away and leave us alone?" Nimble added.

"I don't make deals with anyone," the Fisher shouted. "Just get me out!"

The kits turned yet again to Ereth.

Ereth sighed deeply. He could feel the pain where the fisher had clawed him. And yet, as he looked at the beast in the trap, all he could think of was the fisher's predicament. "Frog freckles," he grumbled. "I suppose we should."

"Of course you should," Marty snarled. "The weak always have an obligation to help the strong. We're the important ones. Besides, I've suffered a great deal. Didn't I just explain, my family is almost extinct. You have an obligation to help me."

Lumbering forward, Ereth approached the cage. After sniffing and studying it carefully, he found the bar Marty had mentioned, the one that would open the trap. Rearing up he pushed down on it. It gave way partly but not enough to release the doors. He looked around at the kits. "Come on," he called.

"Ereth . . ." Flip called, "are . . . you sure we should do this?"

"Come on," Ereth growled, "lend a paw!"

Tumble jumped atop the trap. Nimble reared up from one side, while Flip got close to Ereth.

"When I say three, we'll all push," Ereth said.

"Would you hurry!" Marty snarled.

"One . . . two . . ." Ereth stopped.

From somewhere in the distance came a high-pitched whine. Tumble cocked his ears. "What's that?"

The animals listened.

"Faster, you fools!" Marty shouted. "I must get out!"

The whine grew louder, becoming a growl as it got closer.

"What is that?" Flip asked Ereth.

"Pig pudding," the porcupine swore. "It's the snowmobile. The hunters. They're coming back."

"Let me out of here!" Marty shrieked. "Don't let them get me. You mustn't!"

The sound of the snowmobile grew very loud.

Ereth leaped off the trap. "Into the woods!" he cried to the kits. "Hide! Run!" He scrambled away painfully.

The kits tore after him.

"Don't leave me!" Marty screamed. "Don't let them get me!"

Ereth dove under the low-lying branches of a pine tree. The kits quickly joined him.

"What's going to happen?" a frightened Flip asked.

"Shut up!" Ereth ordered.

The four peered out through the tree branches. They could still see the trap. Marty was thrashing about, trying desperately to free himself.

The sound of the snowmobile had become a roar. The next moment they saw it burst into the clearing in front of the cabin and stop. It was the same machine Ereth had seen before. Sure enough, two men were perched on it. Though they were so bundled up it was hard to see their faces, Ereth recognized the furs they were wearing: they were the same humans he'd dealt with before.

Sure enough, one of them said, "Hey, Wayne, look here. There's blood on the ground."

The man on the backseat leaped off and peered into the snow. "Some animal has been wounded," he said.

"That's my blood, you two-legged lump of wind cheese!" Ereth snarled.

"Shut up!" Tumble whispered.

Ereth gave the fox a dirty look but said no more.

"Whatever it was, it went this way," said the man. He began to follow the trail of Ereth's blood away from the cabin, moving right to the stump where the struggle had taken place. The other man followed.

"Look here, Parker," the first man said. "Must have been some kind of fight. Must have been a whole bunch of animals."

"Tracks go there," the man named Parker said. He began to move toward the trap.

Ereth and the three kits, not even daring to breathe, watched.

"Wayne," Parker called. "I think we got something."

"Good Lord . . . what is it?"

"Not certain. Look at that gorgeous fur. But he sure is mad. Watch out for his claws."

"Hey, that's a fisher!"

"Sweet."

"Lot better than that porcupine we were trying to get. Zoo material. Might give us a lot for it. No one wants to see a porky. But lots of people would like to look at a fisher. Pretty rare."

The two men picked up the trap and began to walk toward the cabin. Once they reached it they opened the door and took the trap inside with them. Then they closed the door with a bang.

At first the animals under the tree said nothing. It was Flip who finally spoke.

Turning to Ereth, he nudged him with his wet nose. "Are you all right?" he asked.

"Did you hear what he said?" Ereth muttered. "Better than a . . . a *porky*!"

"Ereth," Flip repeated, "is your body all right?"

"Oh. Some cuts and bruises. Where did you all come from?"

"The den," Tumble said.

"But . . . your father . . . where is he?"

"Dad?" Flip said. There was a slight look of embarrassment about his face. "He said he had some business to do."

"And he *left*?" Ereth asked, feeling his indignation rise.

"It's okay. He asked us if we minded being left alone," Nimble explained. "We said we didn't."

"He said he only came back to be sure you weren't bothering us," Tumble said.

Flip said, "So the day after you left, he took off."

"It was important business," Tumble interjected with some of his old heat.

"But . . . when will he be coming back?" Ereth asked.

"Oh, sometime in the spring," Nimble said casually.

"Right. He's going to take us hunting," Tumble said.

"He's really great at that," Flip put in.

Ereth thought of saying something. Instead he told them, "You saved my life. And . . . and I didn't think I'd ever see you again."

"You didn't?" Flip said, taken by surprise. "Why?"

"Because . . . oh, toe jam on a toothbrush," Ereth grumbled. "I just didn't, that's all."

"I mean," Nimble said, "Dad is fun, but you're the one who takes care of us. So of course you'd have to see us again."

"The thing is," Tumble added in his sour way, "Dad has more important things to do than take care of kits. But Ereth, you're so old you've got nothing better to do."

A speechless Ereth looked around.

"So can you come back to the den with us?" Nimble asked.

Ereth glowered.

"We found the last trap," Tumble said. "You won't have to worry about that."

"Will you come back?" Flip coaxed.

"No," Ereth said at last.

"*No?*" the kits chorused.

"I'm going home. My home."

"But . . . what about . . . *us?*" Flip whispered.

"You'll be fine without me," Ereth said. "You didn't eat up all that food your mother left you, did you?"

"No."

"Good. It should get you through the winter."

The dismayed foxes stared at Ereth.

"But . . . we'll miss you," Nimble said.

"A lot," Flip said.

To which Tumble added, "Yeah, we will."

"Tumbled toad toes," Ereth grumbled. He looked out through the forest and toward the south—and his home.

"Ereth . . ." Flip said. "Guess what?"

"What?"

"There was something we forgot to tell you."

"What's that?"

Flip looked from Nimble, to Tumble, then back to Ereth. "We wanted to say . . . thank you."

The pain in Ereth's chest was making it hard for him to breathe. "Oh, bobcat beads," he muttered.

"And another thing," Tumble said.

"Stop!" Ereth snapped. "I don't want to hear!"

"We . . . like you. A lot."

Ereth looked away.

"And anyway," Nimble added, "I bet with those scratches that fisher gave you, you'll need us to look after you. Am I right?"

"Right," Flip said, "this time we'll take care of you."

Ereth stared at the three kits, who were sitting in a row. Tongues lolling, eyes full of bright curiosity, large-eared and big-pawed, they seemed so terribly young.

"Busted bug bottoms," Ereth muttered. "You'll never be able to take care of me."

"But if you don't let us try," Nimble said, "you won't ever

know, will you?"

"Yeah," Tumble said.

"Centipede armpits!" Ereth cried. "All I want is to go back to my own smelly log."

The kits looked at one another. It was Flip who said, "Well, then we'll go with you."

"No!"

"But . . . why not?" Flip said.

"If you came to my place, what would you eat?"

"What we always do," Tumble said. "Meat."

"Look here, nibble nose, my best friends are mice."

"Oh," Nimble said.

"If you so much as touch one whisker of one mouse—*one!*— I'll turn you inside out so fast you won't know what direction you're going. If you come with me for a visit you're going to eat nothing but . . . but vegetables."

The foxes exchanged looks.

Tumble grinned. "That's okay with us," he said. "But only when we visit you."

27
Ereth's Birthday

Ereth led the way, the three foxes trotting by his side. With the porcupine limping, they moved slowly. Now and again the foxes darted off, but they never went far and they always came back.

At first they chatted quite a bit, asking Ereth questions about where he lived, how he lived, whom he lived with, along with countless queries about Poppy. Ereth answered very little. To most questions, he said, "You'll see." Or, "None of your business, nit nose."

So the foxes chatted among themselves. It was continual, it was loud, and was not without some bickering. Ereth paid little mind, but waddled slowly, steadily on.

It had taken one day for Ereth to come from his home to Long Lake. The return trip took two days. There were moments he felt he should just turn around and go with the foxes to their den. But he kept reminding himself that he wanted to be in his own dark and smelly home. He also needed to see Poppy.

Of course, as he limped along, he occasionally thought about the salt he'd left behind in the cabin. Perhaps someday he would go back. But as he mused on when that day might be he suddenly stopped.

"What's the matter?" Flip asked him.

"I'm very old," Ereth whispered. Though he found himself glancing over his shoulder from time to time, he said no more.

They arrived home the following day just about noon. It was Columbine, playing about at the foot of the snag, who first saw them coming.

"Uncle Ereth!" she cried with delight. "You're back!"

"Of course I'm back, you dull dab of bobcat widdle. Where else would I be?"

"But . . . you've been gone so . . ." Then Columbine saw the three foxes. Frightened, she turned tail and raced into the snag.

In moments Poppy ran out. She was joined by Rye and the rest of the litter. "Ereth," Poppy cried, "where have you been?"

Ereth wanted to burst out with all that had happened. Instead he said, "Oh, busy."

"But you were gone for a *month*. We were worried."

"You were?"

"Of course we were." Poppy looked over to the three foxes. "Are these friends of yours?"

"Absolutely. This is Tumble, Nimble, and Flip. Guys, this is Poppy. And her husband, Rye. These mice are named Columbine, Mariposa, Snowberry, Walnut, Verbena, Scruboak, Pipsissewa, Crabgrass, Locust, Sassafras, and Ragweed the Second."

"How-do-you-do-Tumble-Nimble-and-Flip," the young

mice chorused.

Rye considered the foxes nervously. "Are they . . . safe?" he asked Ereth.

"Strict vegetarians."

"Oh, okay."

The foxes, remembering all the tales Ereth had told, gazed at the famous Poppy with awe. She was so small, but she had done so much!

It was Poppy who said, "Ereth, did you realize that on the day you went off, it was your birthday?"

"Is that so?" Ereth replied, trying not to frown. "I guess I forgot."

Sassafras ran over to Poppy and whispered into her ear, "Ma! Ereth's . . . you know."

"Oh, my, yes," Poppy said. "You really should."

With that all eleven of the young mice raced back into the hole at the base of the snag.

"It's just a little something Rye and I—and the children— got for your birthday," Poppy explained. "We went to get it for you that morning."

Ereth could feel himself blushing. "Well, it didn't seem to me that . . ."

"The children said they tried to get you to stay but you rushed off."

The young mice reappeared, rolling forward a large lump of salt. The lump being six times the size of any one of the youngsters, all of whom were trying to be helpful, there was much slipping and falling, squeaking and laughing.

"Happy birthday, Uncle Ereth!" they cried in unison when

they finally reached the porcupine.

It was Rye who explained: "You see, Ereth, Poppy and I got it from the salt block at New Farm. Unfortunately, it took us longer to drag it back than we thought it would. By the time we got home you had gone."

"And we had no idea where," Poppy added.

"Then the storm came," Rye said.

"We began to think something might have happened to you," Poppy went on. "Really, Ereth, we were very worried. But we didn't know where to look. When you go off that way you really must leave some word. I . . . I began to think something awful happened to you. I've been very upset."

Eyes glued to the gift, Ereth stood there open-mouthed,

incapable of saying a word. "*Salt . . .*" he muttered finally, already drooling.

"Speech, Uncle Ereth," Sassafras cried. "Birthday boys have to make speeches."

Ereth took a deep breath. "I . . . Oh, pull the chain and grab five mops," he managed to say, even as tears began to roll down his cheeks. "I . . . don't know what to say," he muttered between sobs, "except . . . oh, thank you . . . thank each and every one of you."

The next moment the eleven young mice started to sing "Happy Birthday" in a very ragged chorus. The three foxes joined in with howls of their own.

Ereth could not wait until they were done. He snatched up

the salt and began to lick it in a frenzy of delight.

The mice cheered. The foxes bayed.

And if Ereth's tears made the salt a little saltier than usual, that might explain why, as far as the old porcupine was concerned, it was the best-tasting salt he had ever eaten in his whole, long life.

Indeed, as the years went by and Ereth grew truly old and his quills became gray—and less sharp—and he looked back on all that had happened to him, he had no doubt—not the slightest doubt in all the world—that this birthday turned out to be the very best he ever had.

The new way to get AROUND town.

Make the most of your stay. Go Day by Day!

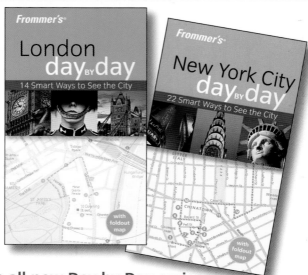

The all-new Day by Day series shows you the best places to visit and the best way to see them.

- Full-color throughout, with hundreds of photos and maps
- Packed with 1–to–3–day itineraries, neighborhood walks, and thematic tours
- Museums, literary haunts, offbeat places, and more
- Star-rated hotel and restaurant listings
- Sturdy foldout map in reclosable plastic wallet
- Foldout front covers with at-a-glance maps and info

The best trips start here. ***Frommer's***®

A Branded Imprint of ⊕**WILEY**
Now you know.